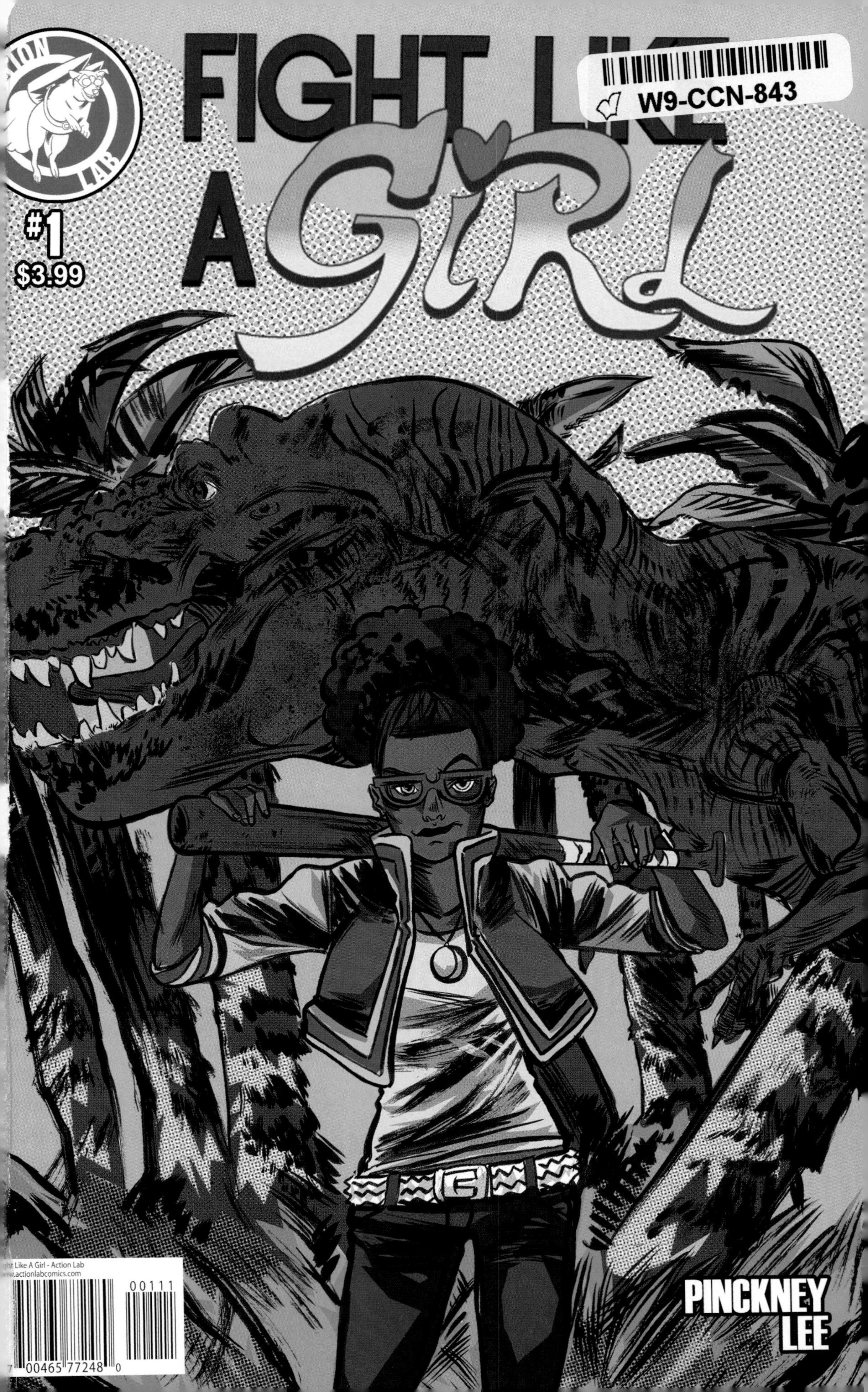
ACTION LAB
FIGHT LIKE A GIRL
#1
$3.99
ght Like A Girl - Action Lab
ww.actionlabcomics.com
00111
7 00465 77248 0
PINCKNEY
LEE
W9-CCN-843

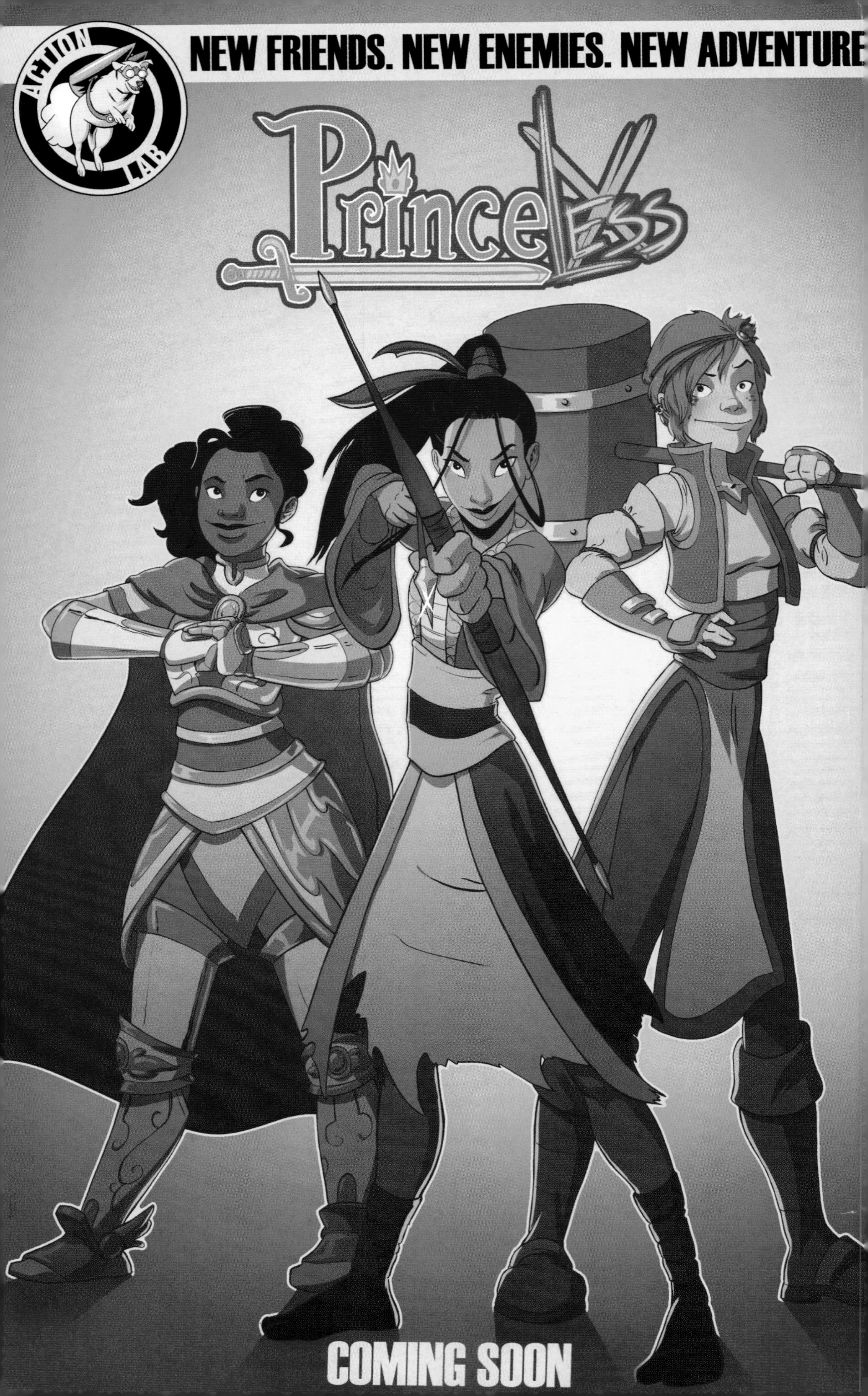
ACTION LAB
NEW FRIENDS. NEW ENEMIES. NEW ADVENTURE
Princeless
COMING SOON

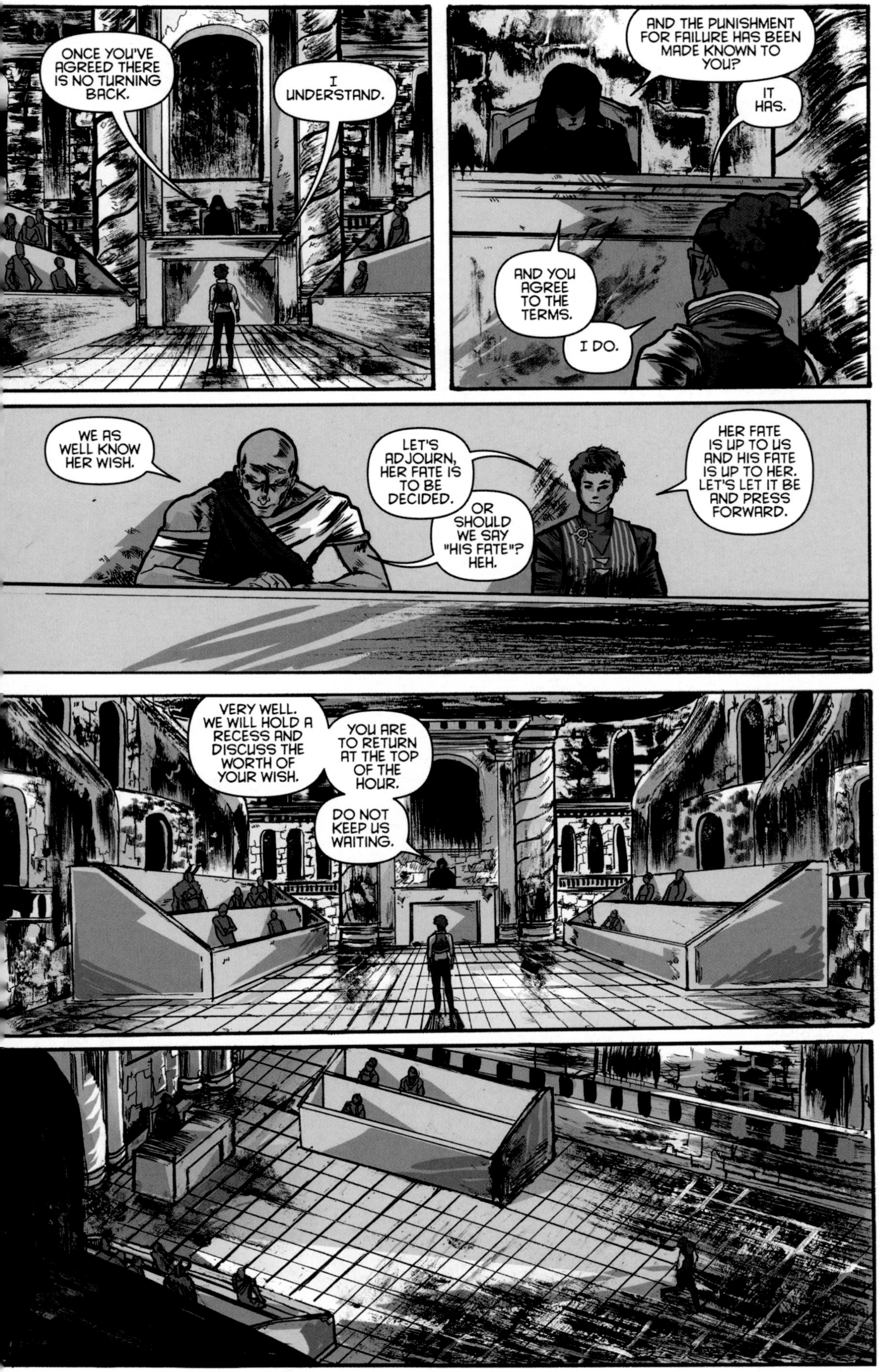

ONCE YOU'VE AGREED THERE IS NO TURNING BACK.
I UNDERSTAND.
AND THE PUNISHMENT FOR FAILURE HAS BEEN MADE KNOWN TO YOU?
IT HAS.
AND YOU AGREE TO THE TERMS.
I DO.
WE AS WELL KNOW HER WISH.
LET'S ADJOURN, HER FATE IS TO BE DECIDED.
OR SHOULD WE SAY "HIS FATE"? HEH.
HER FATE IS UP TO US AND HIS FATE IS UP TO HER. LET'S LET IT BE AND PRESS FORWARD.
VERY WELL. WE WILL HOLD A RECESS AND DISCUSS THE WORTH OF YOUR WISH.
YOU ARE TO RETURN AT THE TOP OF THE HOUR.
DO NOT KEEP US WAITING.

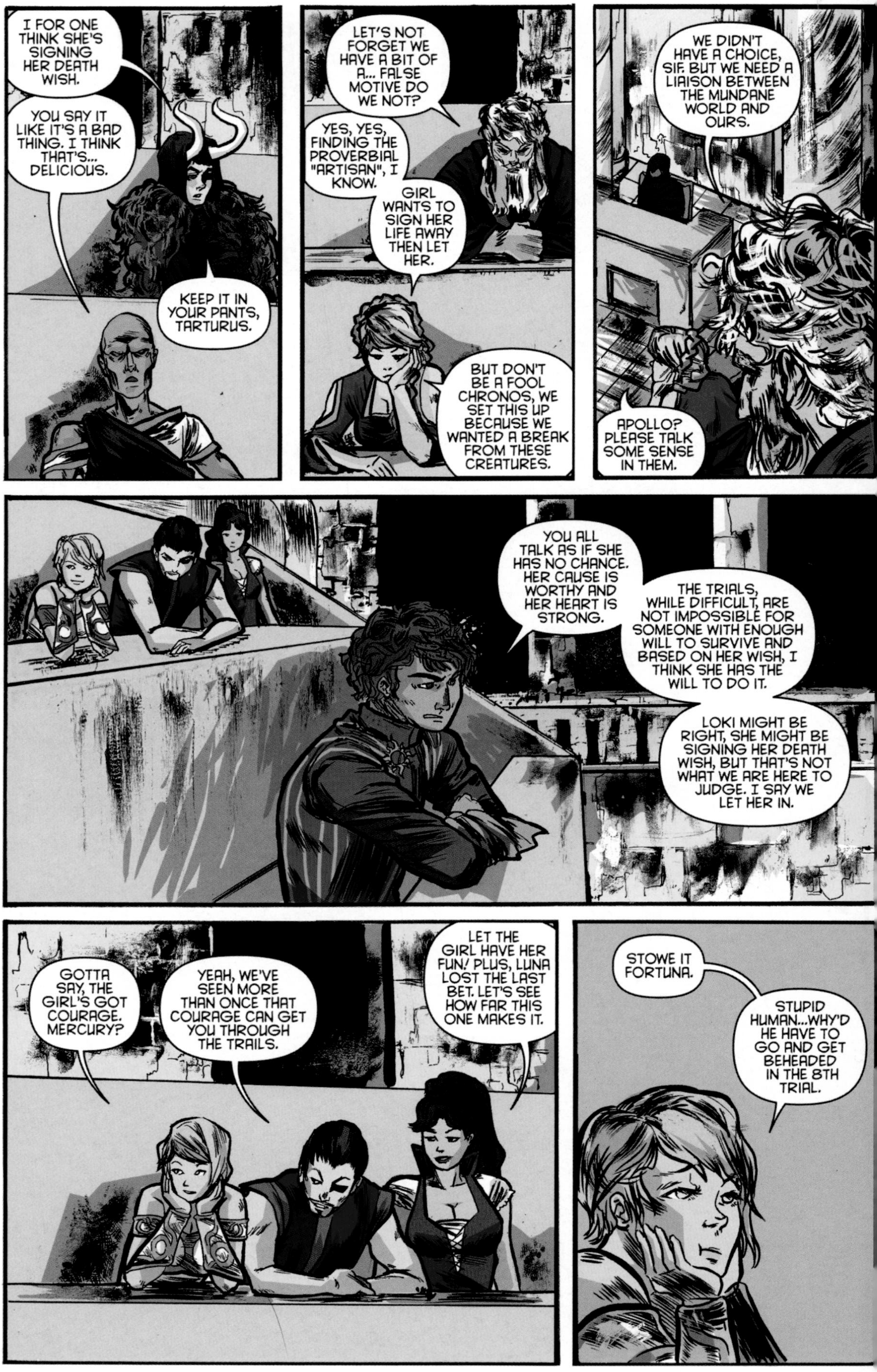

I FOR ONE THINK SHE'S SIGNING HER DEATH WISH.
YOU SAY IT LIKE IT'S A BAD THING. I THINK THAT'S... DELICIOUS.
KEEP IT IN YOUR PANTS, TARTURUS.
LET'S NOT FORGET WE HAVE A BIT OF A... FALSE MOTIVE DO WE NOT?
YES, YES, FINDING THE PROVERBIAL "ARTISAN", I KNOW.
GIRL WANTS TO SIGN HER LIFE AWAY THEN LET HER.
BUT DON'T BE A FOOL CHRONOS, WE SET THIS UP BECAUSE WE WANTED A BREAK FROM THESE CREATURES.
WE DIDN'T HAVE A CHOICE, SIF. BUT WE NEED A LIAISON BETWEEN THE MUNDANE WORLD AND OURS.
APOLLO? PLEASE TALK SOME SENSE IN THEM.
YOU ALL TALK AS IF SHE HAS NO CHANCE. HER CAUSE IS WORTHY AND HER HEART IS STRONG.
THE TRIALS, WHILE DIFFICULT, ARE NOT IMPOSSIBLE FOR SOMEONE WITH ENOUGH WILL TO SURVIVE AND BASED ON HER WISH, I THINK SHE HAS THE WILL TO DO IT.
LOKI MIGHT BE RIGHT, SHE MIGHT BE SIGNING HER DEATH WISH, BUT THAT'S NOT WHAT WE ARE HERE TO JUDGE. I SAY WE LET HER IN.
GOTTA SAY, THE GIRL'S GOT COURAGE. MERCURY?
YEAH, WE'VE SEEN MORE THAN ONCE THAT COURAGE CAN GET YOU THROUGH THE TRAILS.
LET THE GIRL HAVE HER FUN! PLUS, LUNA LOST THE LAST BET. LET'S SEE HOW FAR THIS ONE MAKES IT.
STOWE IT FORTUNA.
STUPID HUMAN...WHY'D HE HAVE TO GO AND GET BEHEADED IN THE 8TH TRIAL.

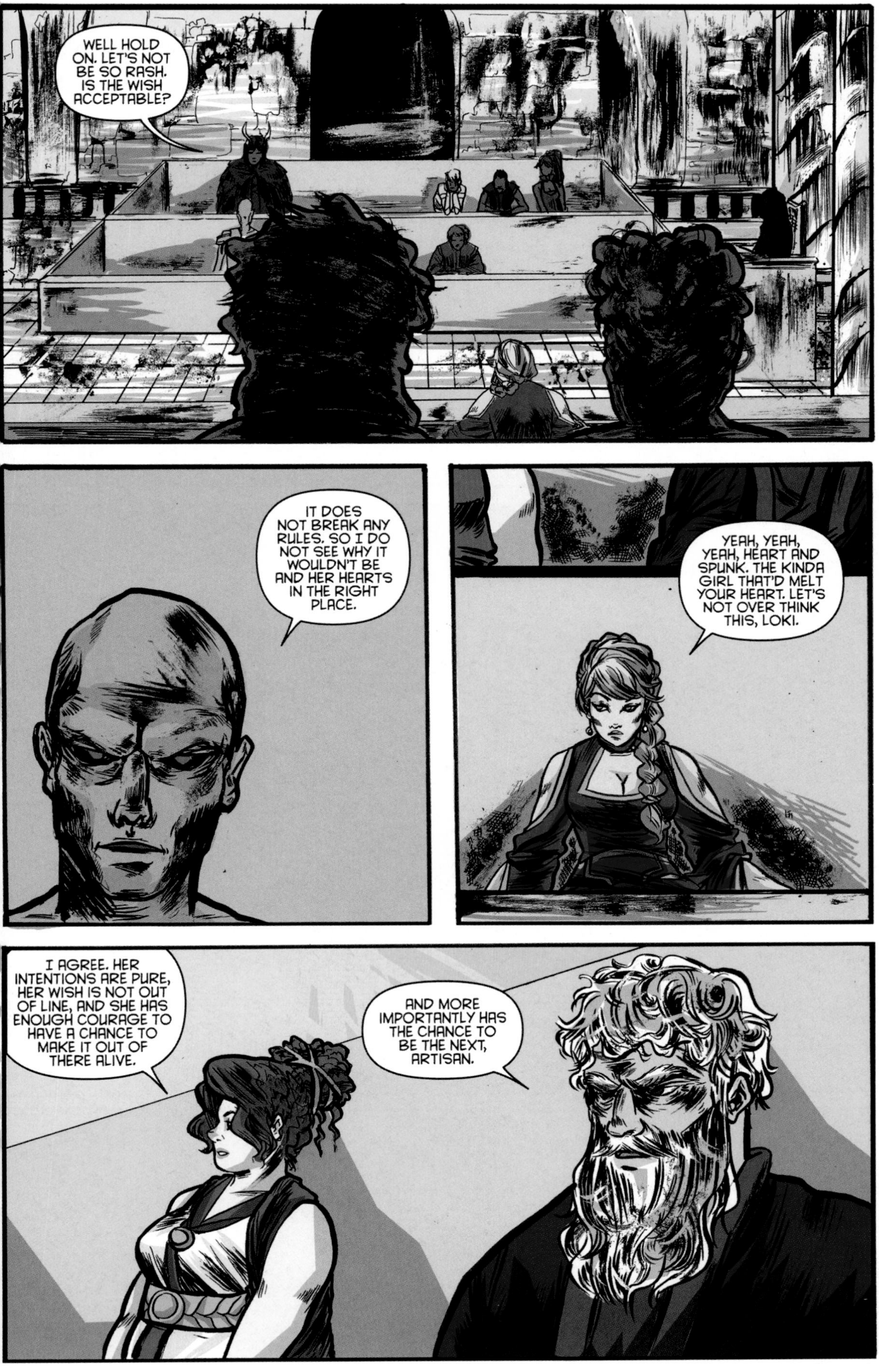
WELL HOLD ON. LET'S NOT BE SO RASH. IS THE WISH ACCEPTABLE?
IT DOES NOT BREAK ANY RULES. SO I DO NOT SEE WHY IT WOULDN'T BE AND HER HEARTS IN THE RIGHT PLACE.
YEAH, YEAH, YEAH, HEART AND SPUNK. THE KINDA GIRL THAT'D MELT YOUR HEART. LET'S NOT OVER THINK THIS, LOKI.
I AGREE. HER INTENTIONS ARE PURE, HER WISH IS NOT OUT OF LINE, AND SHE HAS ENOUGH COURAGE TO HAVE A CHANCE TO MAKE IT OUT OF THERE ALIVE.
AND MORE IMPORTANTLY HAS THE CHANCE TO BE THE NEXT, ARTISAN.

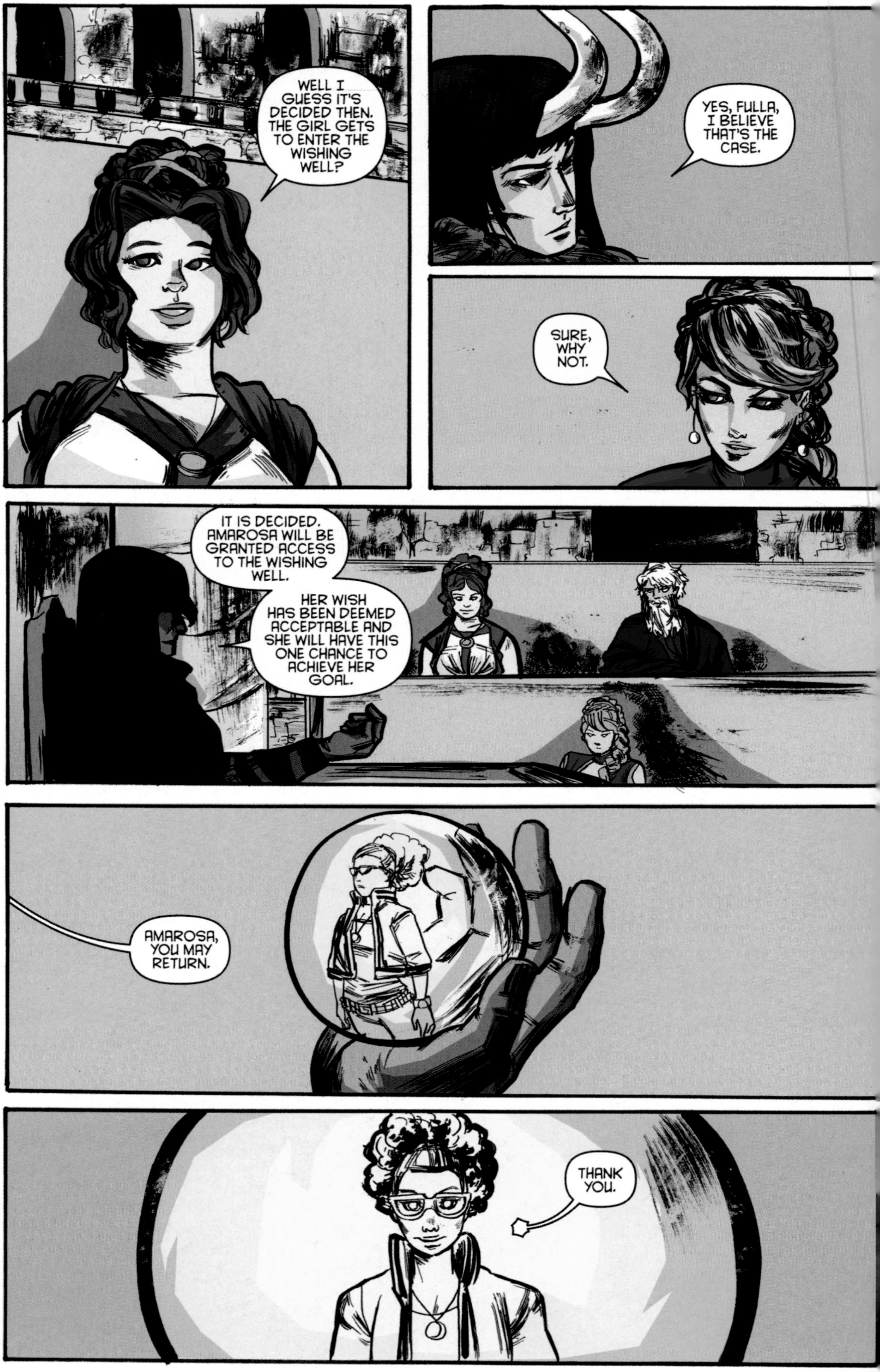
WELL I GUESS IT'S DECIDED THEN. THE GIRL GETS TO ENTER THE WISHING WELL?
YES, FULLA, I BELIEVE THAT'S THE CASE.
SURE, WHY NOT.
IT IS DECIDED. AMAROSA WILL BE GRANTED ACCESS TO THE WISHING WELL.
HER WISH HAS BEEN DEEMED ACCEPTABLE AND SHE WILL HAVE THIS ONE CHANCE TO ACHIEVE HER GOAL.
AMAROSA, YOU MAY RETURN.
THANK YOU.

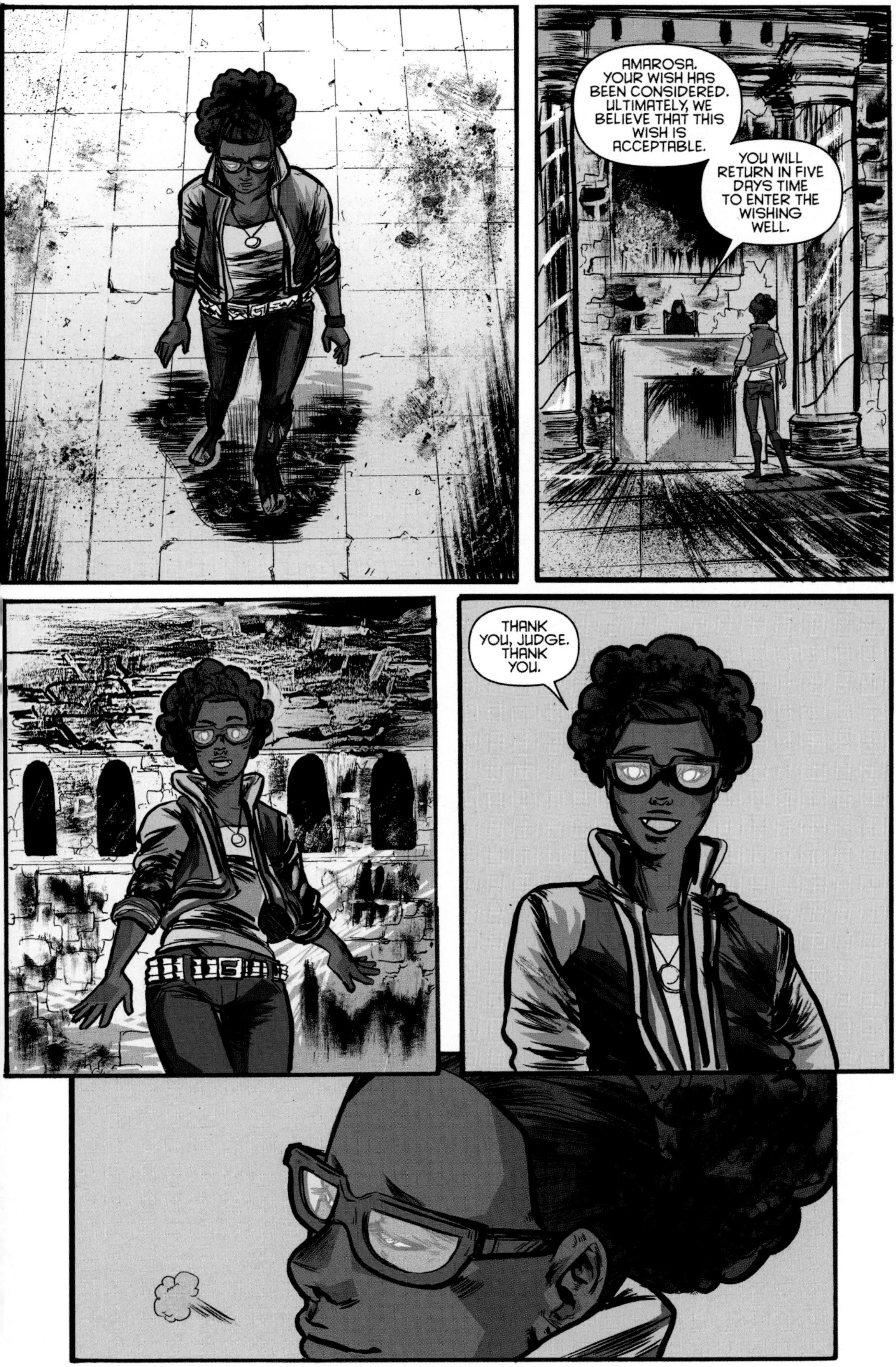
AMAROSA. YOUR WISH HAS BEEN CONSIDERED. ULTIMATELY, WE BELIEVE THAT THIS WISH IS ACCEPTABLE.
YOU WILL RETURN IN FIVE DAYS TIME TO ENTER THE WISHING WELL.
THANK YOU, JUDGE. THANK YOU.

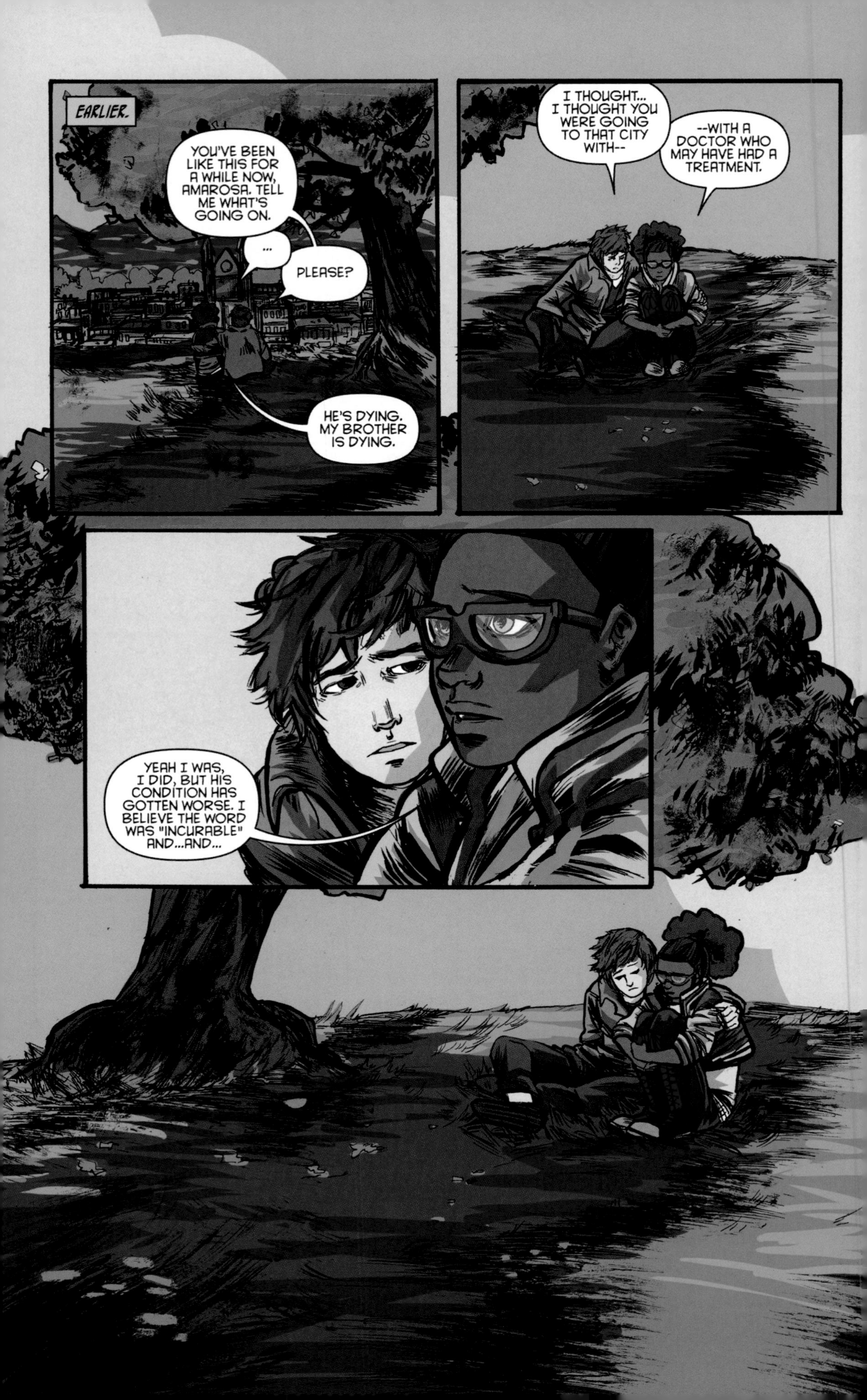
EARLIER.
YOU'VE BEEN LIKE THIS FOR A WHILE NOW, AMAROSA. TELL ME WHAT'S GOING ON.
...
PLEASE?
HE'S DYING. MY BROTHER IS DYING.
I THOUGHT... I THOUGHT YOU WERE GOING TO THAT CITY WITH--
--WITH A DOCTOR WHO MAY HAVE HAD A TREATMENT.
YEAH I WAS, I DID, BUT HIS CONDITION HAS GOTTEN WORSE. I BELIEVE THE WORD WAS "INCURABLE" AND...AND...

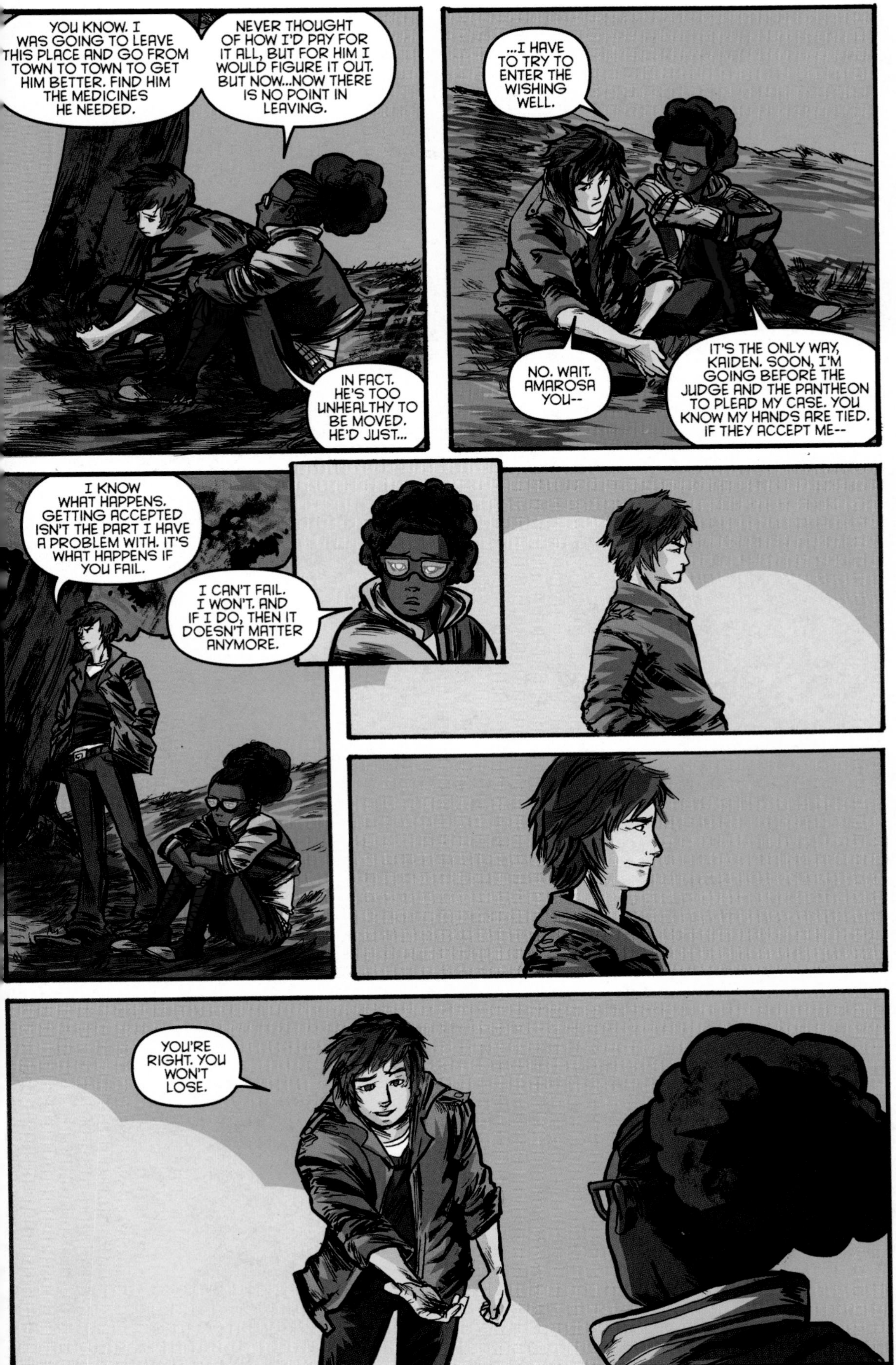
YOU KNOW. I WAS GOING TO LEAVE THIS PLACE AND GO FROM TOWN TO TOWN TO GET HIM BETTER. FIND HIM THE MEDICINES HE NEEDED.
NEVER THOUGHT OF HOW I'D PAY FOR IT ALL, BUT FOR HIM I WOULD FIGURE IT OUT. BUT NOW...NOW THERE IS NO POINT IN LEAVING.
IN FACT. HE'S TOO UNHEALTHY TO BE MOVED. HE'D JUST...
...I HAVE TO TRY TO ENTER THE WISHING WELL.
NO. WAIT. AMAROSA YOU--
IT'S THE ONLY WAY, KAIDEN. SOON, I'M GOING BEFORE THE JUDGE AND THE PANTHEON TO PLEAD MY CASE. YOU KNOW MY HANDS ARE TIED. IF THEY ACCEPT ME--
I KNOW WHAT HAPPENS. GETTING ACCEPTED ISN'T THE PART I HAVE A PROBLEM WITH. IT'S WHAT HAPPENS IF YOU FAIL.
I CAN'T FAIL. I WON'T. AND IF I DO, THEN IT DOESN'T MATTER ANYMORE.
YOU'RE RIGHT. YOU WON'T LOSE.

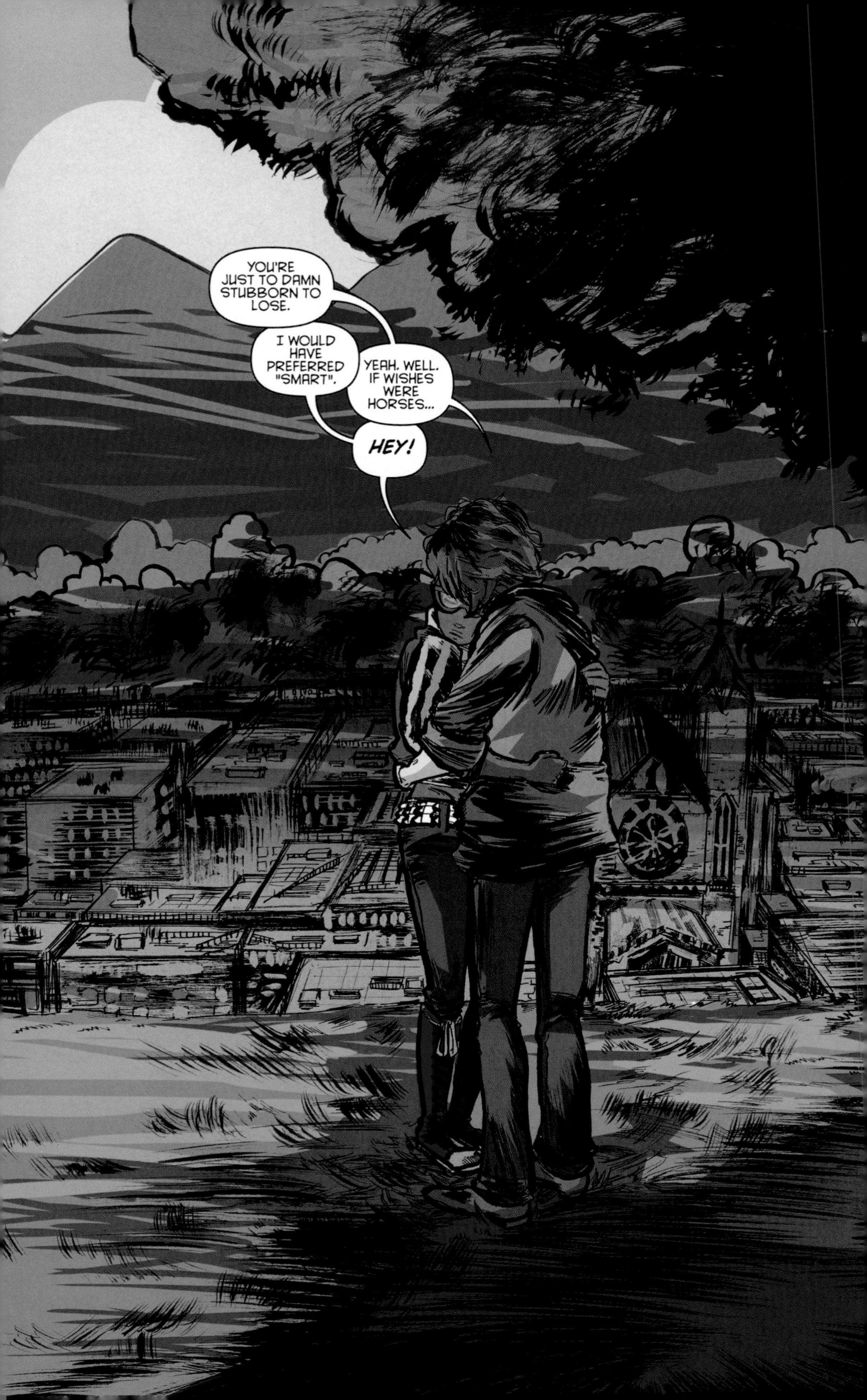
YOU'RE JUST TO DAMN STUBBORN TO LOSE.
I WOULD HAVE PREFERRED "SMART".
YEAH. WELL. IF WISHES WERE HORSES...
HEY!

CHAPTER ONE

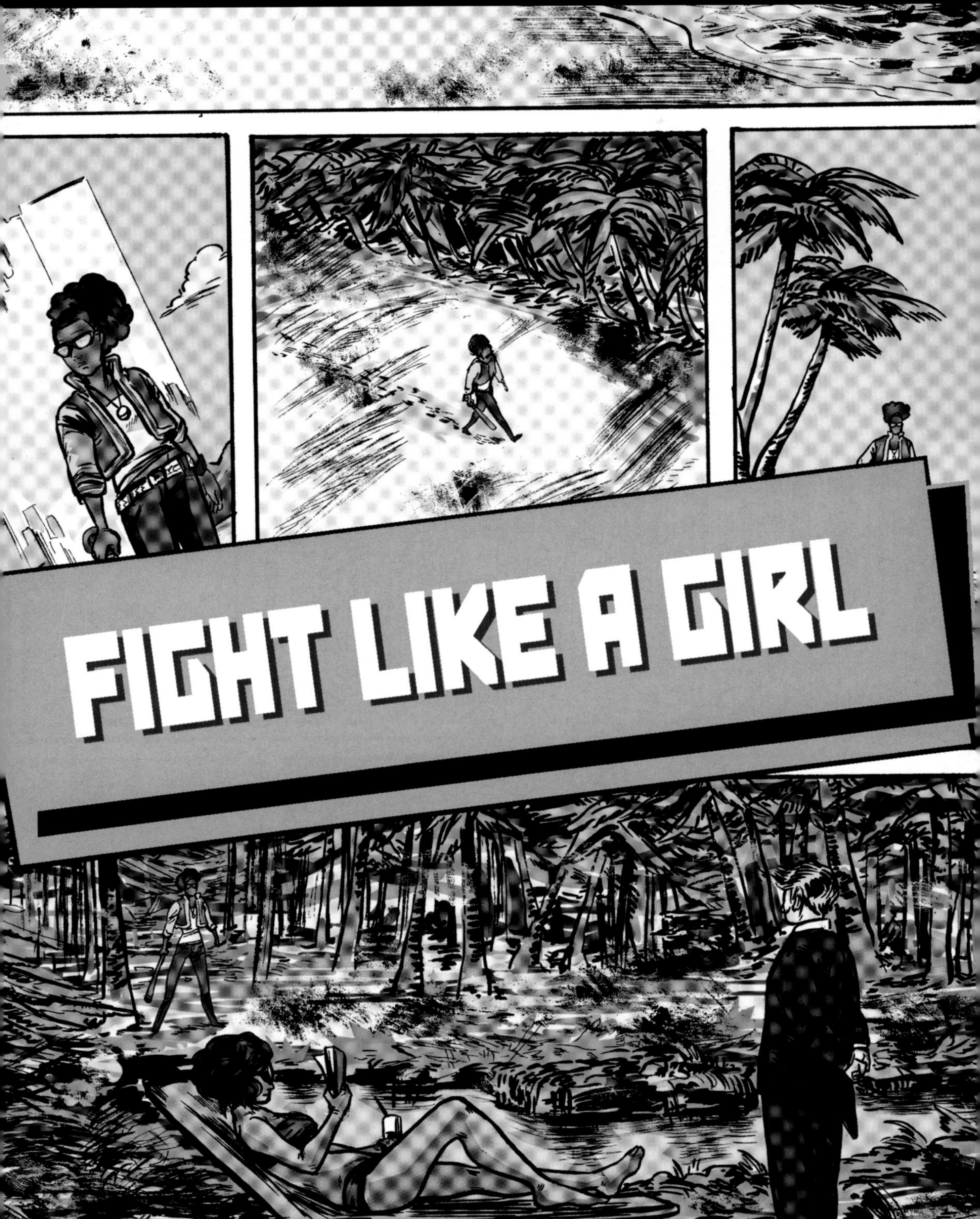
FIGHT LIKE A GIRL

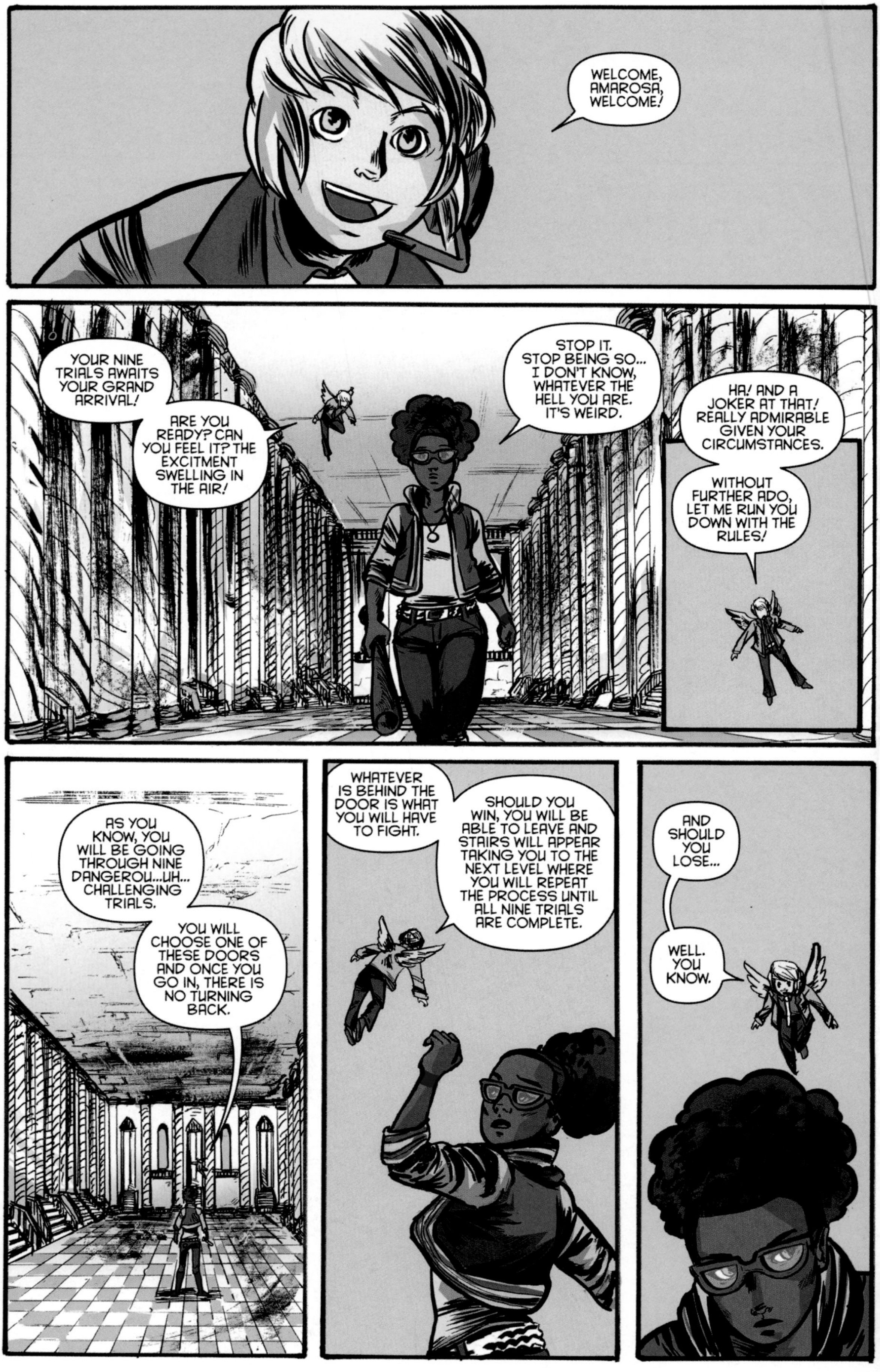
WELCOME, AMAROSA, WELCOME!
YOUR NINE TRIALS AWAITS YOUR GRAND ARRIVAL!
ARE YOU READY? CAN YOU FEEL IT? THE EXCITMENT SWELLING IN THE AIR!
STOP IT. STOP BEING SO... I DON'T KNOW, WHATEVER THE HELL YOU ARE. IT'S WEIRD.
HA! AND A JOKER AT THAT! REALLY ADMIRABLE GIVEN YOUR CIRCUMSTANCES.
WITHOUT FURTHER ADO, LET ME RUN YOU DOWN WITH THE RULES!
AS YOU KNOW, YOU WILL BE GOING THROUGH NINE DANGEROU...UH... CHALLENGING TRIALS.
YOU WILL CHOOSE ONE OF THESE DOORS AND ONCE YOU GO IN, THERE IS NO TURNING BACK.
WHATEVER IS BEHIND THE DOOR IS WHAT YOU WILL HAVE TO FIGHT.
SHOULD YOU WIN, YOU WILL BE ABLE TO LEAVE AND STAIRS WILL APPEAR TAKING YOU TO THE NEXT LEVEL WHERE YOU WILL REPEAT THE PROCESS UNTIL ALL NINE TRIALS ARE COMPLETE.
AND SHOULD YOU LOSE...
WELL. YOU KNOW.

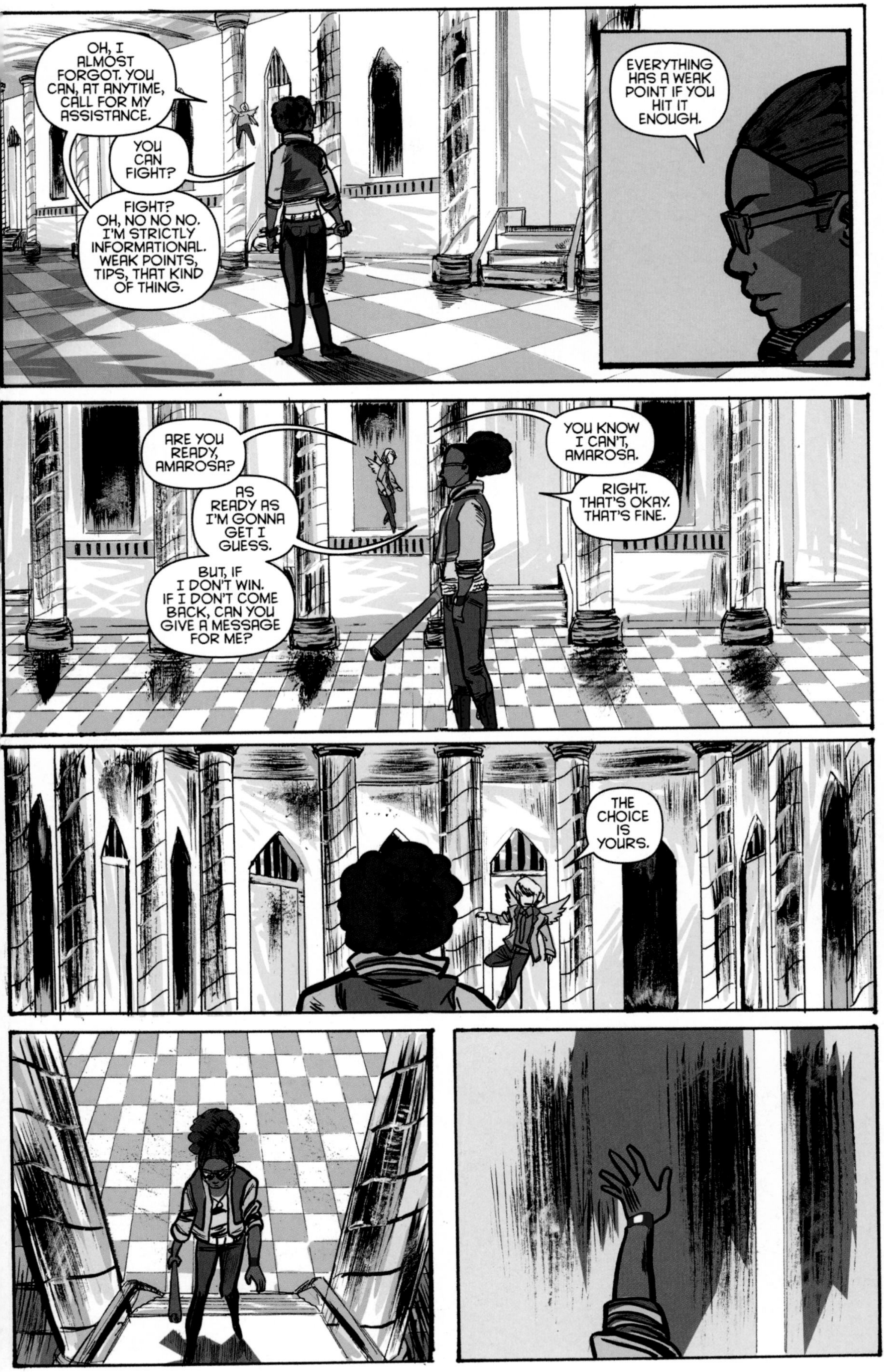
OH, I ALMOST FORGOT. YOU CAN, AT ANYTIME, CALL FOR MY ASSISTANCE.
YOU CAN FIGHT?
FIGHT? OH, NO NO NO. I'M STRICTLY INFORMATIONAL. WEAK POINTS, TIPS, THAT KIND OF THING.
EVERYTHING HAS A WEAK POINT IF YOU HIT IT ENOUGH.
ARE YOU READY, AMAROSA?
AS READY AS I'M GONNA GET I GUESS.
BUT, IF I DON'T WIN. IF I DON'T COME BACK, CAN YOU GIVE A MESSAGE FOR ME?
YOU KNOW I CAN'T, AMAROSA.
RIGHT. THAT'S OKAY. THAT'S FINE.
THE CHOICE IS YOURS.

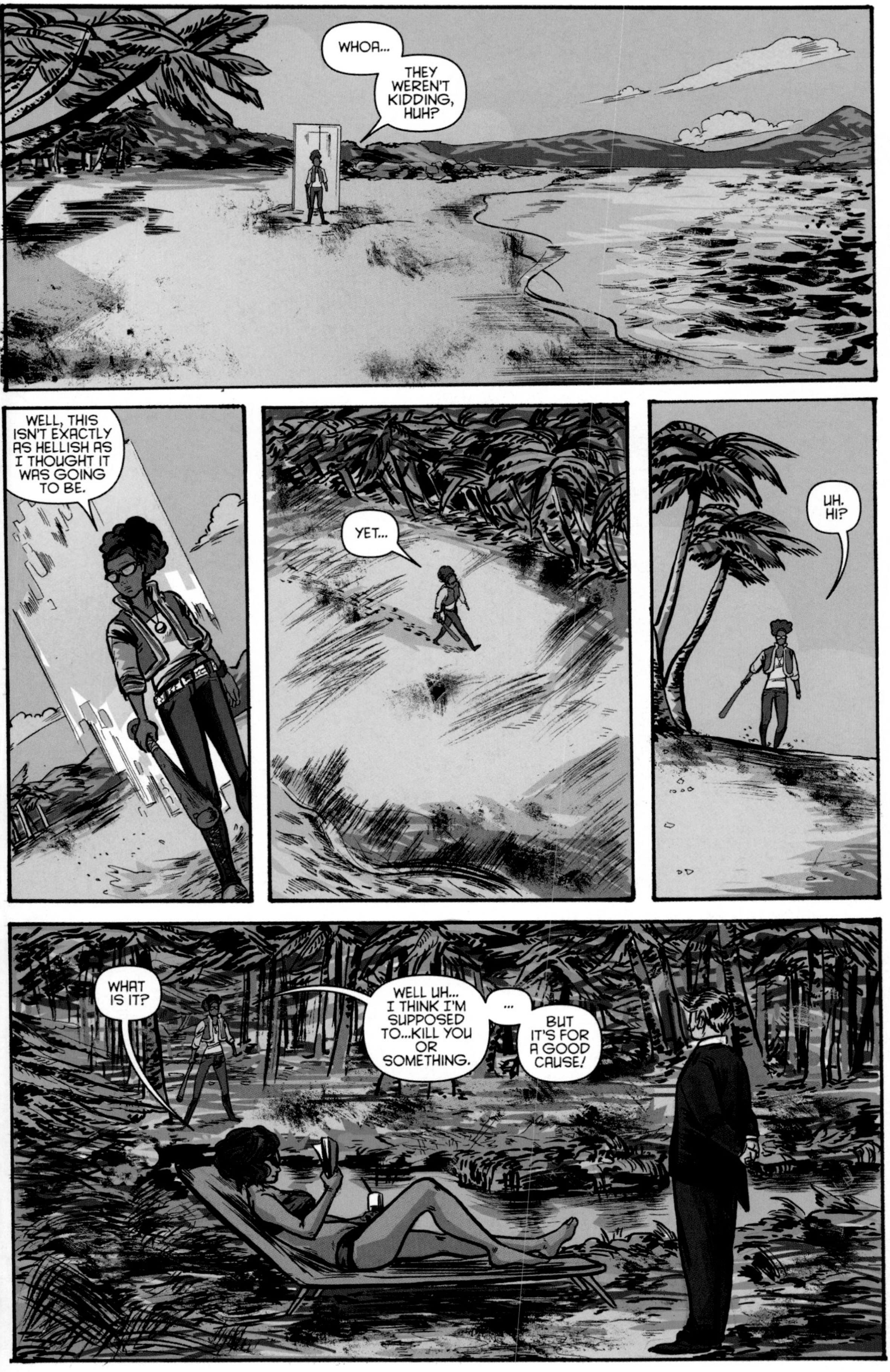
WHOA...
THEY WEREN'T KIDDING, HUH?
WELL, THIS ISN'T EXACTLY AS HELLISH AS I THOUGHT IT WAS GOING TO BE.
YET...
UH. HI?
WHAT IS IT?
WELL UH... I THINK I'M SUPPOSED TO...KILL YOU OR SOMETHING.
...
BUT IT'S FOR A GOOD CAUSE!

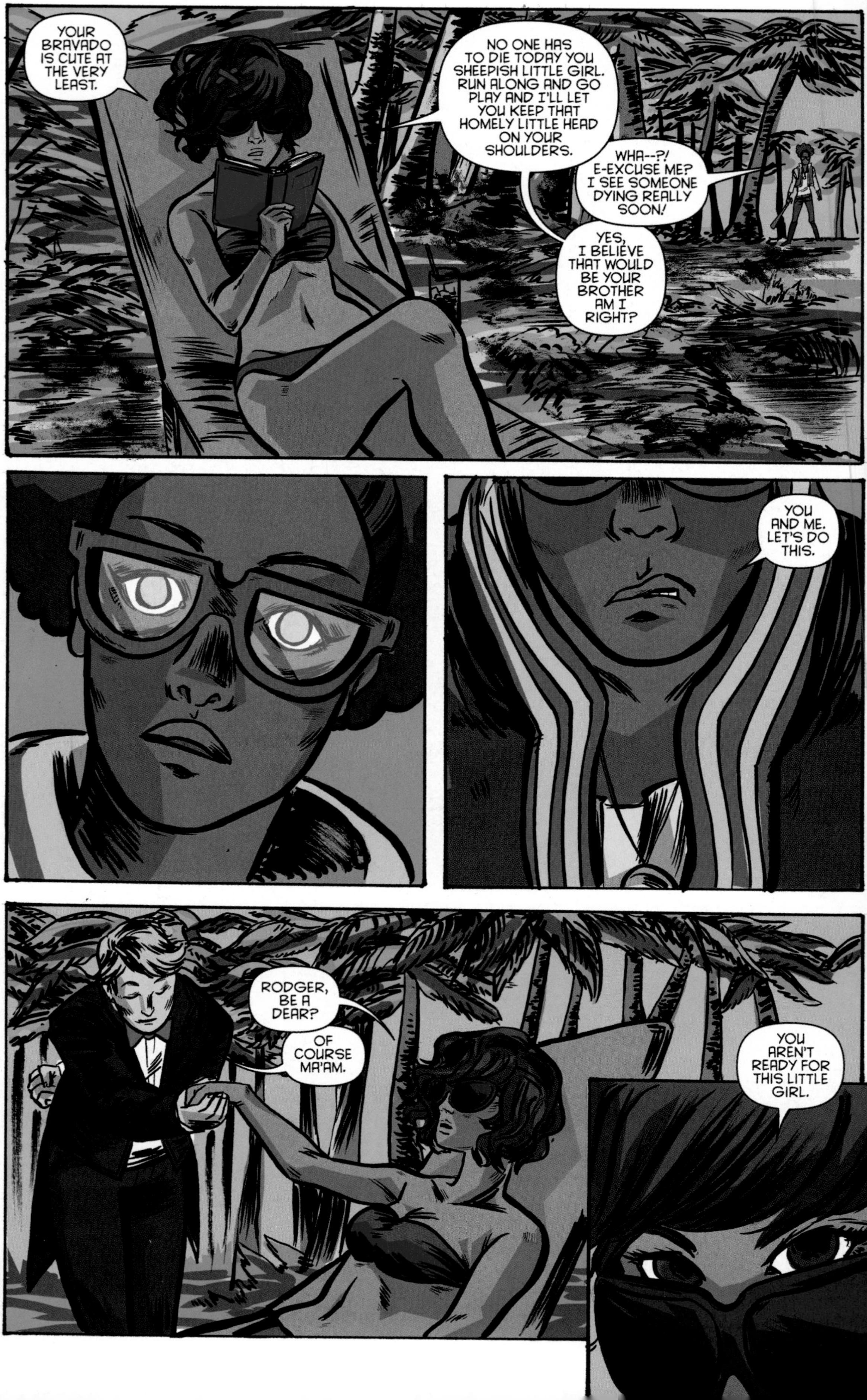
YOUR BRAVADO IS CUTE AT THE VERY LEAST.
NO ONE HAS TO DIE TODAY YOU SHEEPISH LITTLE GIRL. RUN ALONG AND GO PLAY AND I'LL LET YOU KEEP THAT HOMELY LITTLE HEAD ON YOUR SHOULDERS.
WHA--?! E-EXCUSE ME? I SEE SOMEONE DYING REALLY SOON!
YES, I BELIEVE THAT WOULD BE YOUR BROTHER AM I RIGHT?
YOU AND ME. LET'S DO THIS.
RODGER, BE A DEAR?
OF COURSE MA'AM.
YOU AREN'T READY FOR THIS LITTLE GIRL.

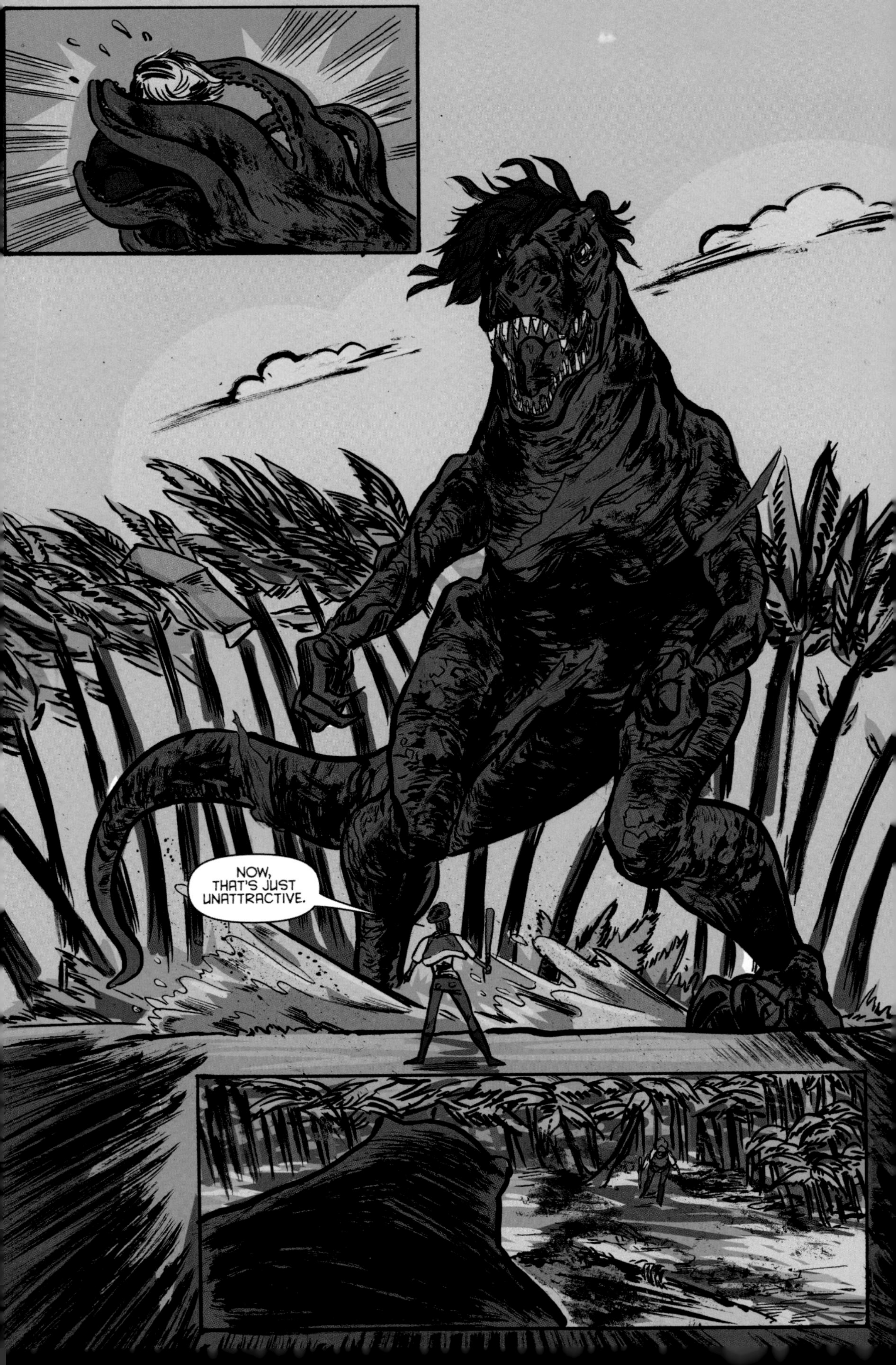
NOW, THAT'S JUST UNATTRACTIVE.

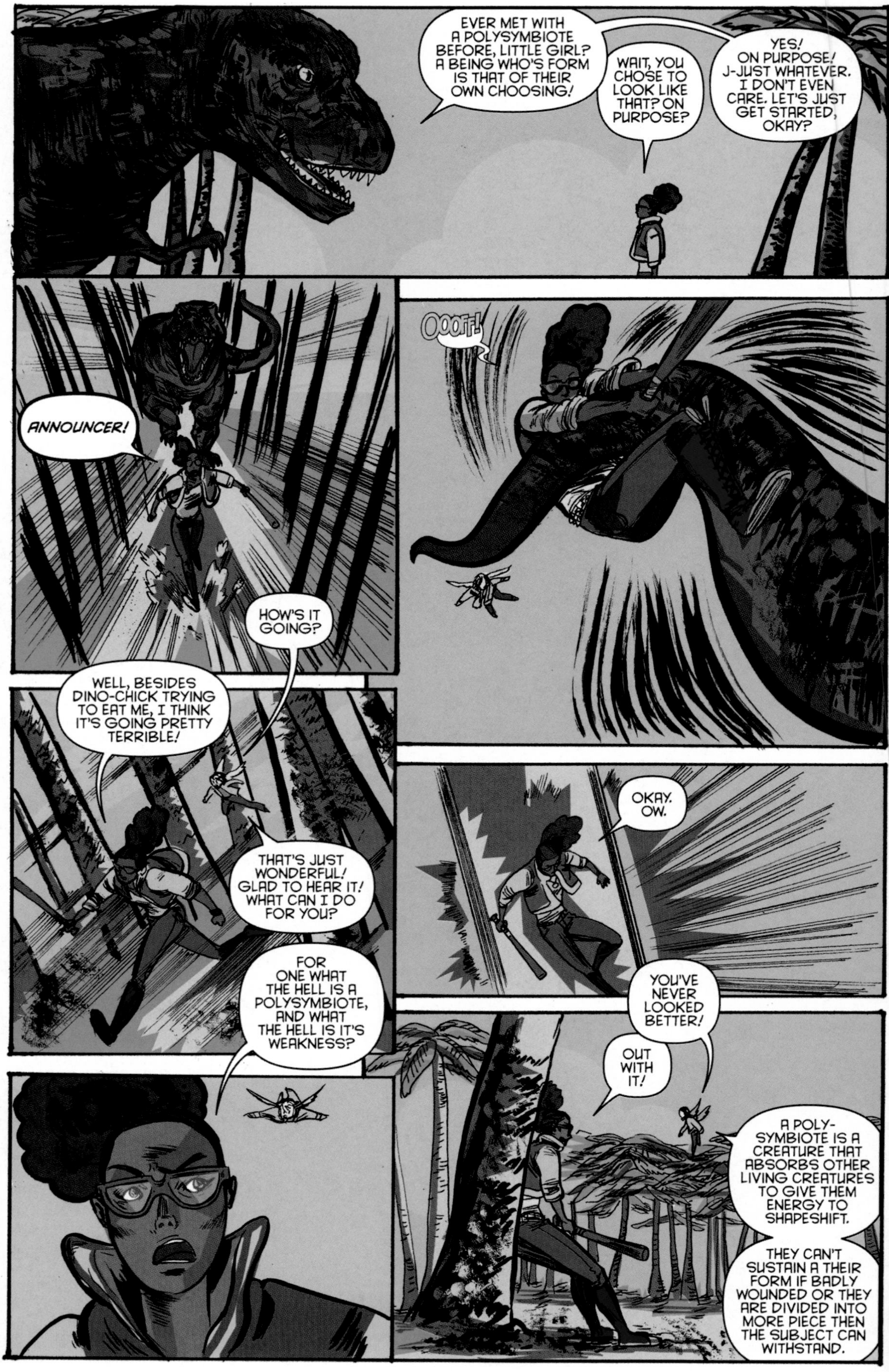
EVER MET WITH A POLYSYMBIOTE BEFORE, LITTLE GIRL? A BEING WHO'S FORM IS THAT OF THEIR OWN CHOOSING!
WAIT, YOU CHOSE TO LOOK LIKE THAT? ON PURPOSE?
YES! ON PURPOSE! J-JUST WHATEVER. I DON'T EVEN CARE. LET'S JUST GET STARTED, OKAY?
ANNOUNCER!
OOOFF!
HOW'S IT GOING?
WELL, BESIDES DINO-CHICK TRYING TO EAT ME, I THINK IT'S GOING PRETTY TERRIBLE!
THAT'S JUST WONDERFUL! GLAD TO HEAR IT! WHAT CAN I DO FOR YOU?
OKAY. OW.
FOR ONE WHAT THE HELL IS A POLYSYMBIOTE, AND WHAT THE HELL IS IT'S WEAKNESS?
YOU'VE NEVER LOOKED BETTER!
OUT WITH IT!
A POLY-SYMBIOTE IS A CREATURE THAT ABSORBS OTHER LIVING CREATURES TO GIVE THEM ENERGY TO SHAPESHIFT.
THEY CAN'T SUSTAIN A THEIR FORM IF BADLY WOUNDED OR THEY ARE DIVIDED INTO MORE PIECE THEN THE SUBJECT CAN WITHSTAND.

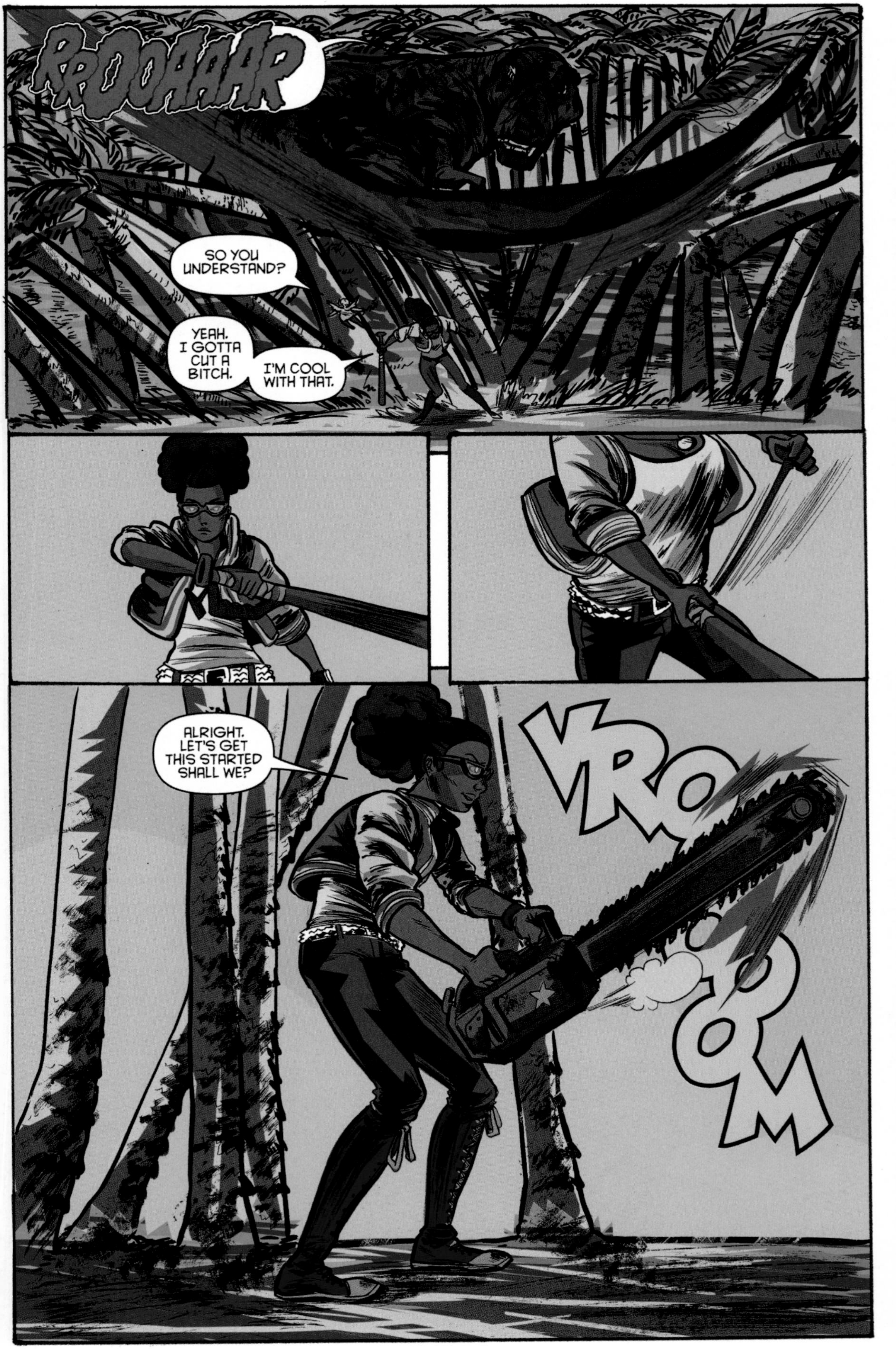
RROOAAAR
SO YOU UNDERSTAND?
YEAH. I GOTTA CUT A BITCH.
I'M COOL WITH THAT.
ALRIGHT. LET'S GET THIS STARTED SHALL WE?
VROOOOOM

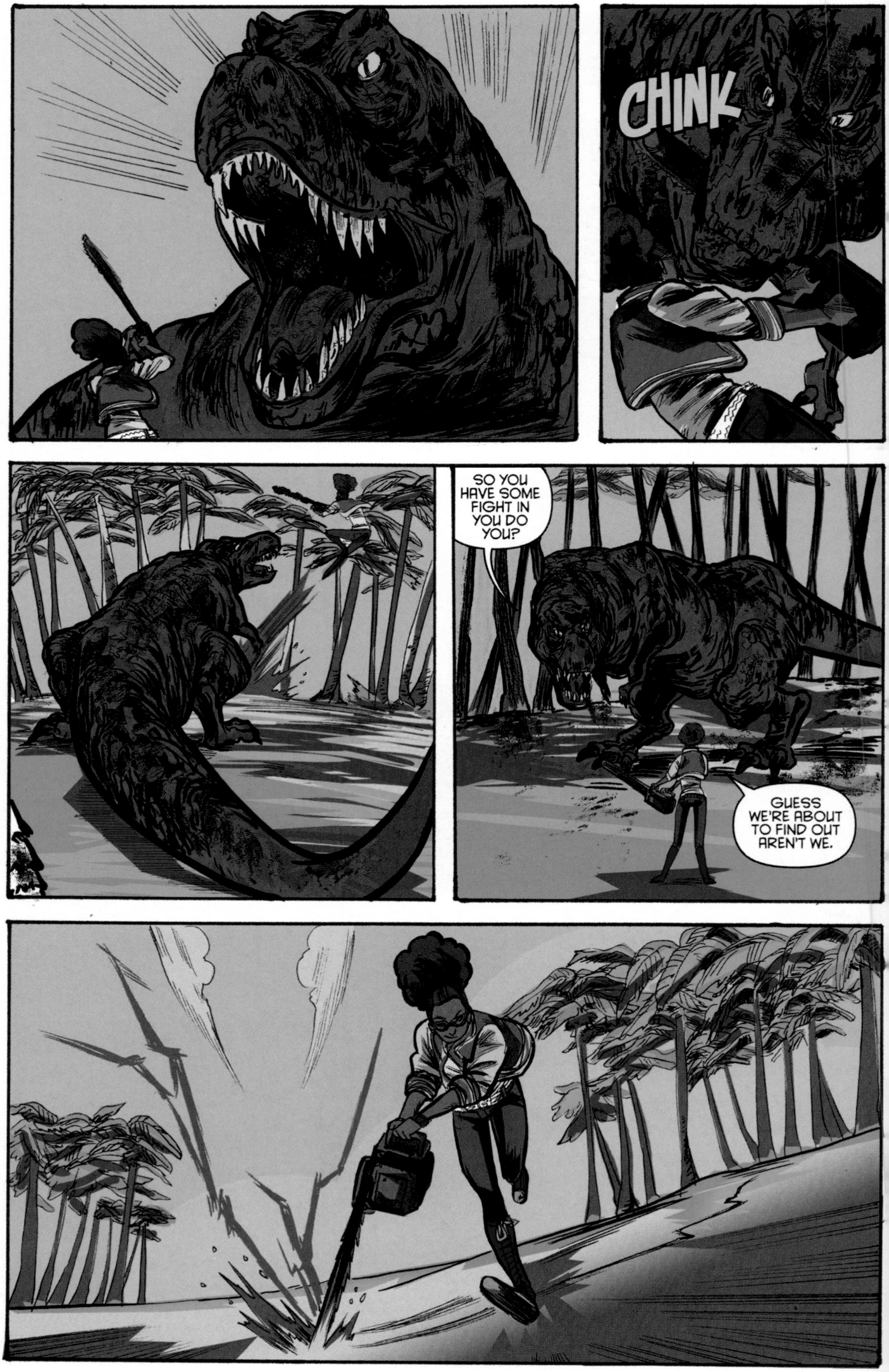
CHINK
SO YOU HAVE SOME FIGHT IN YOU DO YOU?
GUESS WE'RE ABOUT TO FIND OUT AREN'T WE.

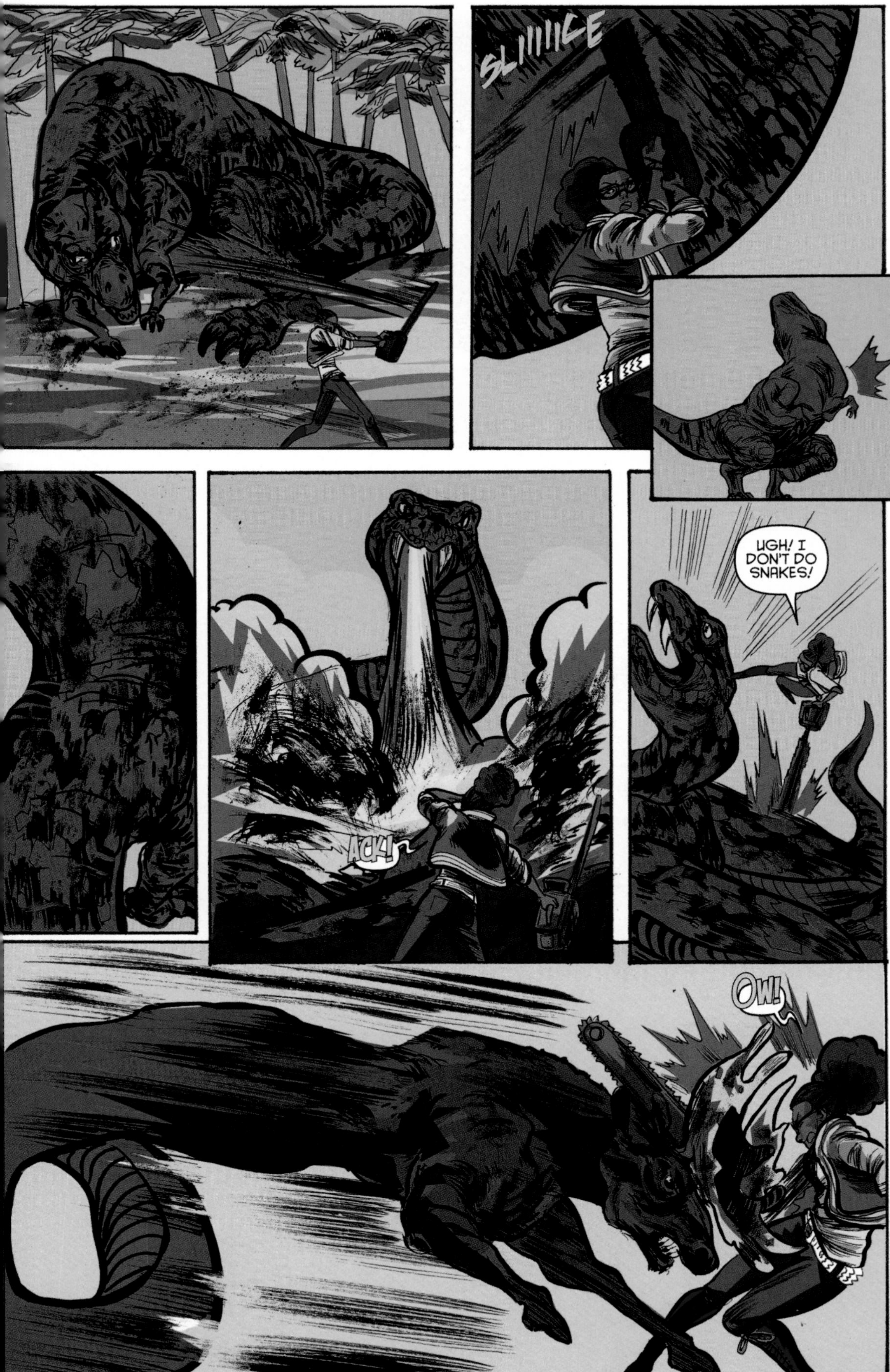
SLIIIIICE
ACK!
UGH! I DON'T DO SNAKES!
OW!

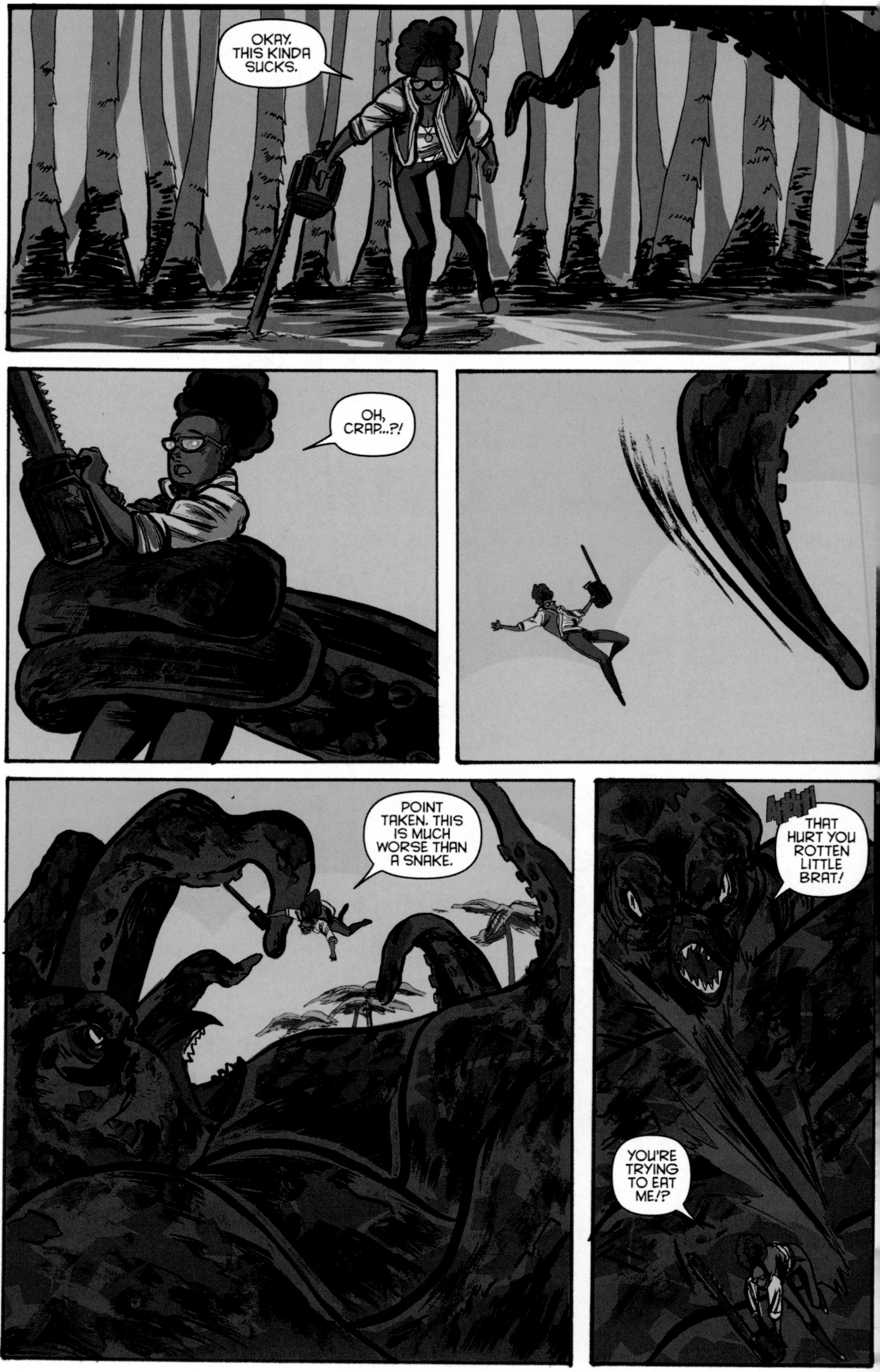
OKAY. THIS KINDA SUCKS.
OH, CRAP...?!
POINT TAKEN. THIS IS MUCH WORSE THAN A SNAKE.
THAT HURT YOU ROTTEN LITTLE BRAT!
YOU'RE TRYING TO EAT ME!?

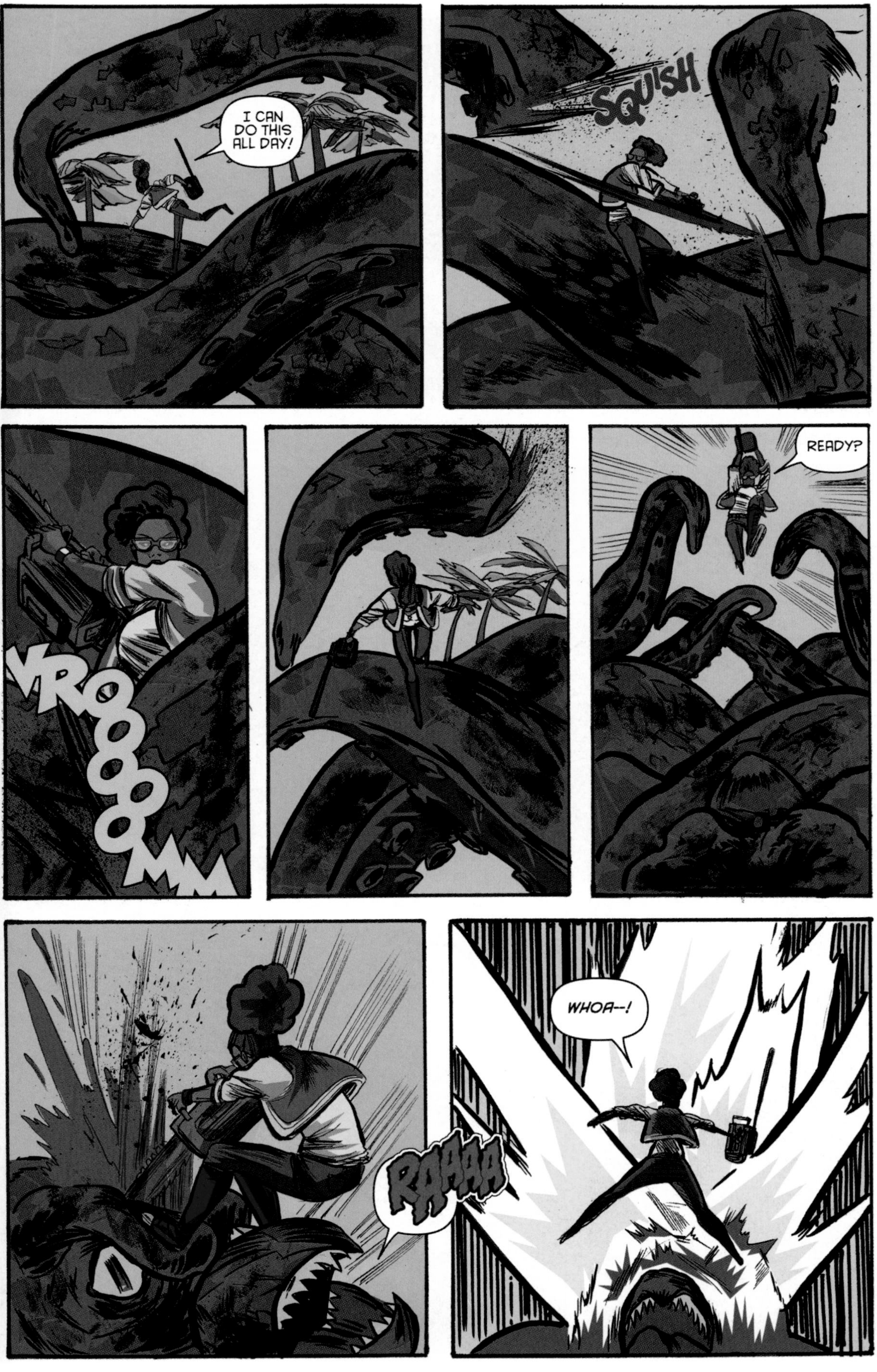
I CAN DO THIS ALL DAY!
SQUISH
VROOOOOMMM
READY?
RAAAA
WHOA--!

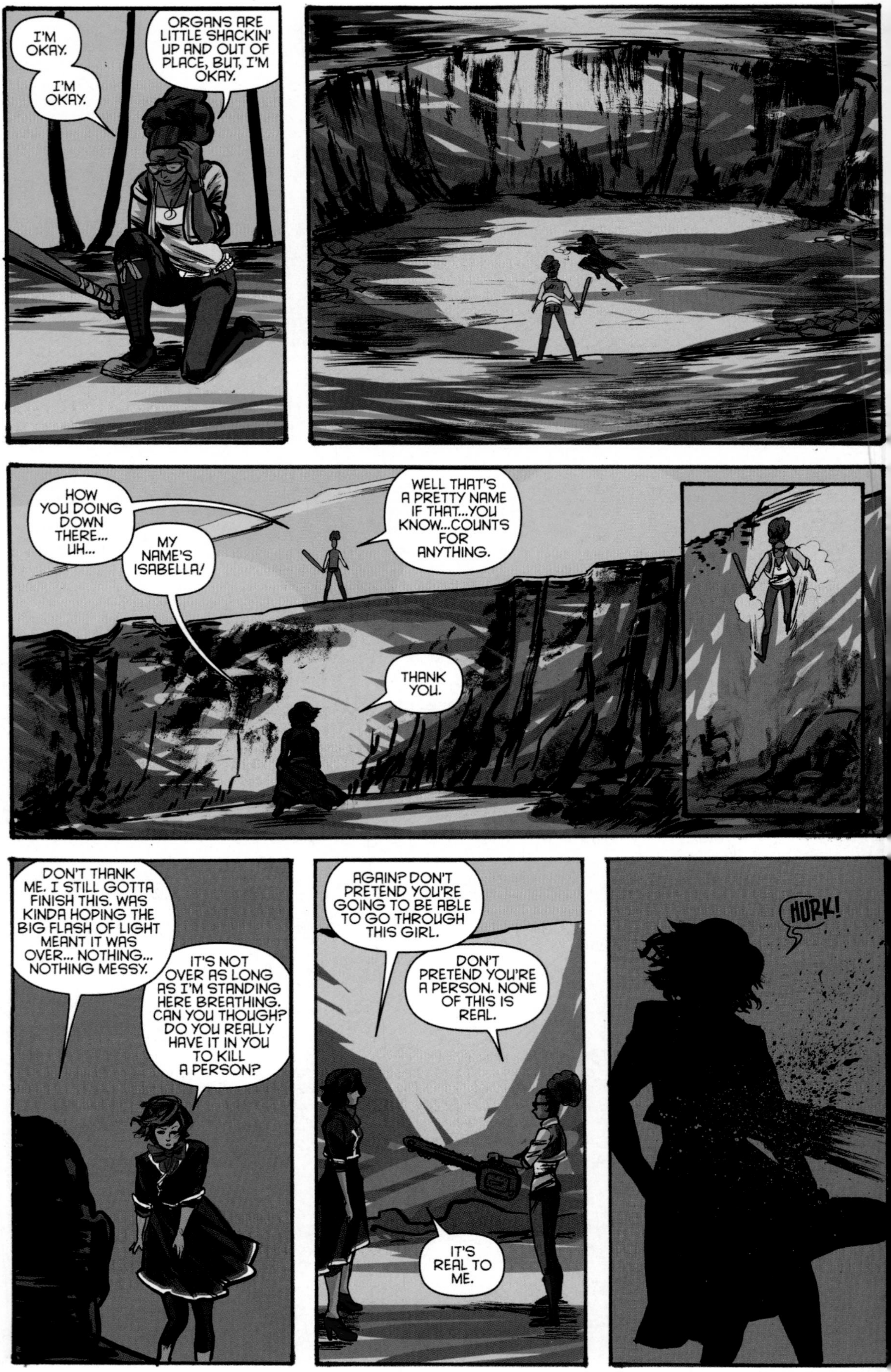
I'M OKAY.
I'M OKAY.
ORGANS ARE LITTLE SHACKIN' UP AND OUT OF PLACE, BUT, I'M OKAY.
HOW YOU DOING DOWN THERE... UH...
MY NAME'S ISABELLA!
WELL THAT'S A PRETTY NAME IF THAT...YOU KNOW...COUNTS FOR ANYTHING.
THANK YOU.
DON'T THANK ME. I STILL GOTTA FINISH THIS. WAS KINDA HOPING THE BIG FLASH OF LIGHT MEANT IT WAS OVER... NOTHING... NOTHING MESSY.
IT'S NOT OVER AS LONG AS I'M STANDING HERE BREATHING. CAN YOU THOUGH? DO YOU REALLY HAVE IT IN YOU TO KILL A PERSON?
AGAIN? DON'T PRETEND YOU'RE GOING TO BE ABLE TO GO THROUGH THIS GIRL.
DON'T PRETEND YOU'RE A PERSON. NONE OF THIS IS REAL.
IT'S REAL TO ME.
HURK!

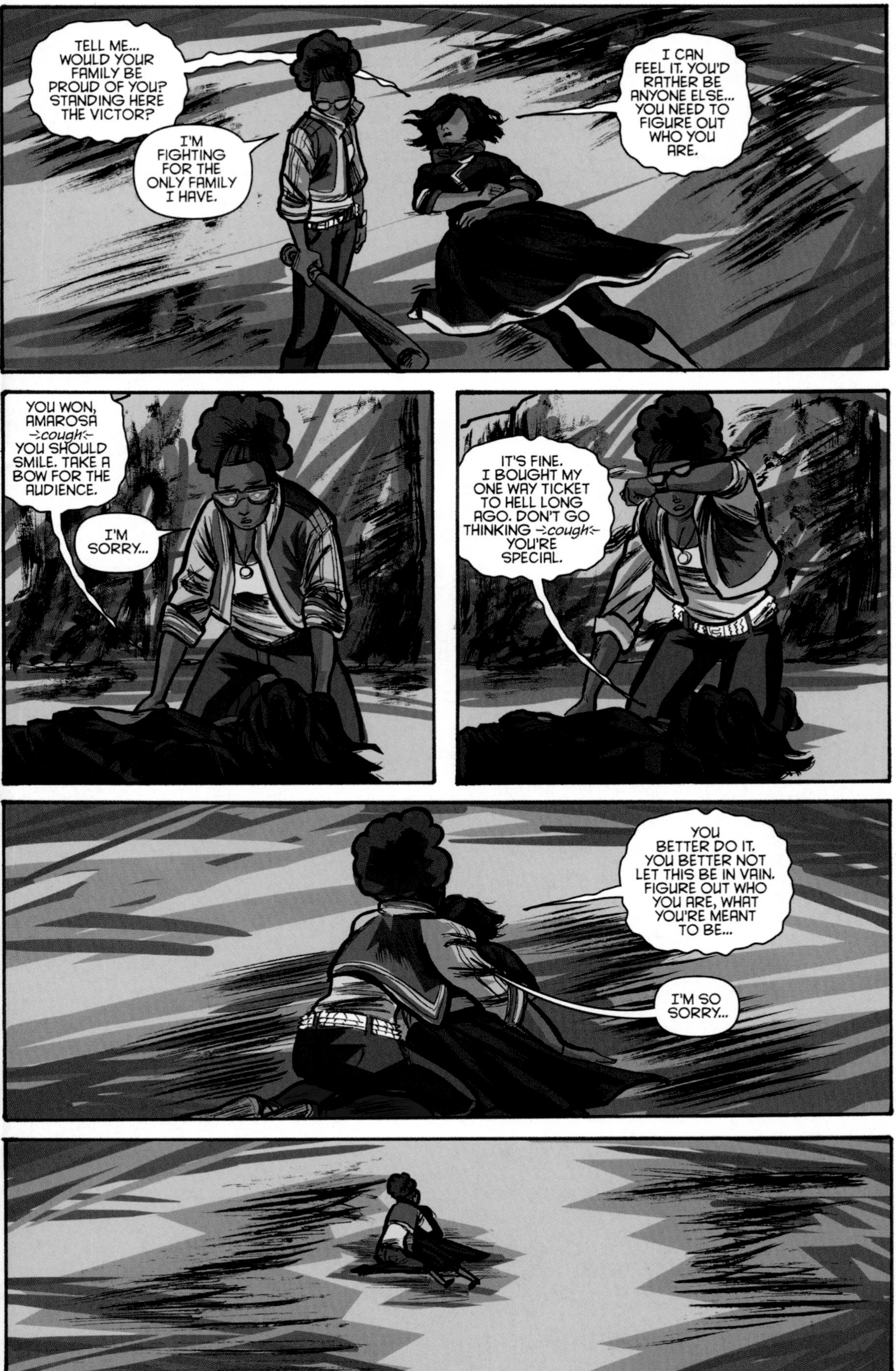
TELL ME... WOULD YOUR FAMILY BE PROUD OF YOU? STANDING HERE THE VICTOR?
I'M FIGHTING FOR THE ONLY FAMILY I HAVE.
I CAN FEEL IT. YOU'D RATHER BE ANYONE ELSE... YOU NEED TO FIGURE OUT WHO YOU ARE.
YOU WON, AMAROSA -cough- YOU SHOULD SMILE. TAKE A BOW FOR THE AUDIENCE.
I'M SORRY...
IT'S FINE. I BOUGHT MY ONE WAY TICKET TO HELL LONG AGO. DON'T GO THINKING -cough- YOU'RE SPECIAL.
YOU BETTER DO IT. YOU BETTER NOT LET THIS BE IN VAIN. FIGURE OUT WHO YOU ARE, WHAT YOU'RE MEANT TO BE...
I'M SO SORRY...

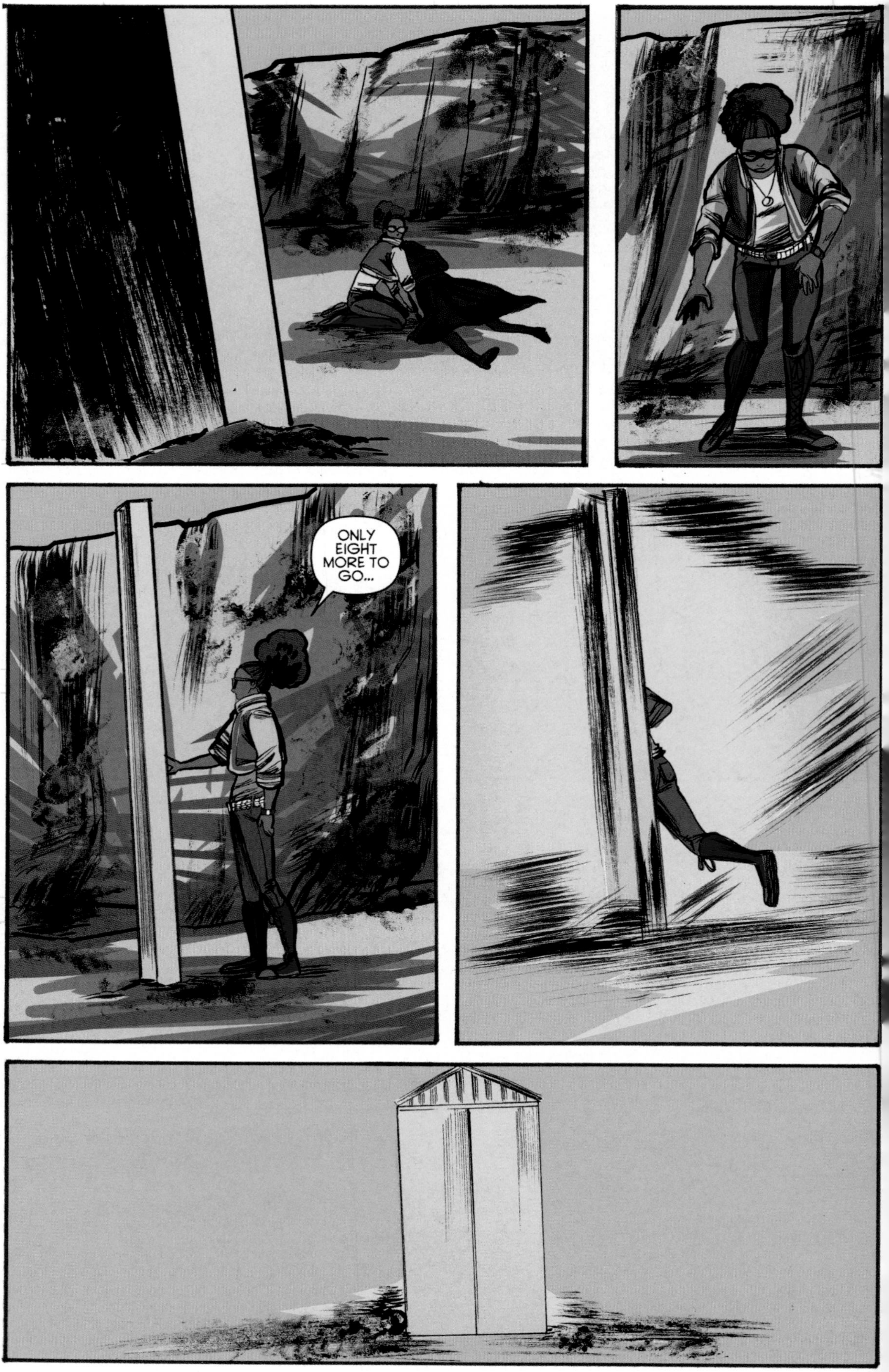
ONLY EIGHT MORE TO GO...

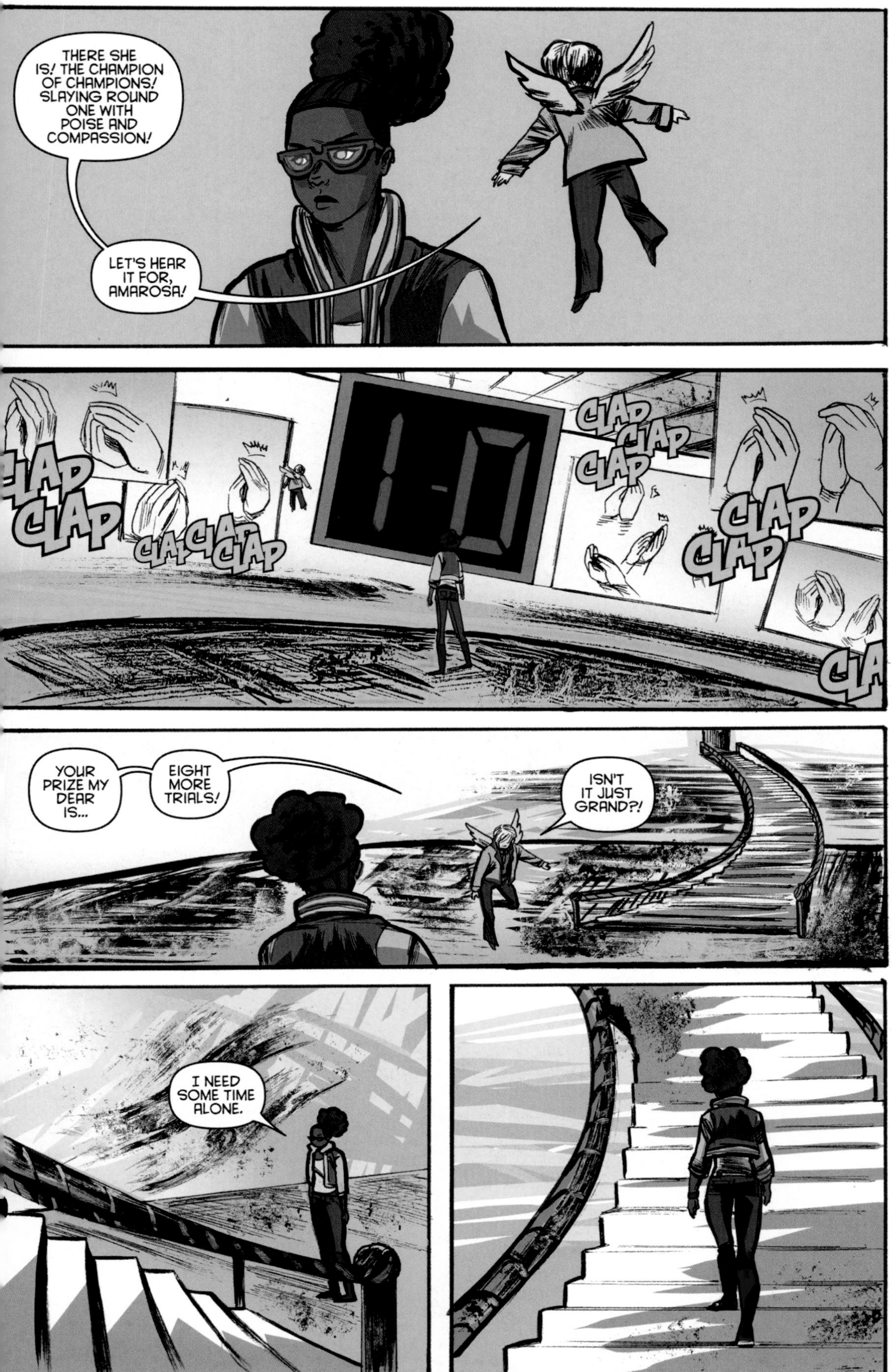
THERE SHE IS! THE CHAMPION OF CHAMPIONS! SLAYING ROUND ONE WITH POISE AND COMPASSION!
LET'S HEAR IT FOR, AMAROSA!
CLAP CLAP
CLAP CLAP CLAP
1-0
CLAP CLAP CLAP
CLAP CLAP
YOUR PRIZE MY DEAR IS...
EIGHT MORE TRIALS!
ISN'T IT JUST GRAND?!
I NEED SOME TIME ALONE.

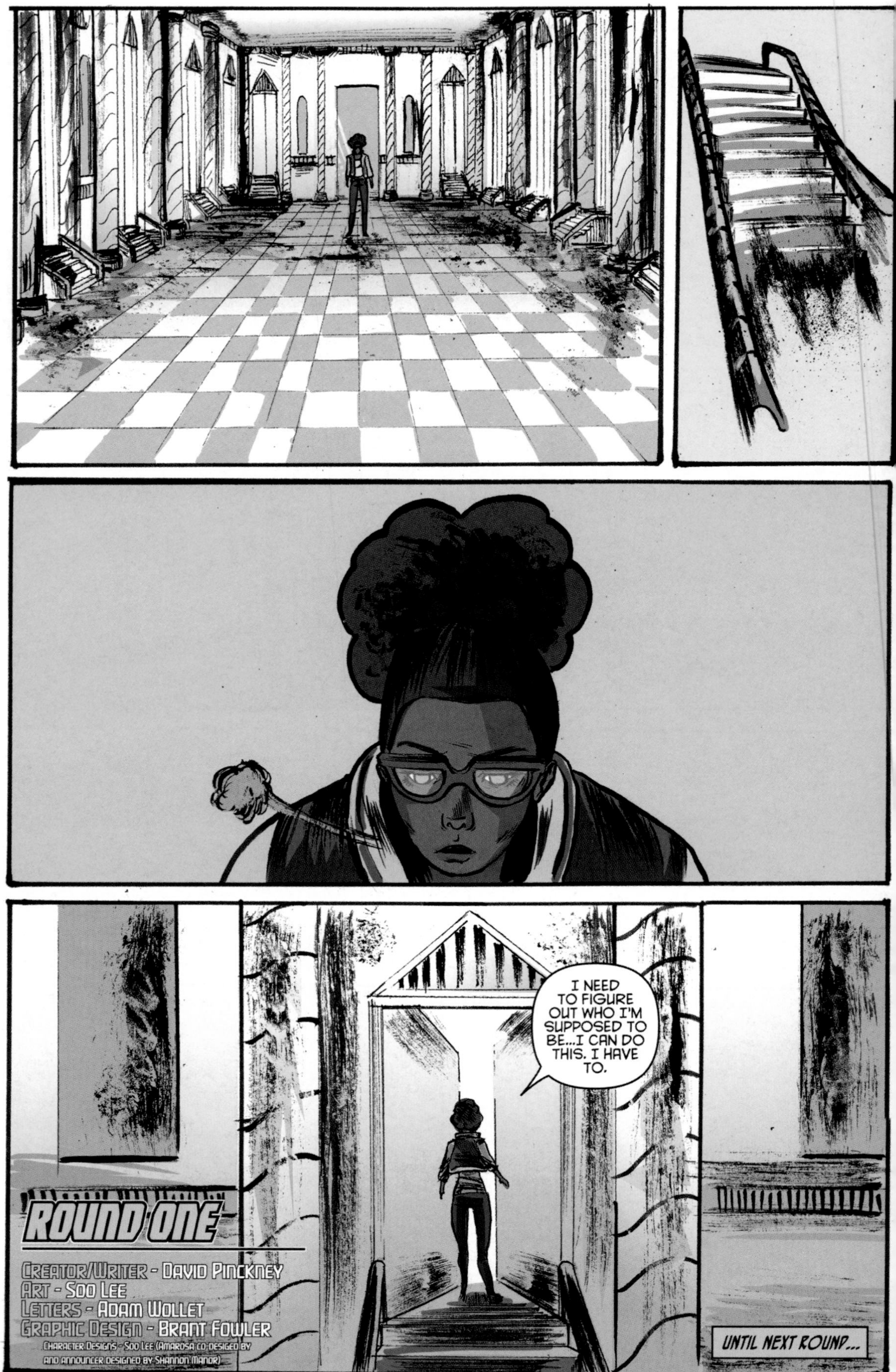
I NEED TO FIGURE OUT WHO I'M SUPPOSED TO BE...I CAN DO THIS. I HAVE TO.
ROUND ONE
CREATOR/WRITER - DAVID PINCKNEY
ART - SOO LEE
LETTERS - ADAM WOLLET
GRAPHIC DESIGN - BRANT FOWLER
CHARACTER DESIGNS - SOO LEE (AMAROSA CO-DESIGED BY AND ANNOUNCER DESIGNED BY SHANNON MANOR)
UNTIL NEXT ROUND...

Bryan Seaton: Publisher - Kevin Freeman: President - Creative Director: Dave Dwonch - Editor In Chief: Shawn Gabborin
Co-Directors of Marketing: Jamal Igle & Kelly Dale - Social Media Director: Jim Dietz - Knock Out: Chad Cicconi - Submissions Editor: Colleen Boyd

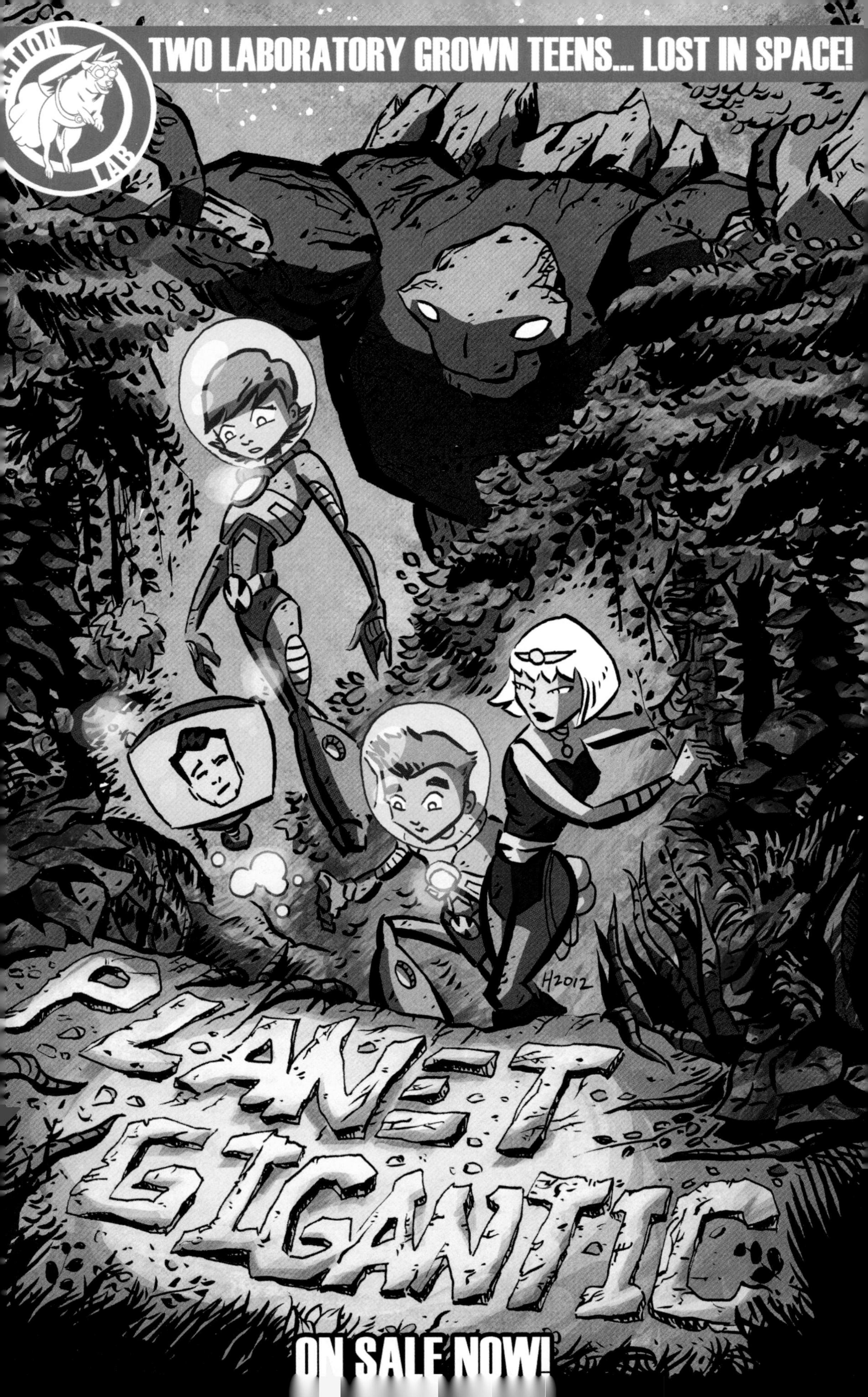
TWO LABORATORY GROWN TEENS... LOST IN SPACE!
PLANET GIGANTIC
H2012
ON SALE NOW!

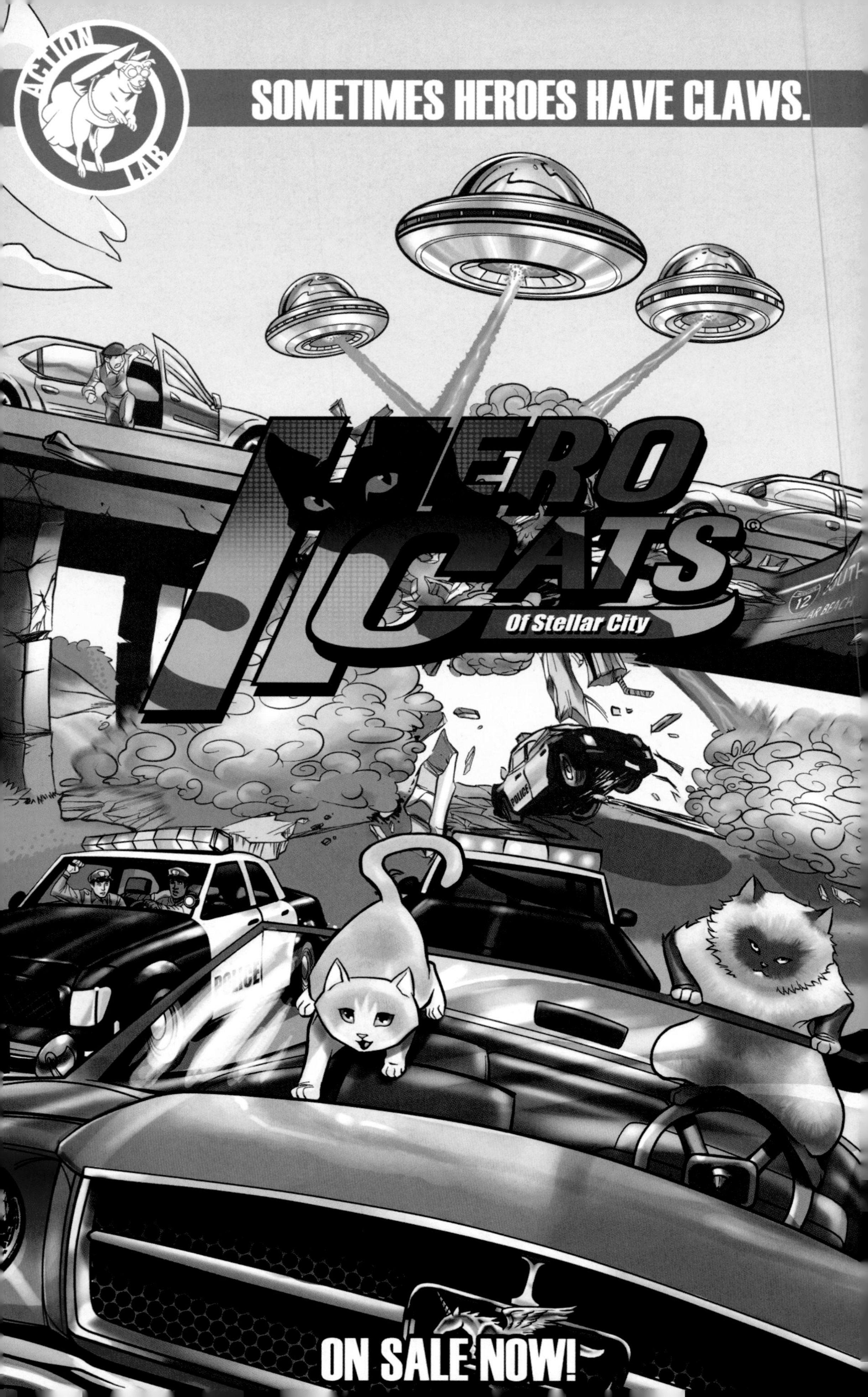
ACTION LAB
SOMETIMES HEROES HAVE CLAWS.
HERO CATS
Of Stellar City
POLICE
ON SALE NOW!

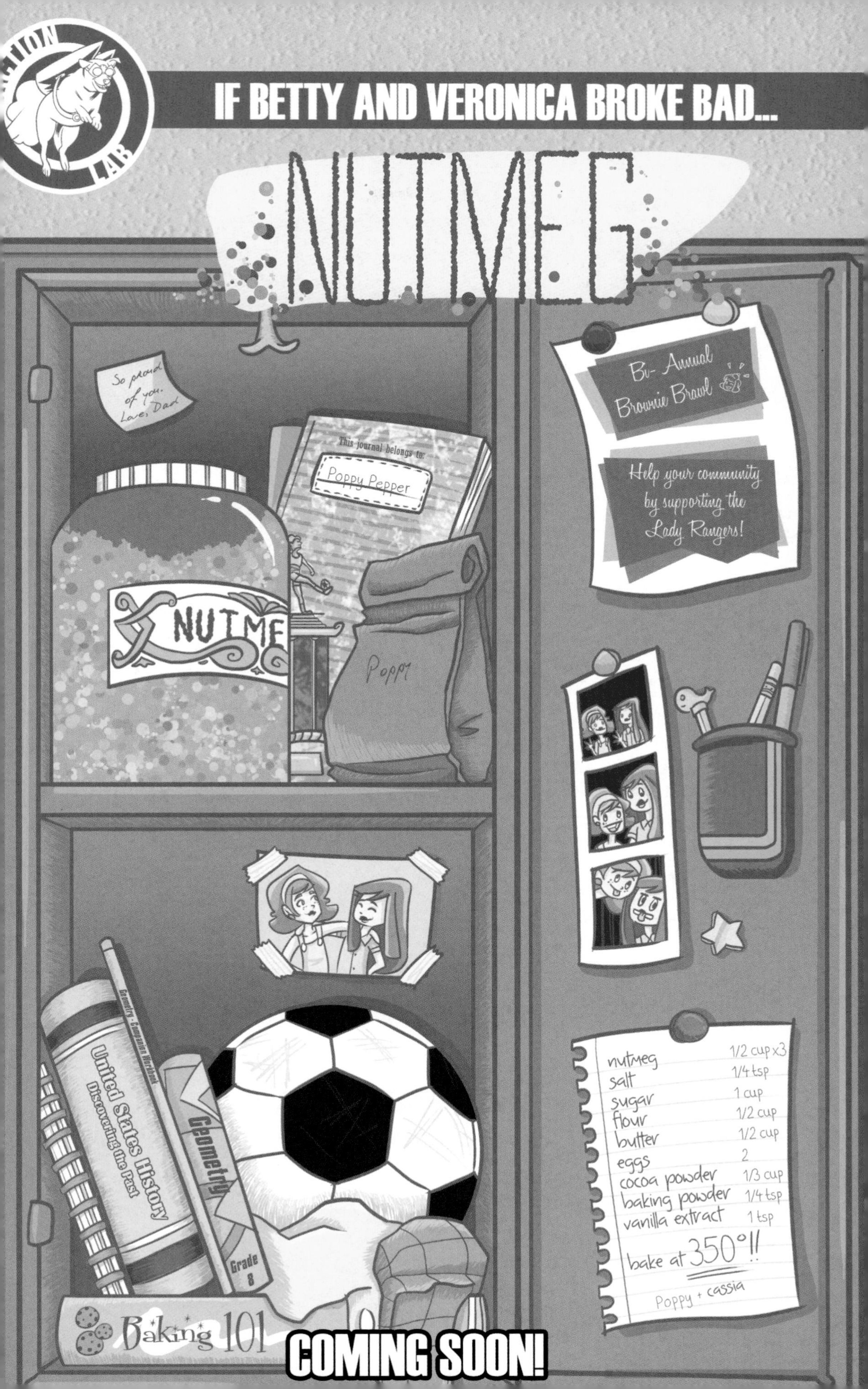
ACTION LAB
IF BETTY AND VERONICA BROKE BAD...
NUTMEG
So proud of you. Love, Dad
This journal belongs to: Poppy Pepper
NUTME
Poppy
Bi-Annual Brownie Brawl
Help your community by supporting the Lady Rangers!
Geometry · Companion Workbook
United States History
Discovering the Past
Geometry
Grade 8
Baking 101
nutmeg 1/2 cup x3
salt 1/4 tsp
sugar 1 cup
flour 1/2 cup
butter 1/2 cup
eggs 2
cocoa powder 1/3 cup
baking powder 1/4 tsp
vanilla extract 1 tsp
bake at 350°!!
Poppy + cassia
COMING SOON!

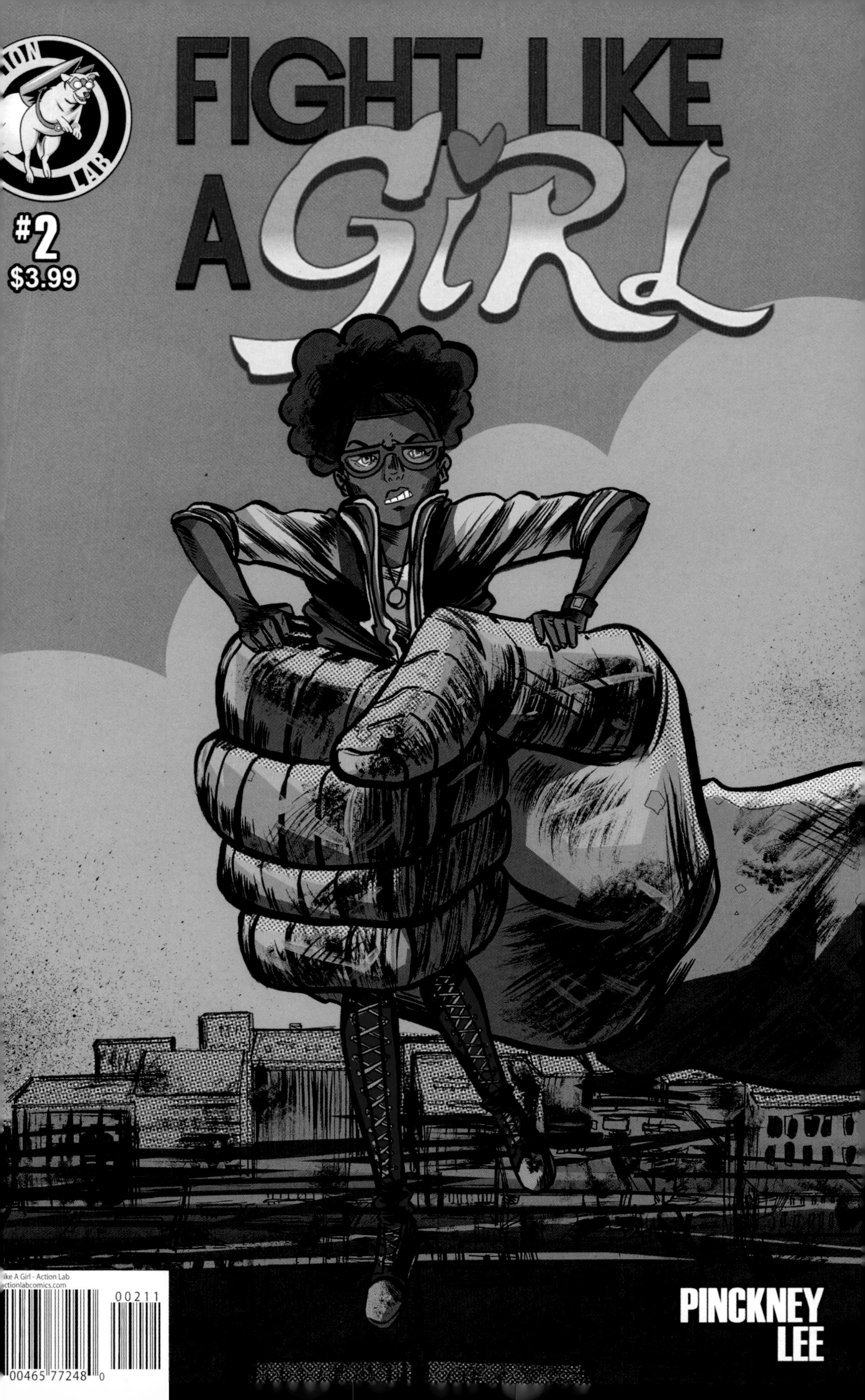
FIGHT LIKE
A GIRL
#2
$3.99
PINCKNEY
LEE
ike A Girl - Action Lab
ctionlabcomics.com
00211
00465 77248 0

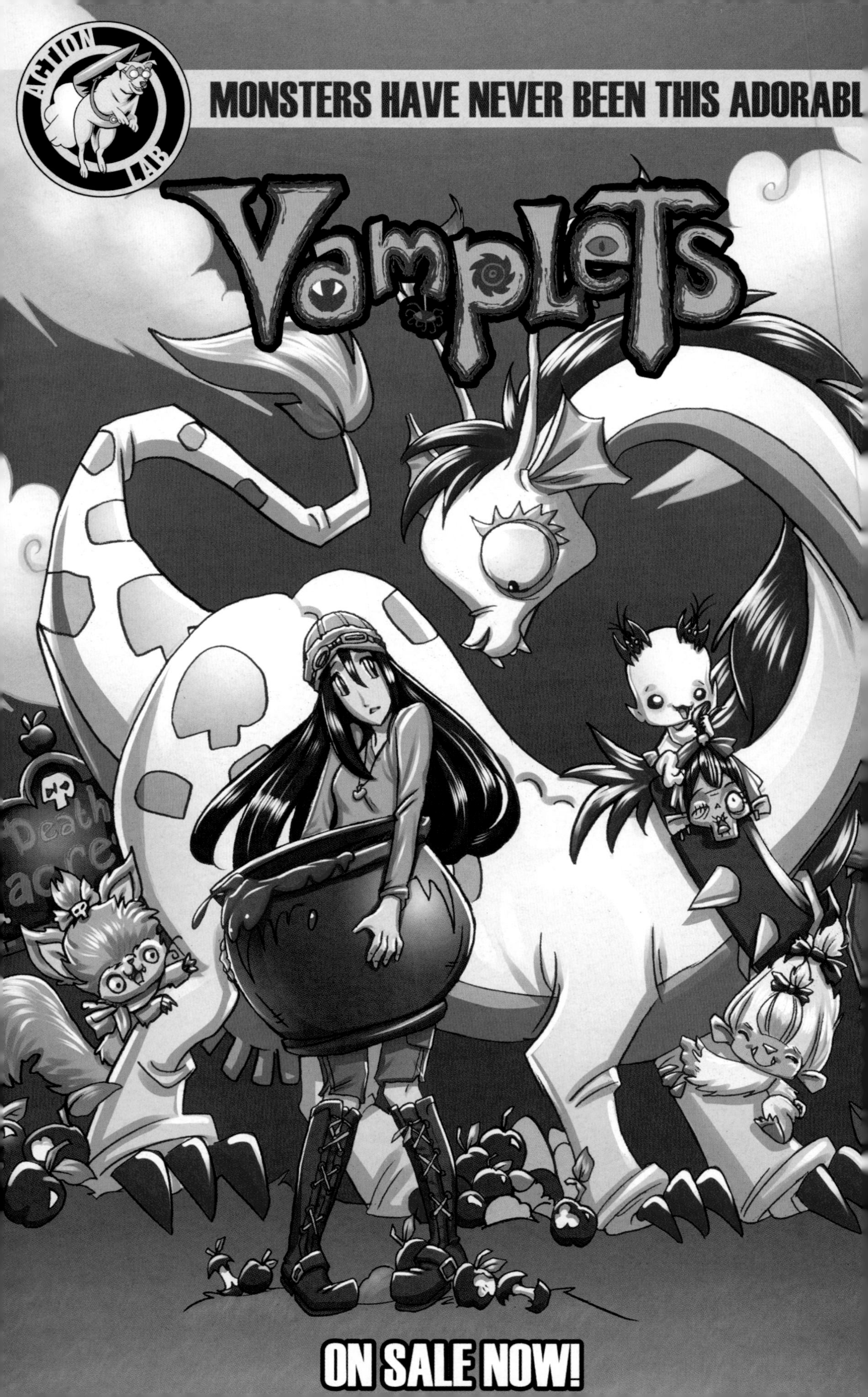

ACTION LAB
MONSTERS HAVE NEVER BEEN THIS ADORABL
VAMPLETS
Death acre
ON SALE NOW!

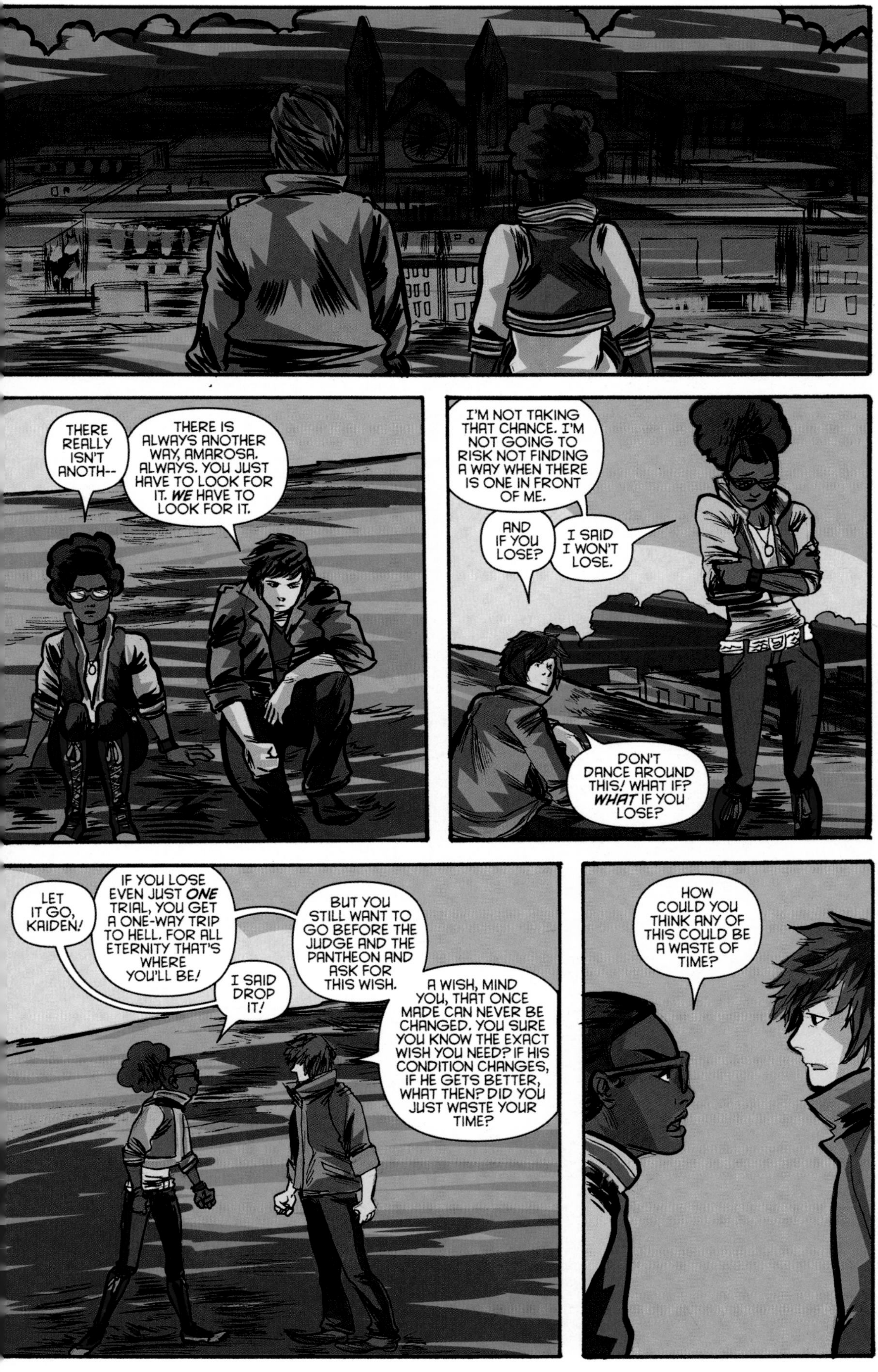
THERE REALLY ISN'T ANOTH--
THERE IS ALWAYS ANOTHER WAY, AMAROSA. ALWAYS. YOU JUST HAVE TO LOOK FOR IT. WE HAVE TO LOOK FOR IT.
I'M NOT TAKING THAT CHANCE. I'M NOT GOING TO RISK NOT FINDING A WAY WHEN THERE IS ONE IN FRONT OF ME.
AND IF YOU LOSE?
I SAID I WON'T LOSE.
DON'T DANCE AROUND THIS! WHAT IF? WHAT IF YOU LOSE?
LET IT GO, KAIDEN!
IF YOU LOSE EVEN JUST ONE TRIAL, YOU GET A ONE-WAY TRIP TO HELL. FOR ALL ETERNITY THAT'S WHERE YOU'LL BE!
I SAID DROP IT!
BUT YOU STILL WANT TO GO BEFORE THE JUDGE AND THE PANTHEON AND ASK FOR THIS WISH.
A WISH, MIND YOU, THAT ONCE MADE CAN NEVER BE CHANGED. YOU SURE YOU KNOW THE EXACT WISH YOU NEED? IF HIS CONDITION CHANGES, IF HE GETS BETTER, WHAT THEN? DID YOU JUST WASTE YOUR TIME?
HOW COULD YOU THINK ANY OF THIS COULD BE A WASTE OF TIME?

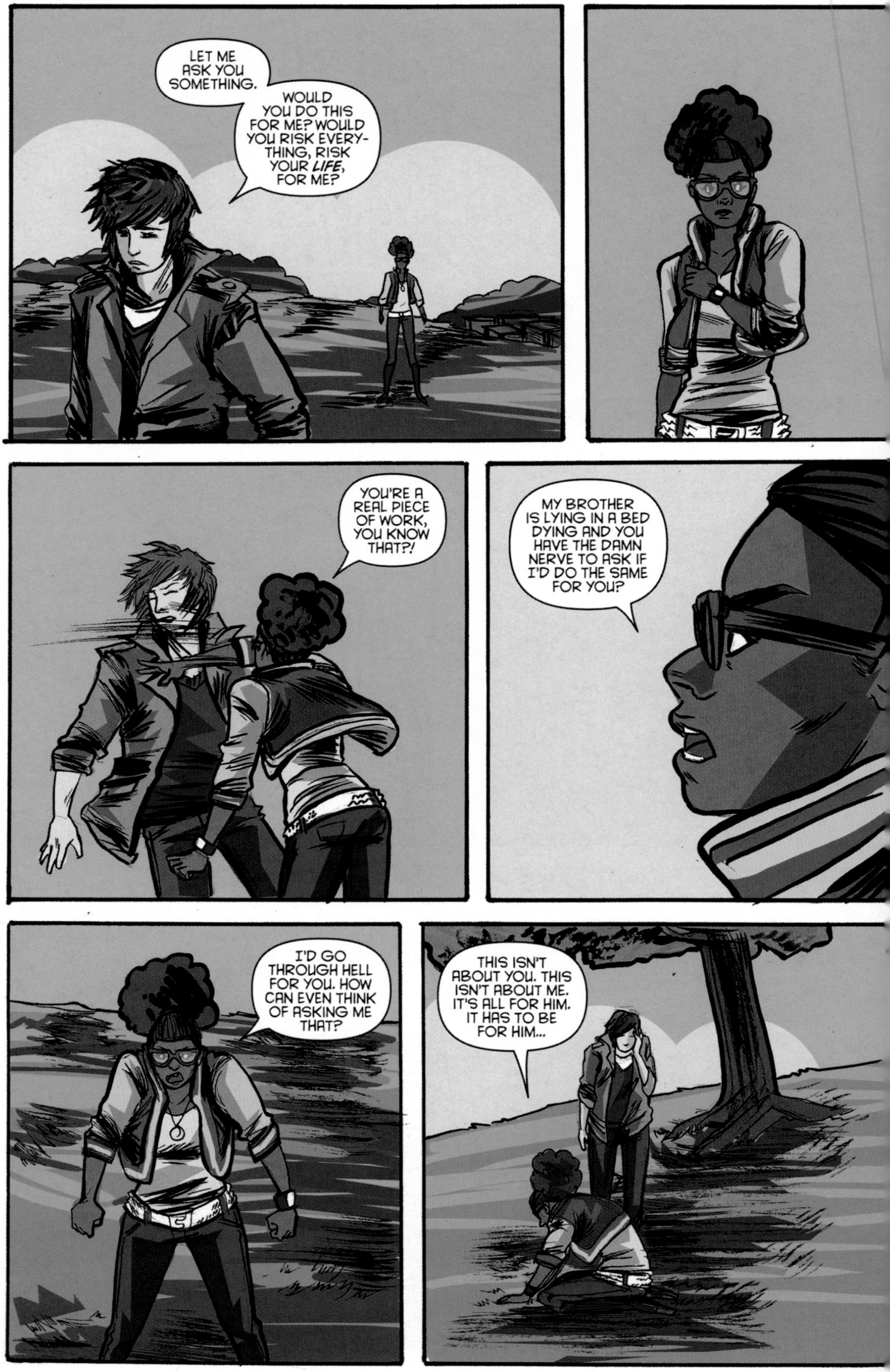
LET ME ASK YOU SOMETHING.
WOULD YOU DO THIS FOR ME? WOULD YOU RISK EVERY-THING, RISK YOUR *LIFE*, FOR ME?
YOU'RE A REAL PIECE OF WORK, YOU KNOW THAT?!
MY BROTHER IS LYING IN A BED DYING AND YOU HAVE THE DAMN NERVE TO ASK IF I'D DO THE SAME FOR YOU?
I'D GO THROUGH HELL FOR YOU. HOW CAN EVEN THINK OF ASKING ME THAT?
THIS ISN'T ABOUT YOU. THIS ISN'T ABOUT ME. IT'S ALL FOR HIM. IT HAS TO BE FOR HIM...

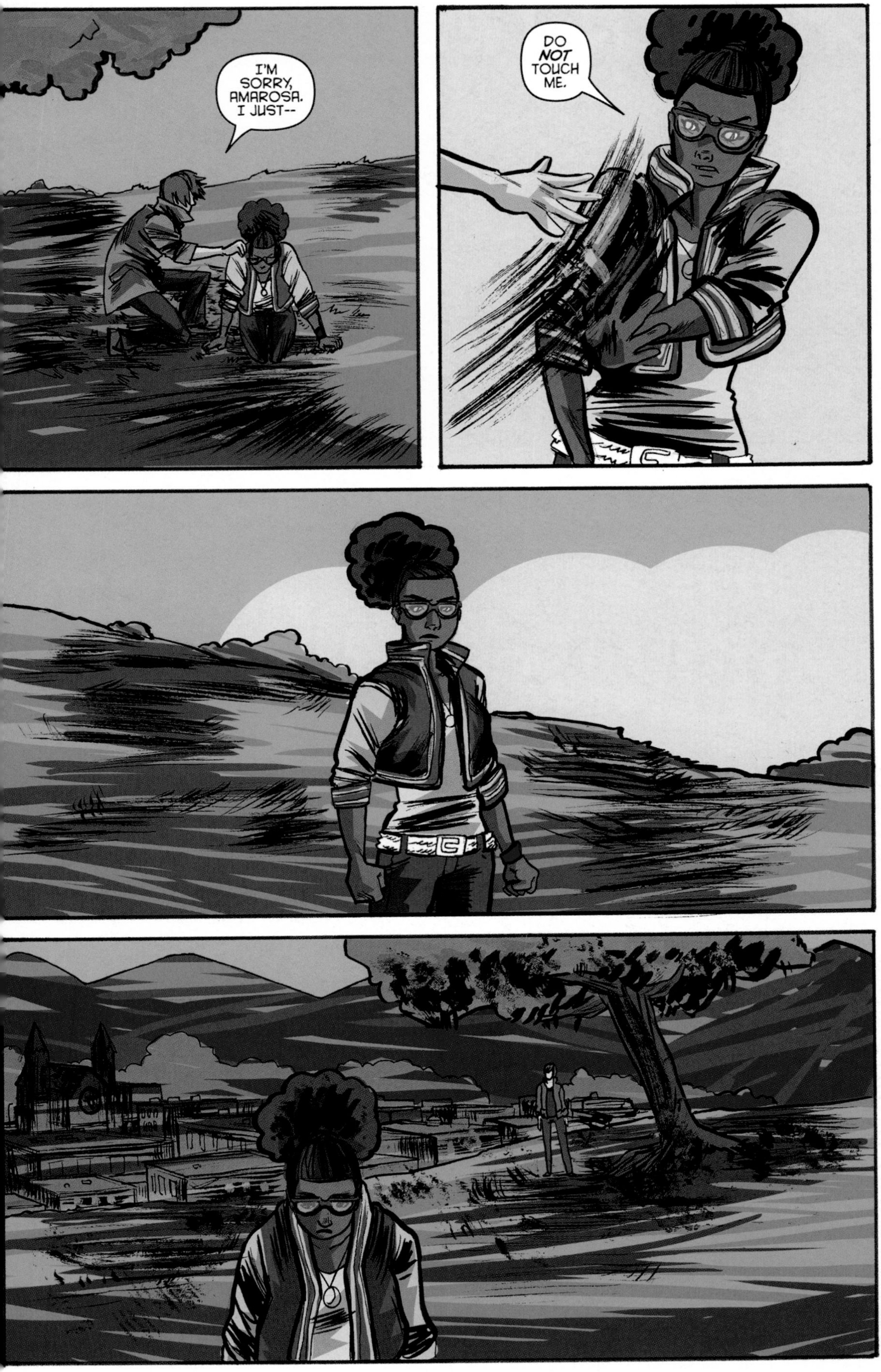

I'M SORRY, AMAROSA. I JUST--
DO *NOT* TOUCH ME.

CHAPTER TWO

ROCK 'EM, SOCK 'EM

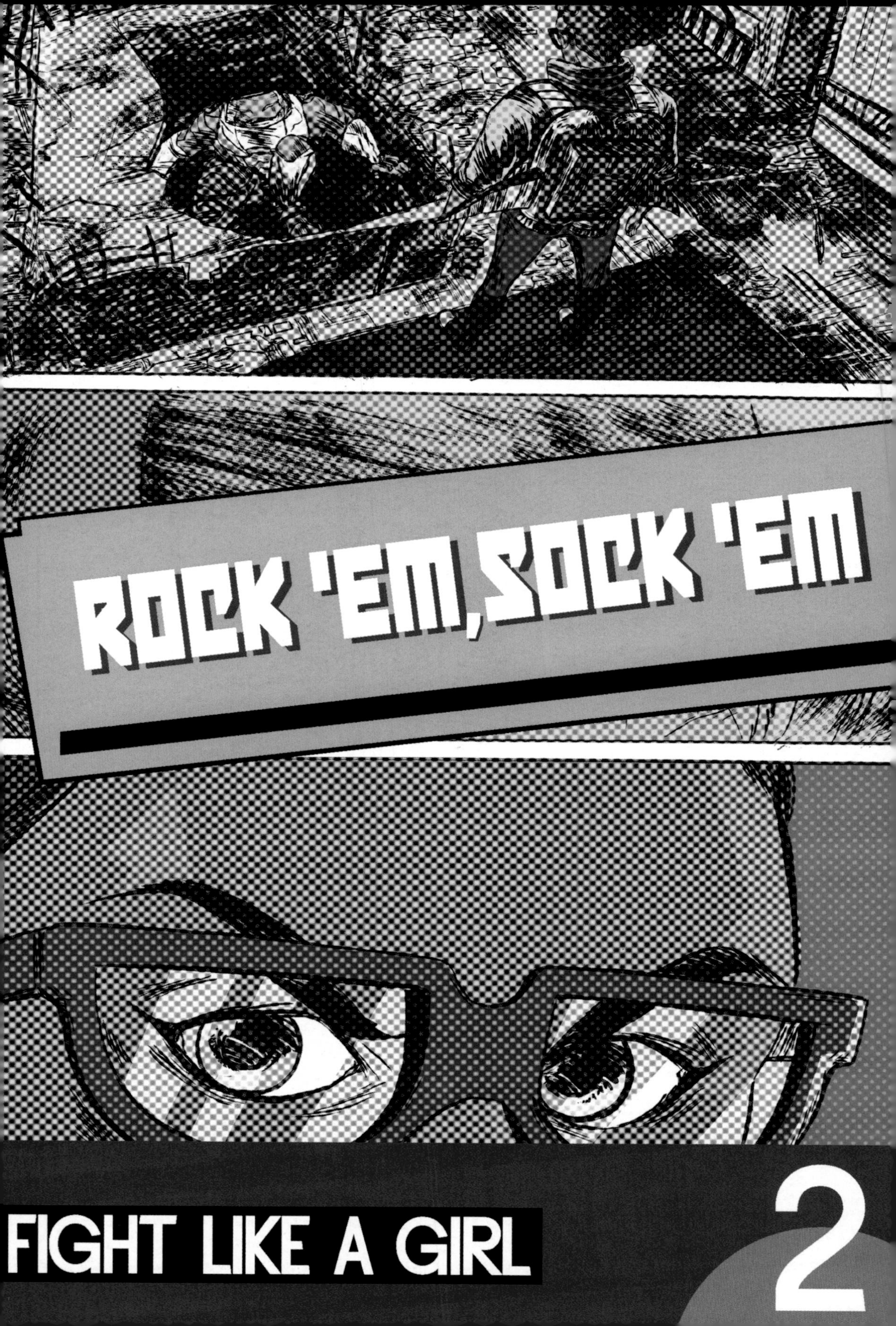

FIGHT LIKE A GIRL

2

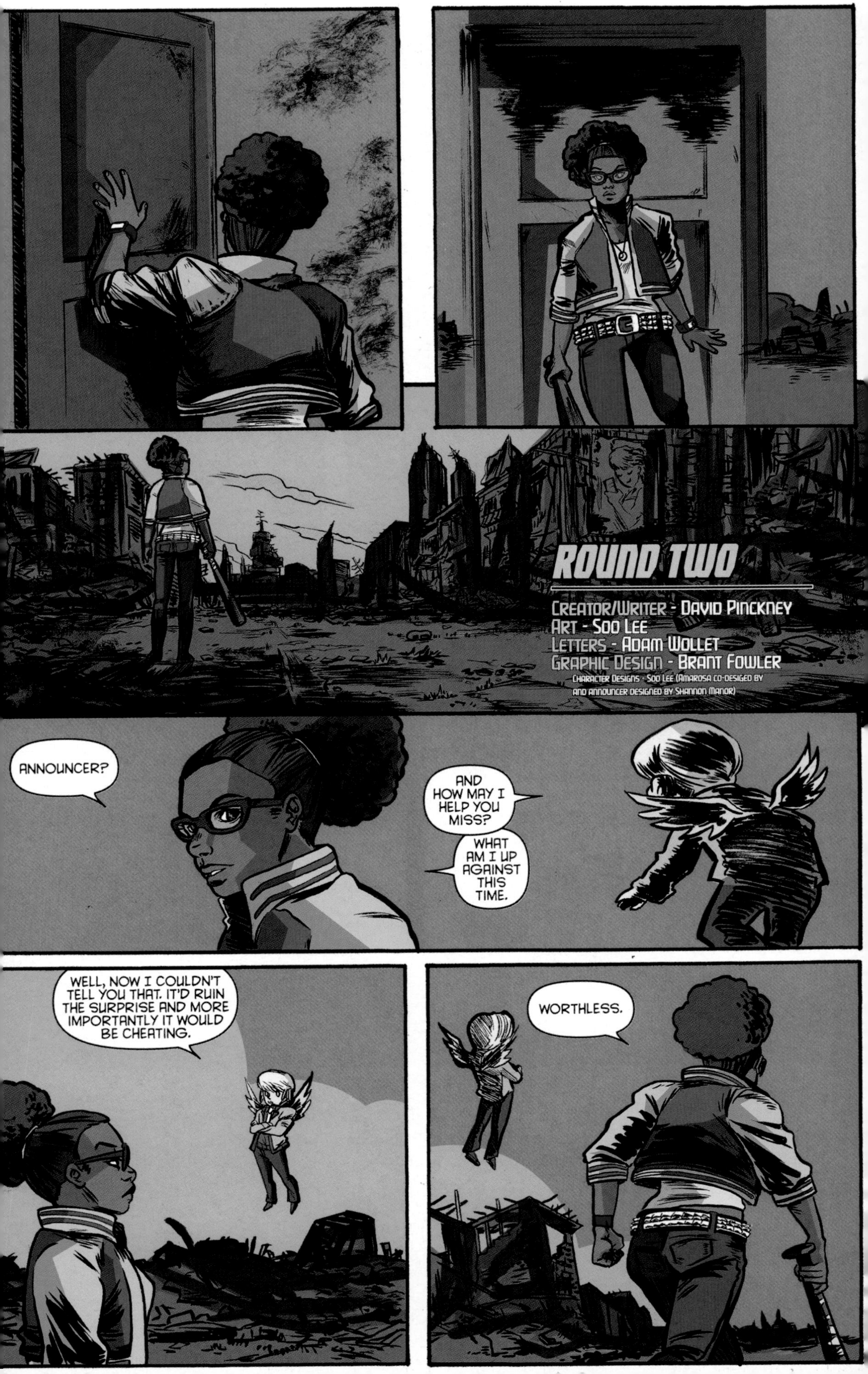
ROUND TWO
CREATOR/WRITER - DAVID PINCKNEY
ART - SOO LEE
LETTERS - ADAM WOLLET
GRAPHIC DESIGN - BRANT FOWLER
CHARACTER DESIGNS - SOO LEE (AMAROSA CO-DESIGED BY AND ANNOUNCER DESIGNED BY SHANNON MANOR)
ANNOUNCER?
AND HOW MAY I HELP YOU MISS?
WHAT AM I UP AGAINST THIS TIME.
WELL, NOW I COULDN'T TELL YOU THAT. IT'D RUIN THE SURPRISE AND MORE IMPORTANTLY IT WOULD BE CHEATING.
WORTHLESS.

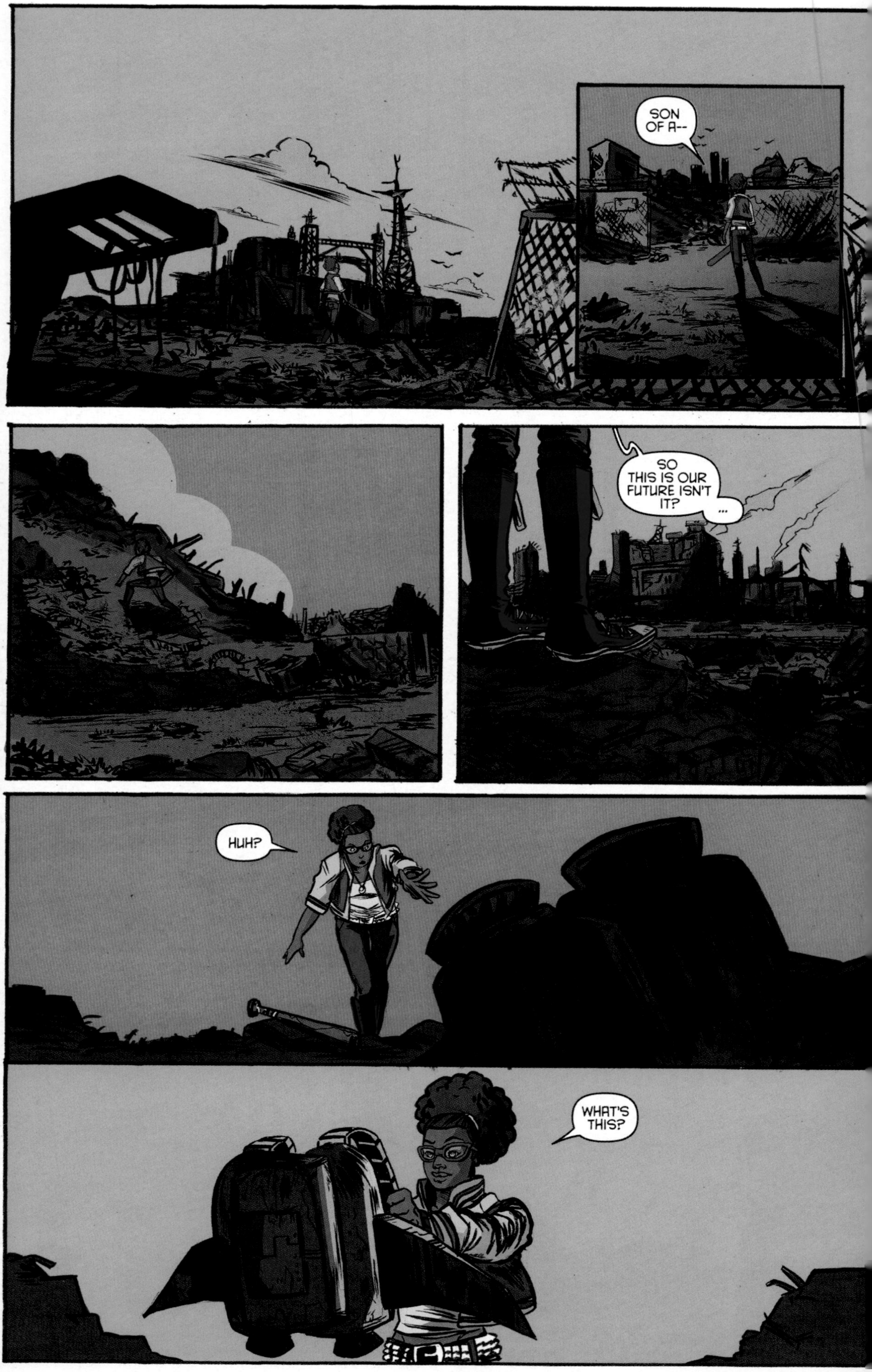
SON OF A--
SO THIS IS OUR FUTURE ISN'T IT?
...
HUH?
WHAT'S THIS?

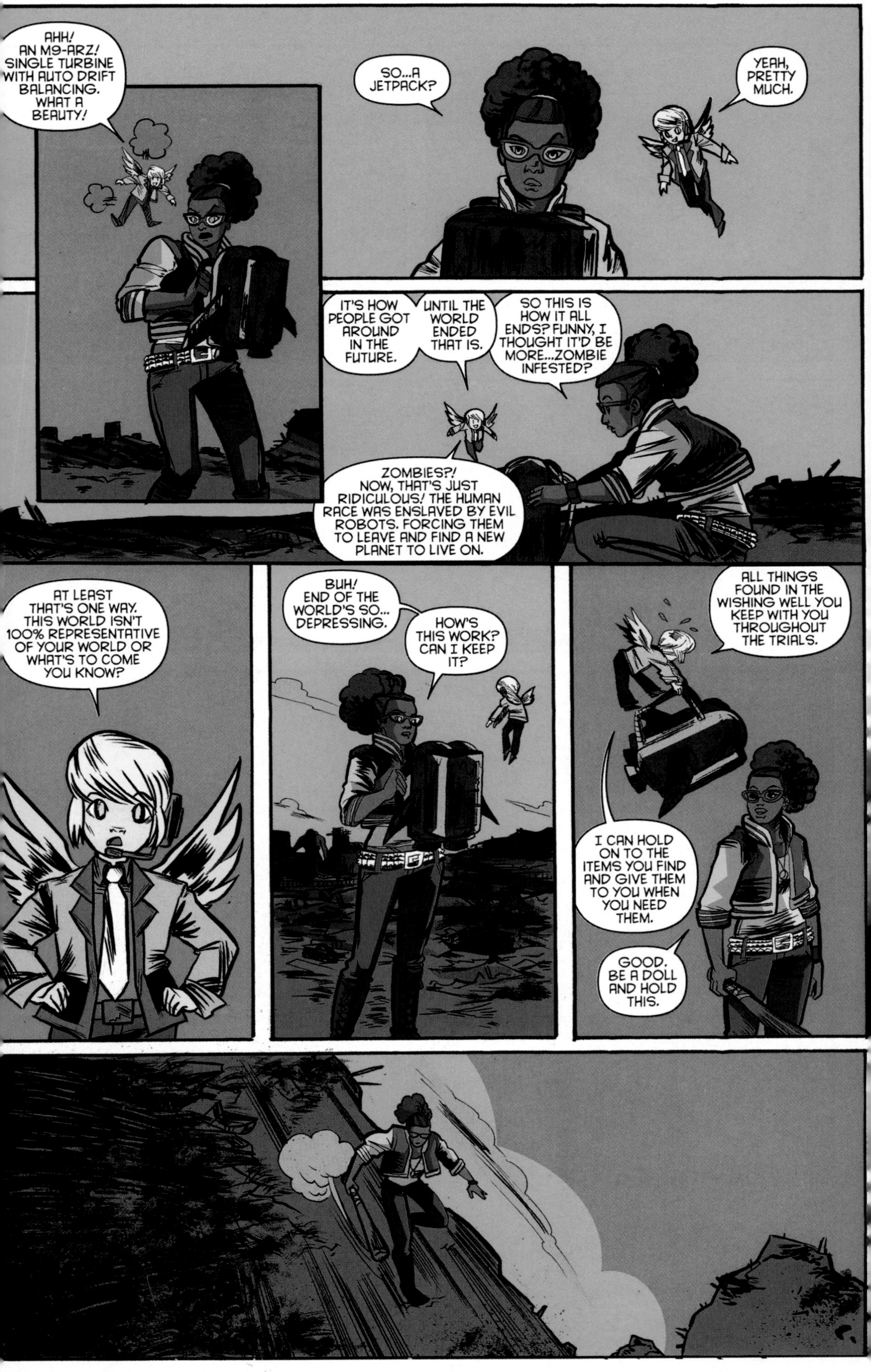
AHH! AN M9-ARZ! SINGLE TURBINE WITH AUTO DRIFT BALANCING. WHAT A BEAUTY!
SO...A JETPACK?
YEAH, PRETTY MUCH.
IT'S HOW PEOPLE GOT AROUND IN THE FUTURE.
UNTIL THE WORLD ENDED THAT IS.
SO THIS IS HOW IT ALL ENDS? FUNNY, I THOUGHT IT'D BE MORE...ZOMBIE INFESTED?
ZOMBIES?! NOW, THAT'S JUST RIDICULOUS! THE HUMAN RACE WAS ENSLAVED BY EVIL ROBOTS. FORCING THEM TO LEAVE AND FIND A NEW PLANET TO LIVE ON.
AT LEAST THAT'S ONE WAY. THIS WORLD ISN'T 100% REPRESENTATIVE OF YOUR WORLD OR WHAT'S TO COME YOU KNOW?
BUH! END OF THE WORLD'S SO... DEPRESSING.
HOW'S THIS WORK? CAN I KEEP IT?
ALL THINGS FOUND IN THE WISHING WELL YOU KEEP WITH YOU THROUGHOUT THE TRIALS.
I CAN HOLD ON TO THE ITEMS YOU FIND AND GIVE THEM TO YOU WHEN YOU NEED THEM.
GOOD. BE A DOLL AND HOLD THIS.

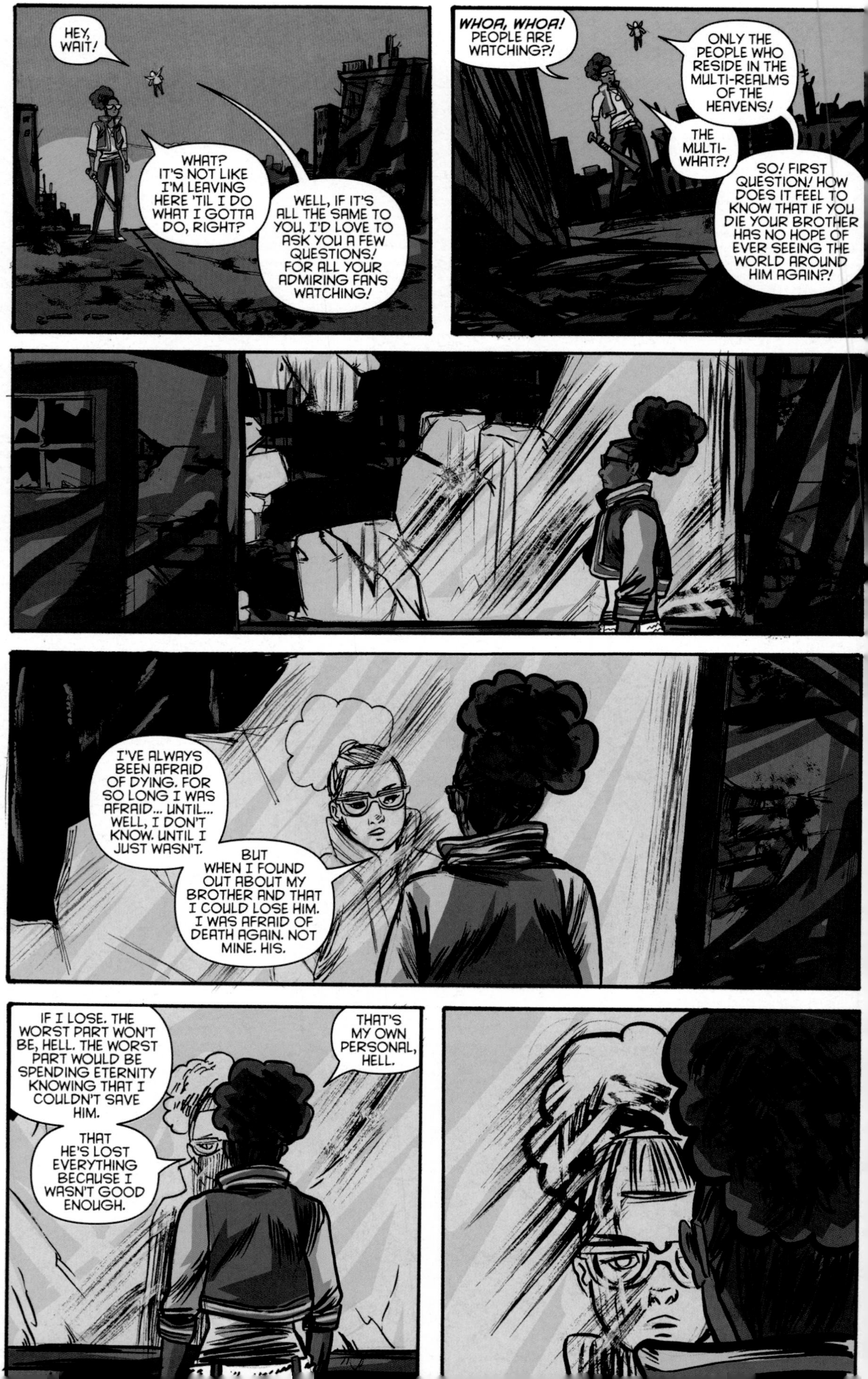
HEY, WAIT!
WHAT? IT'S NOT LIKE I'M LEAVING HERE 'TIL I DO WHAT I GOTTA DO, RIGHT?
WELL, IF IT'S ALL THE SAME TO YOU, I'D LOVE TO ASK YOU A FEW QUESTIONS! FOR ALL YOUR ADMIRING FANS WATCHING!
WHOA, WHOA! PEOPLE ARE WATCHING?!
ONLY THE PEOPLE WHO RESIDE IN THE MULTI-REALMS OF THE HEAVENS!
THE MULTI-WHAT?!
SO! FIRST QUESTION! HOW DOES IT FEEL TO KNOW THAT IF YOU DIE YOUR BROTHER HAS NO HOPE OF EVER SEEING THE WORLD AROUND HIM AGAIN?!
I'VE ALWAYS BEEN AFRAID OF DYING. FOR SO LONG I WAS AFRAID... UNTIL... WELL, I DON'T KNOW. UNTIL I JUST WASN'T.
BUT WHEN I FOUND OUT ABOUT MY BROTHER AND THAT I COULD LOSE HIM. I WAS AFRAID OF DEATH AGAIN. NOT MINE. HIS.
IF I LOSE. THE WORST PART WON'T BE, HELL. THE WORST PART WOULD BE SPENDING ETERNITY KNOWING THAT I COULDN'T SAVE HIM.
THAT HE'S LOST EVERYTHING BECAUSE I WASN'T GOOD ENOUGH.
THAT'S MY OWN PERSONAL, HELL.

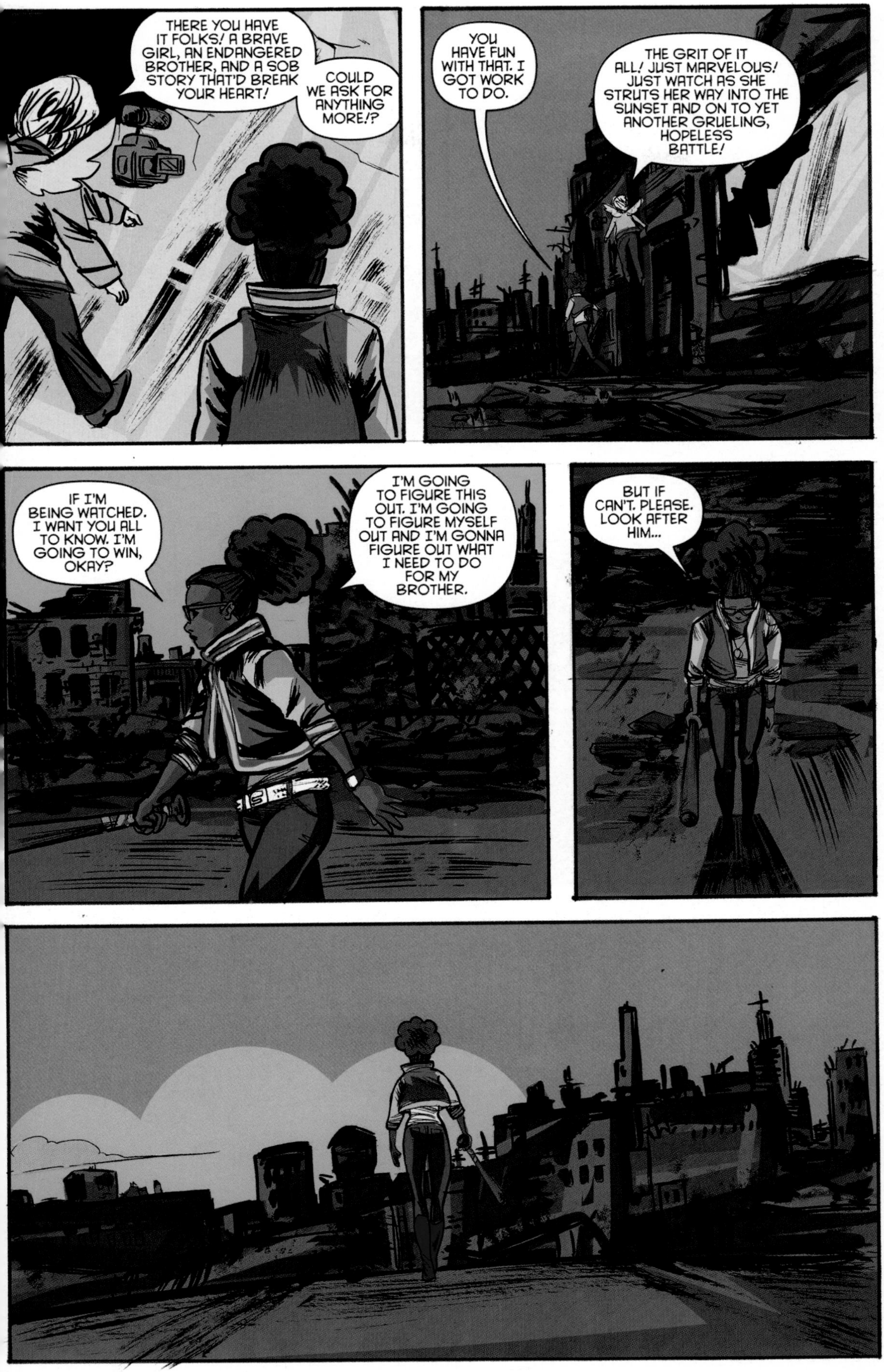

THERE YOU HAVE IT FOLKS! A BRAVE GIRL, AN ENDANGERED BROTHER, AND A SOB STORY THAT'D BREAK YOUR HEART!
COULD WE ASK FOR ANYTHING MORE!?
YOU HAVE FUN WITH THAT. I GOT WORK TO DO.
THE GRIT OF IT ALL! JUST MARVELOUS! JUST WATCH AS SHE STRUTS HER WAY INTO THE SUNSET AND ON TO YET ANOTHER GRUELING, HOPELESS BATTLE!
IF I'M BEING WATCHED. I WANT YOU ALL TO KNOW. I'M GOING TO WIN, OKAY?
I'M GOING TO FIGURE THIS OUT. I'M GOING TO FIGURE MYSELF OUT AND I'M GONNA FIGURE OUT WHAT I NEED TO DO FOR MY BROTHER.
BUT IF CAN'T. PLEASE. LOOK AFTER HIM...

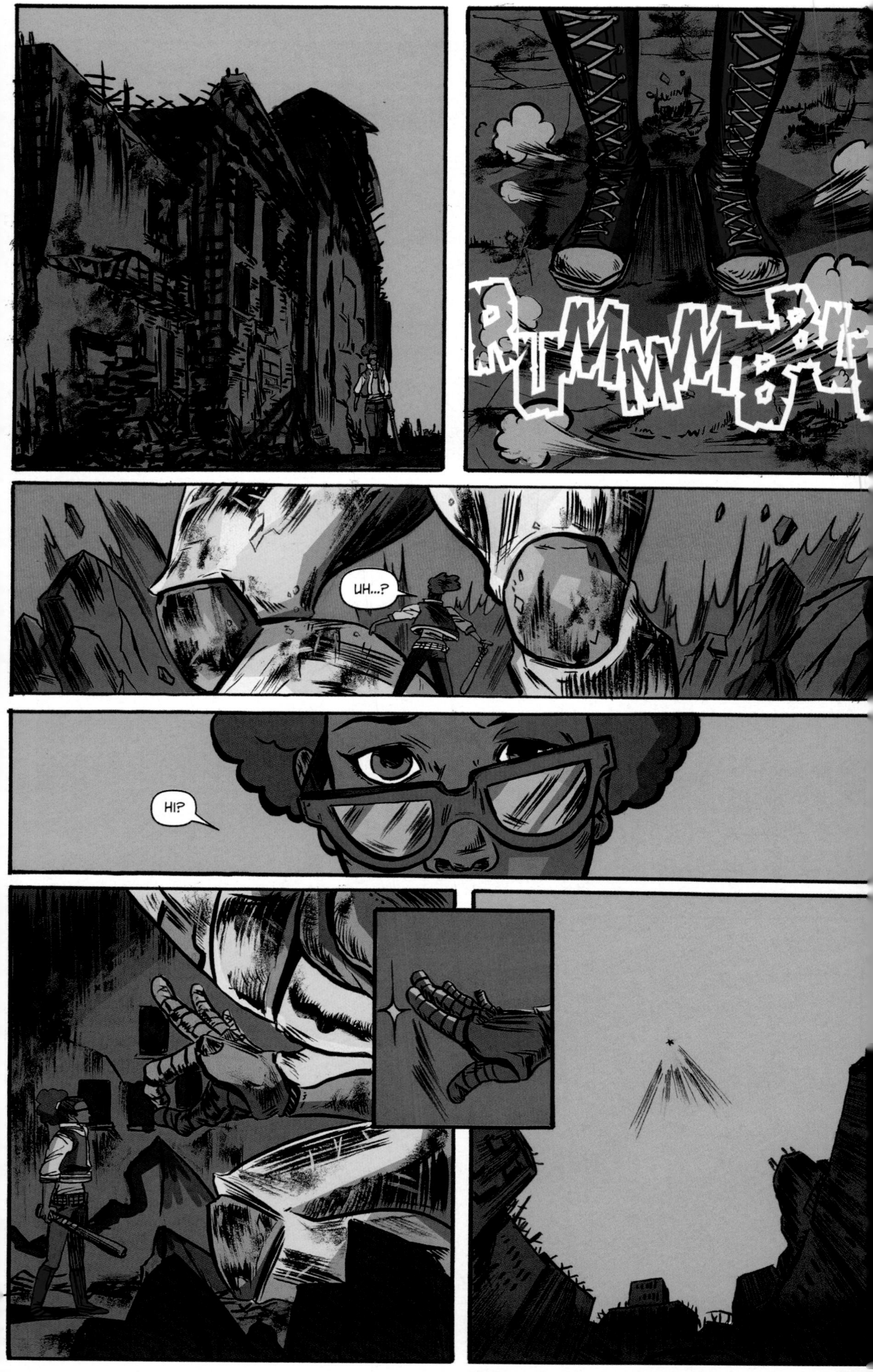
UH...?
HI?

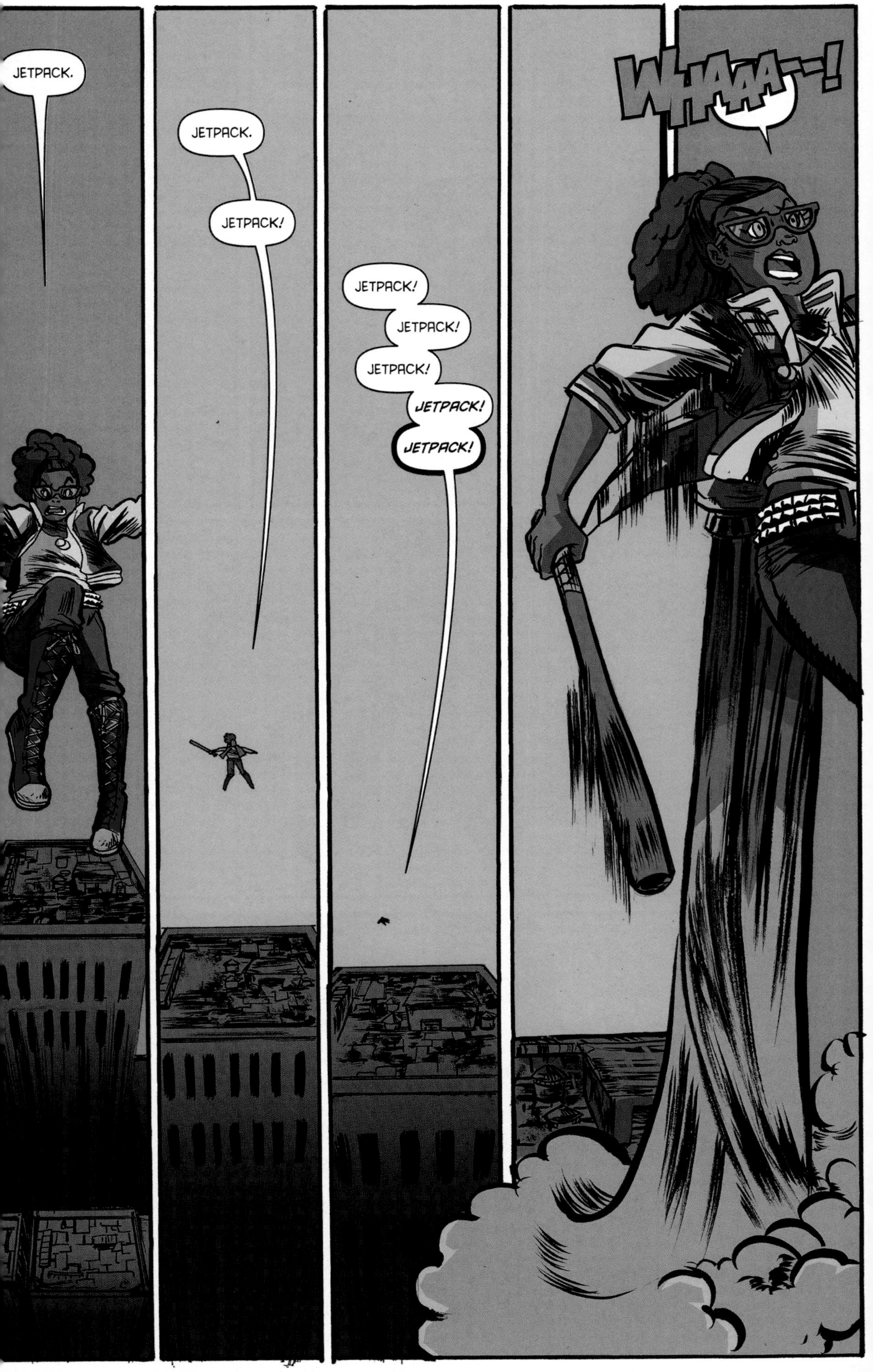
JETPACK.
JETPACK.
JETPACK!
JETPACK!
JETPACK!
JETPACK!
JETPACK!
JETPACK!
WHAAA--!

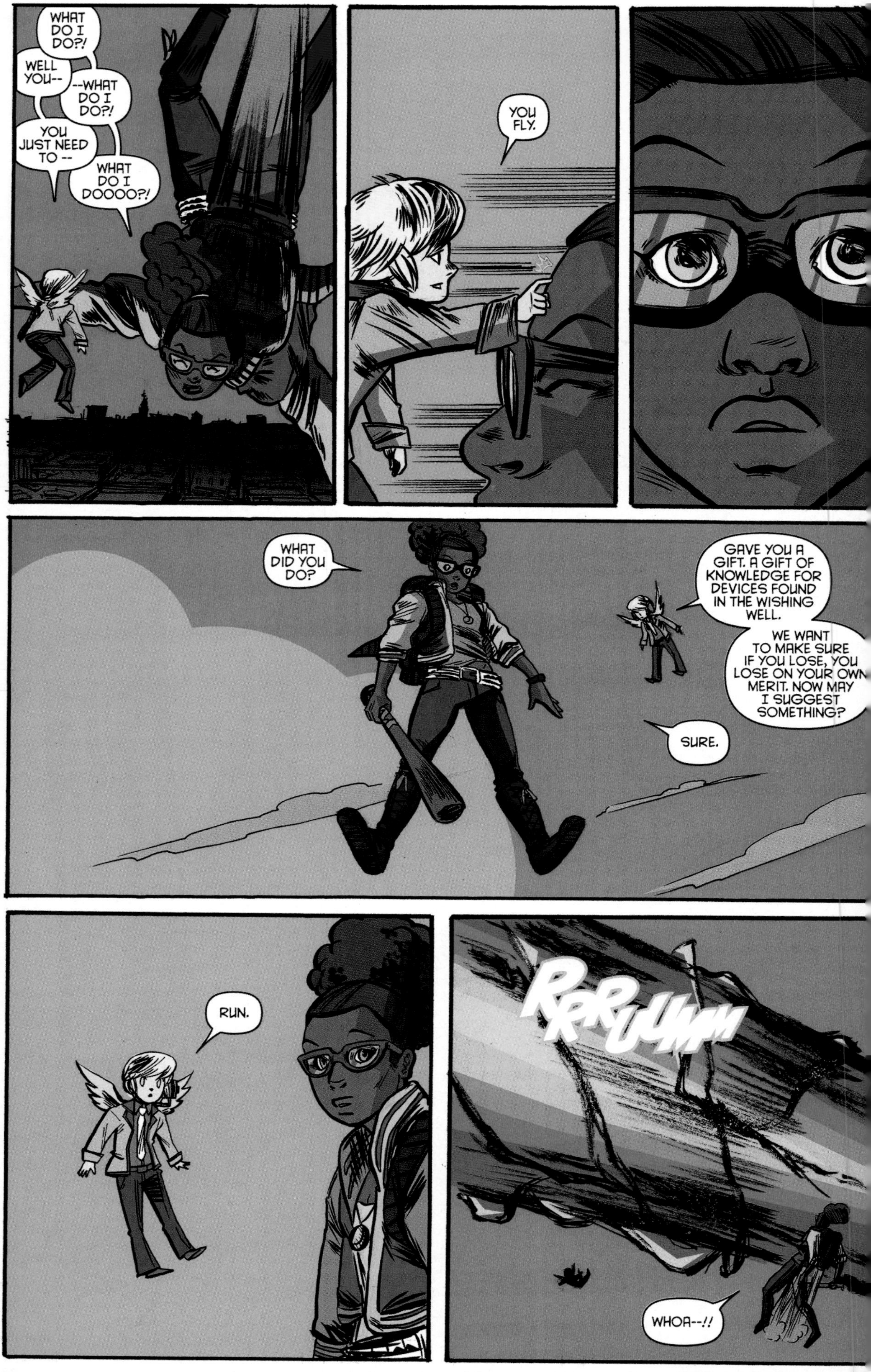
WHAT DO I DO?!
WELL YOU--
--WHAT DO I DO?!
YOU JUST NEED TO --
WHAT DO I DOOOO?!
YOU FLY.
WHAT DID YOU DO?
GAVE YOU A GIFT. A GIFT OF KNOWLEDGE FOR DEVICES FOUND IN THE WISHING WELL.
WE WANT TO MAKE SURE IF YOU LOSE, YOU LOSE ON YOUR OWN MERIT. NOW MAY I SUGGEST SOMETHING?
SURE.
RUN.
RRRUUMM
WHOA--!!

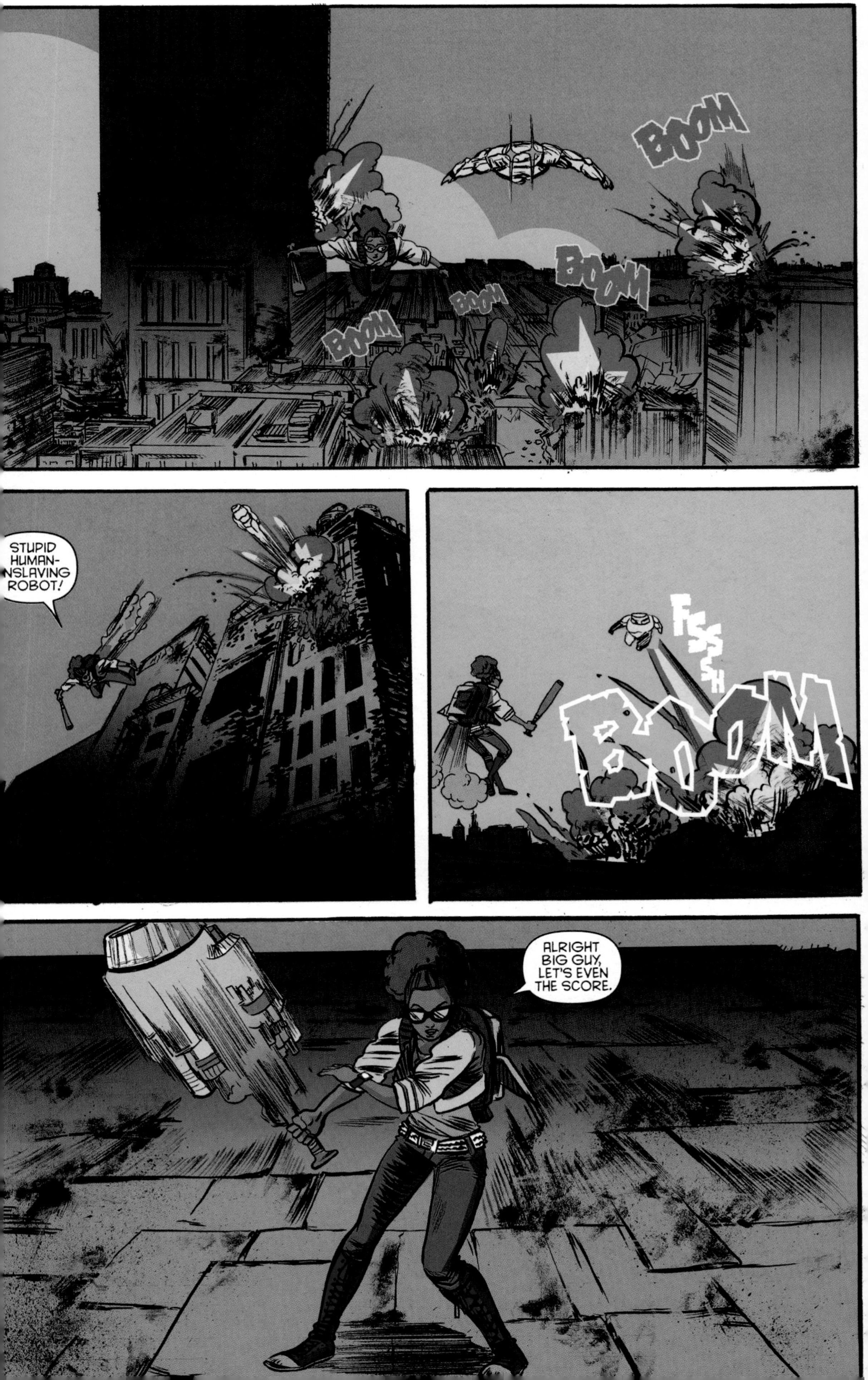
BOOM
BOOM
BOOM
BOOM
STUPID HUMAN-NSLAVING ROBOT!
FSSSH
BOOM
ALRIGHT BIG GUY, LET'S EVEN THE SCORE.

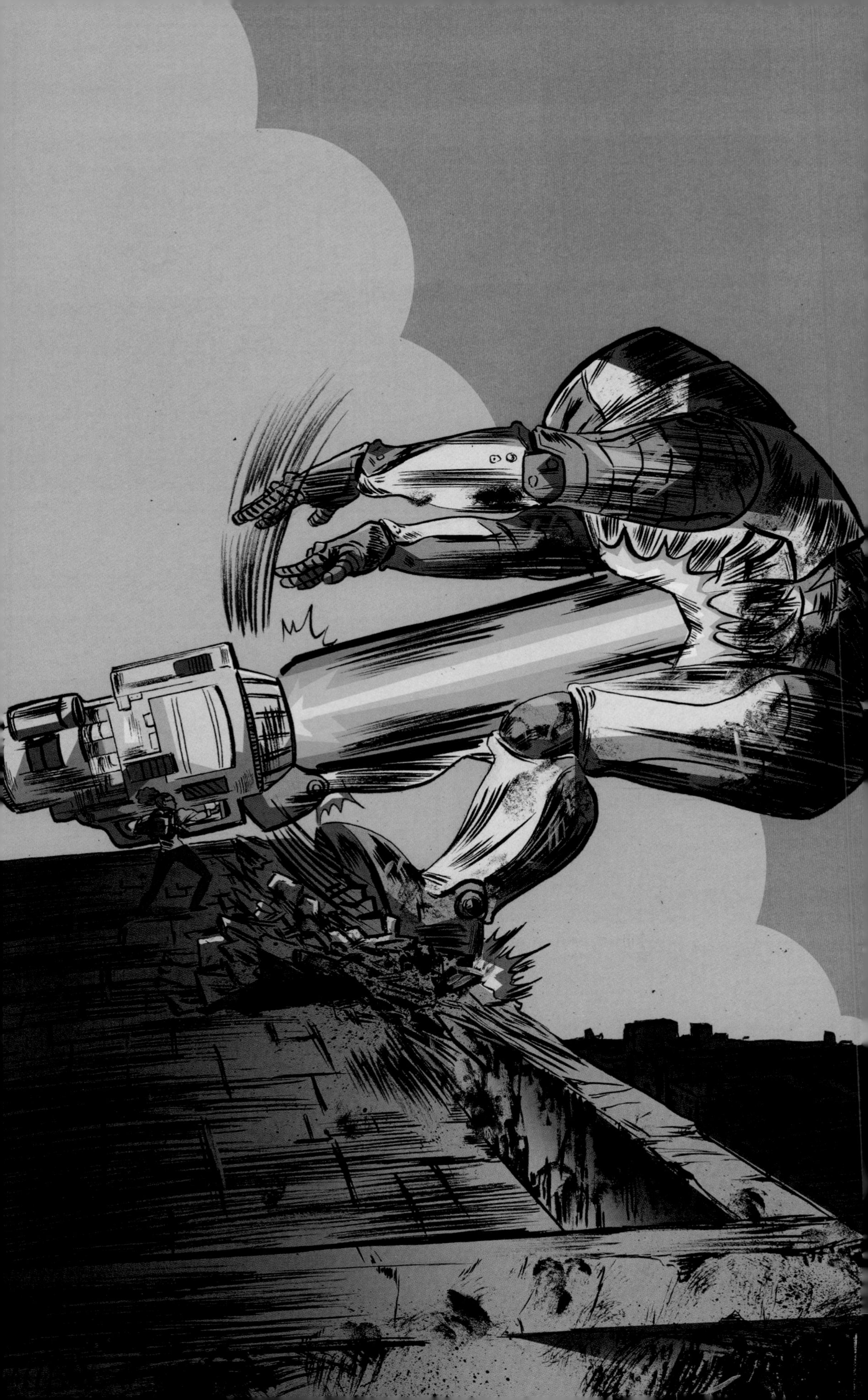

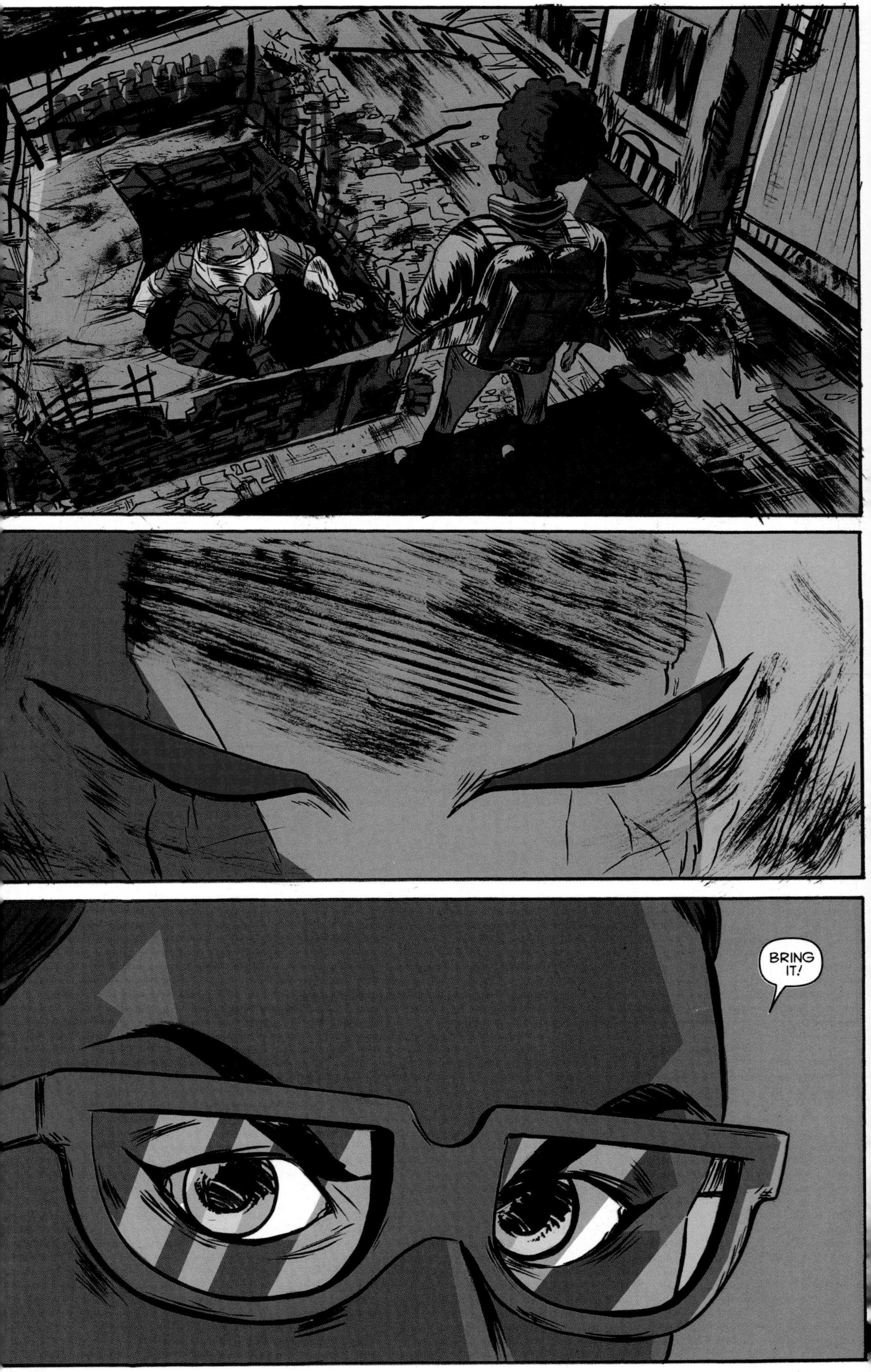
BRING IT!

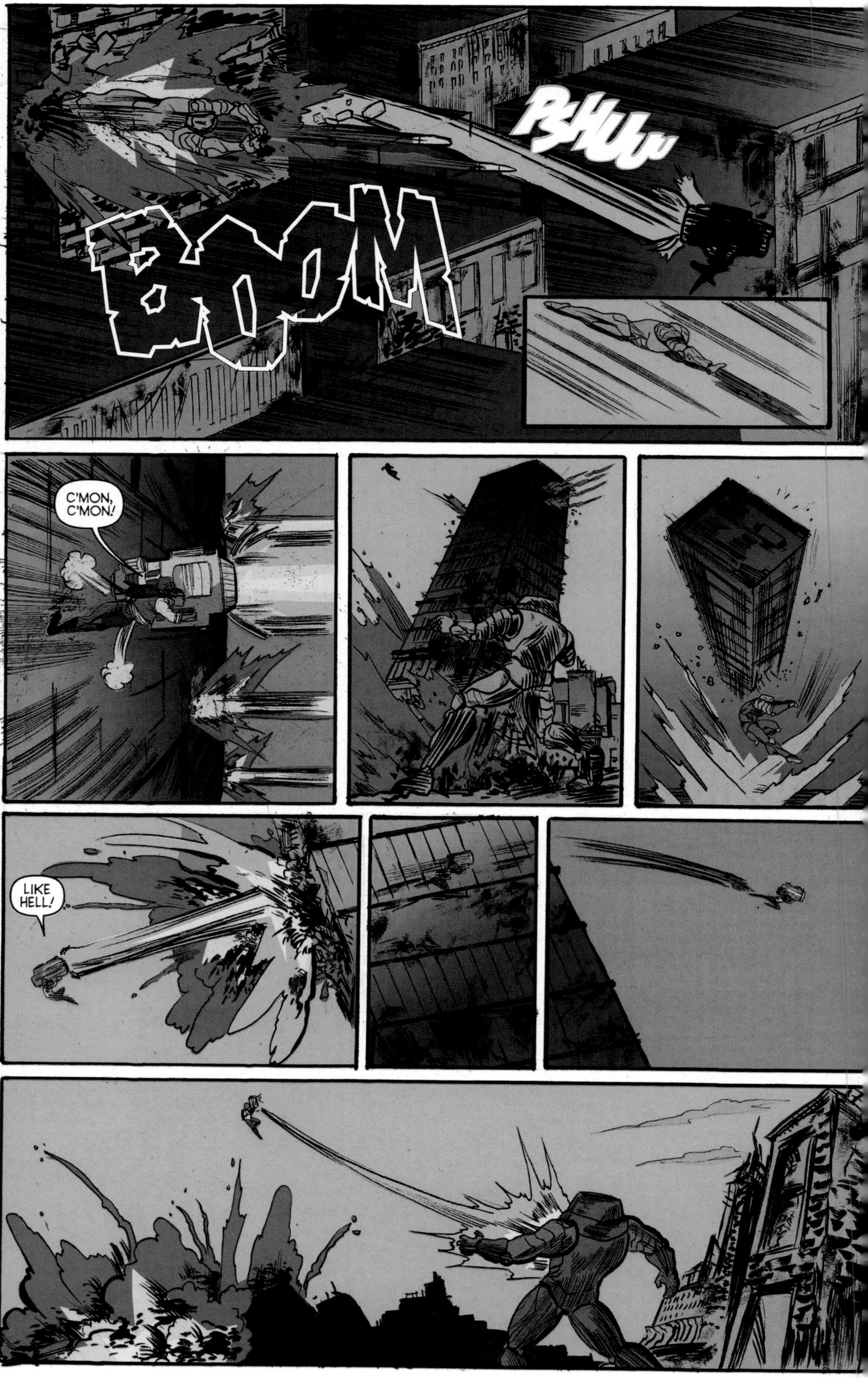
PSHUUU
BOOM
C'MON, C'MON!
LIKE HELL!

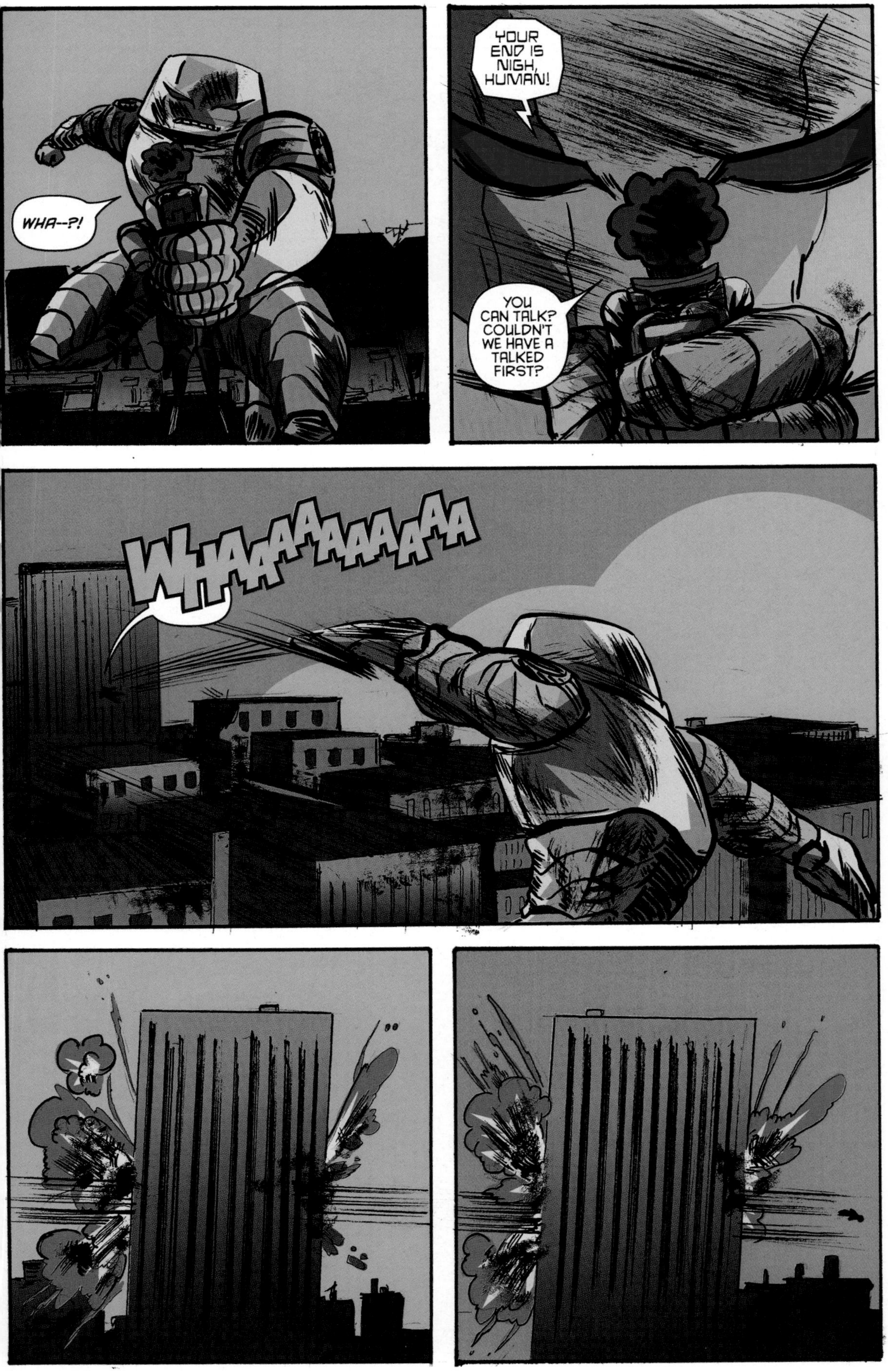
WHA--?!
YOUR END IS NIGH, HUMAN!
YOU CAN TALK? COULDN'T WE HAVE A TALKED FIRST?
WHAAAAAAAAAA

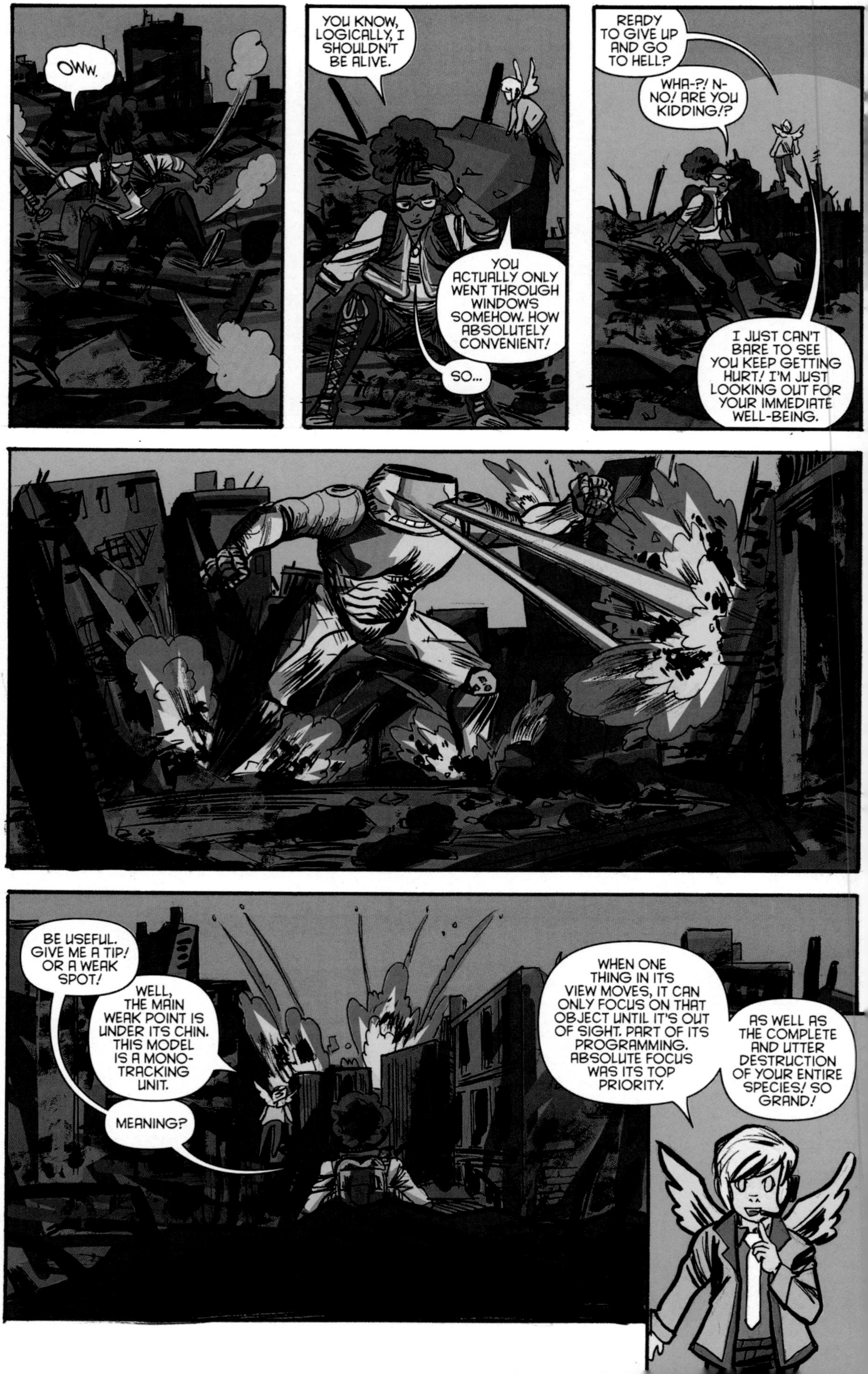
OWW.
YOU KNOW, LOGICALLY, I SHOULDN'T BE ALIVE.
YOU ACTUALLY ONLY WENT THROUGH WINDOWS SOMEHOW. HOW ABSOLUTELY CONVENIENT!
SO...
READY TO GIVE UP AND GO TO HELL?
WHA-?! N-NO! ARE YOU KIDDING!?
I JUST CAN'T BARE TO SEE YOU KEEP GETTING HURT! I'M JUST LOOKING OUT FOR YOUR IMMEDIATE WELL-BEING.
BE USEFUL. GIVE ME A TIP! OR A WEAK SPOT!
WELL, THE MAIN WEAK POINT IS UNDER ITS CHIN. THIS MODEL IS A MONO-TRACKING UNIT.
MEANING?
WHEN ONE THING IN ITS VIEW MOVES, IT CAN ONLY FOCUS ON THAT OBJECT UNTIL IT'S OUT OF SIGHT. PART OF ITS PROGRAMMING. ABSOLUTE FOCUS WAS ITS TOP PRIORITY.
AS WELL AS THE COMPLETE AND UTTER DESTRUCTION OF YOUR ENTIRE SPECIES! SO GRAND!

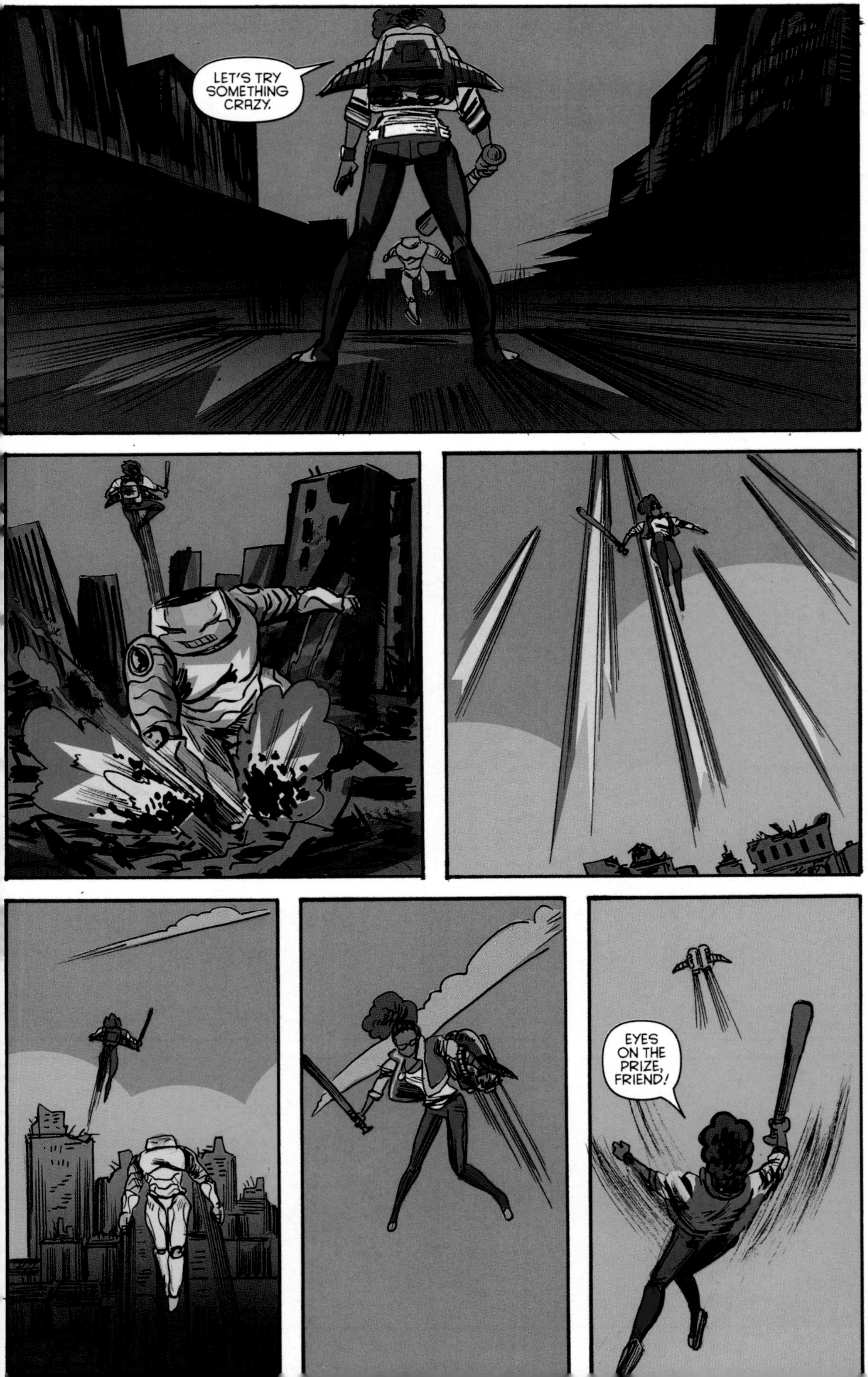
LET'S TRY SOMETHING CRAZY.
EYES ON THE PRIZE, FRIEND!

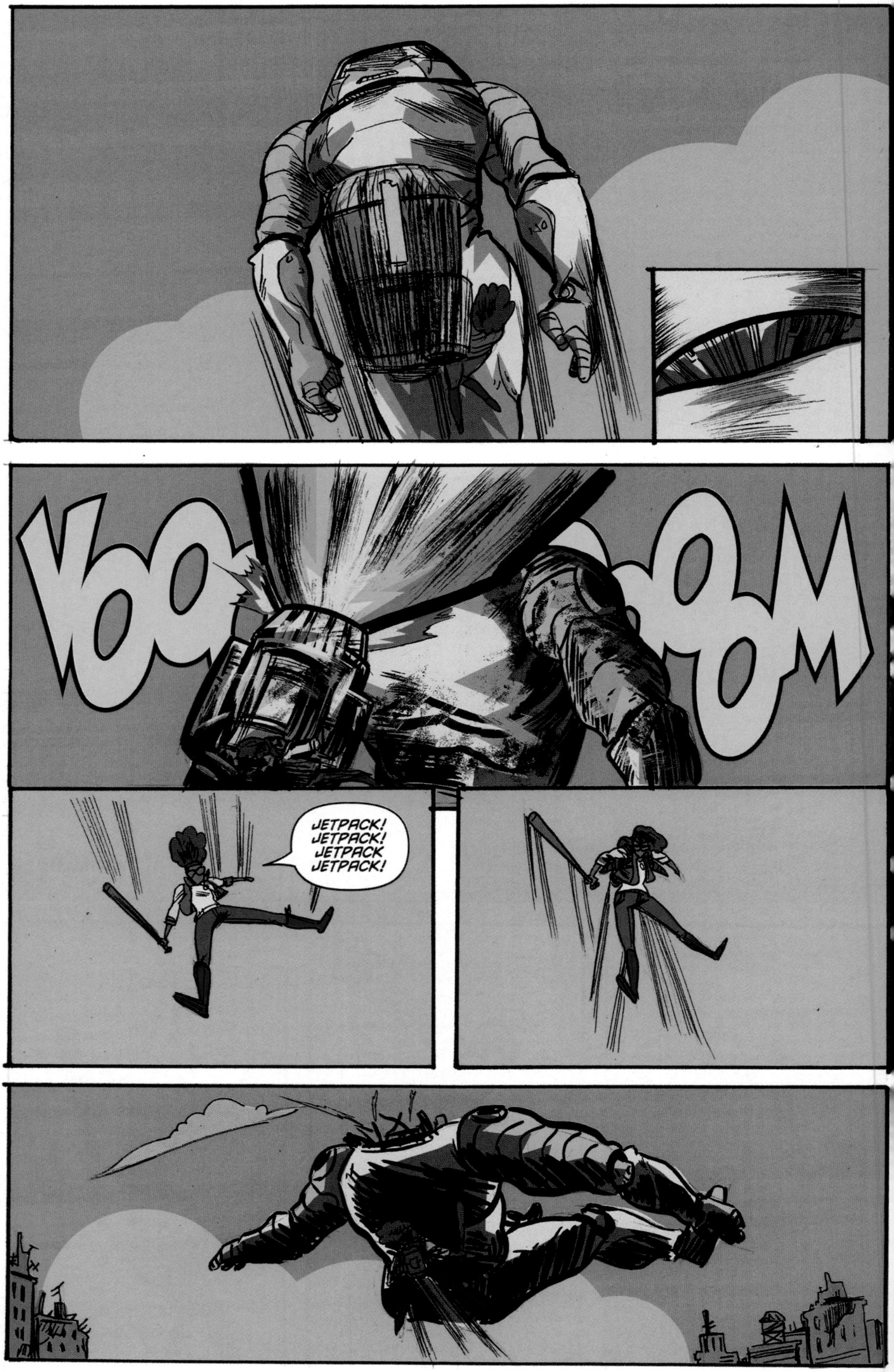
VOOOOM
JETPACK! JETPACK! JETPACK JETPACK!

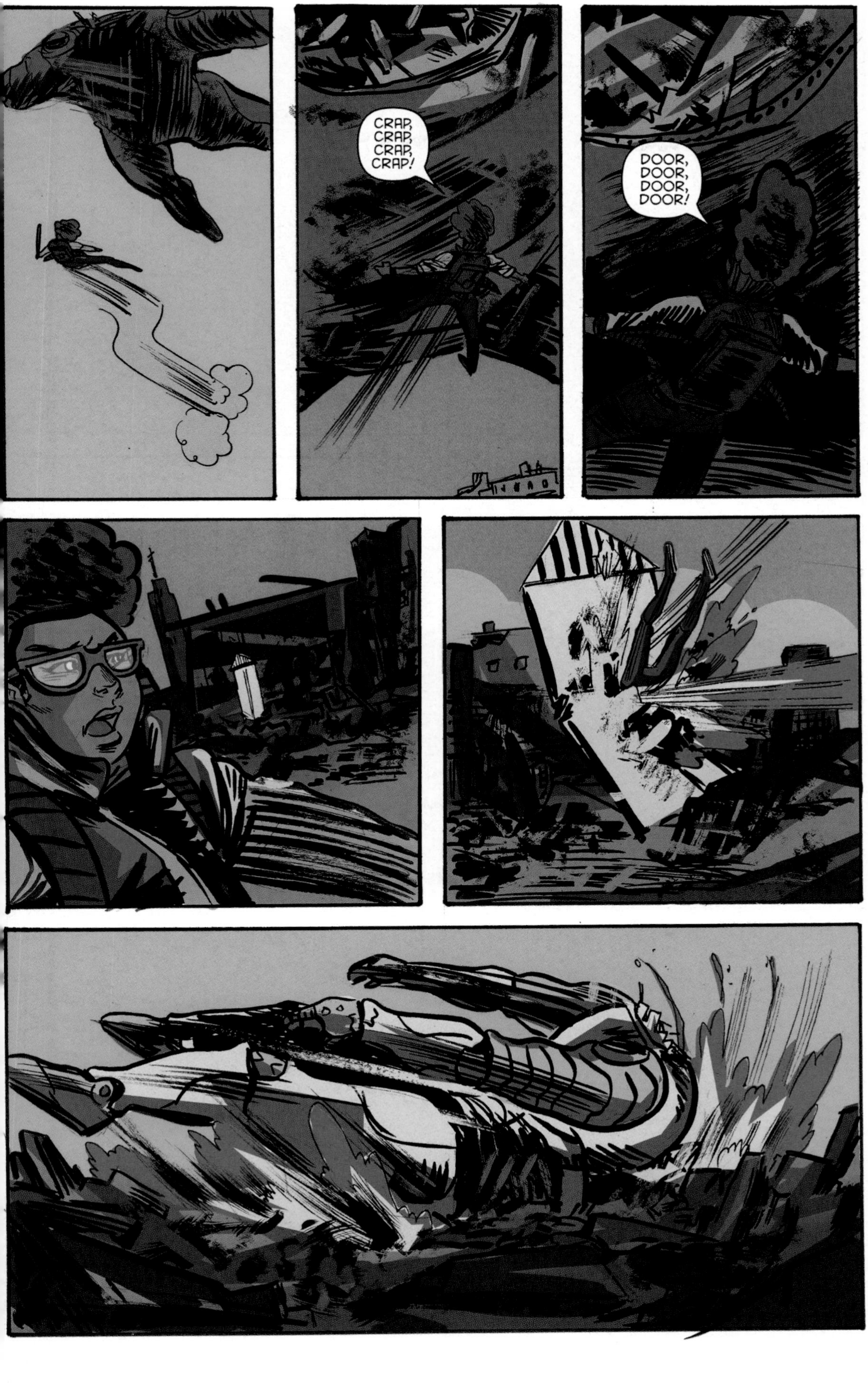
CRAP, CRAP, CRAP, CRAP!
DOOR, DOOR, DOOR, DOOR!

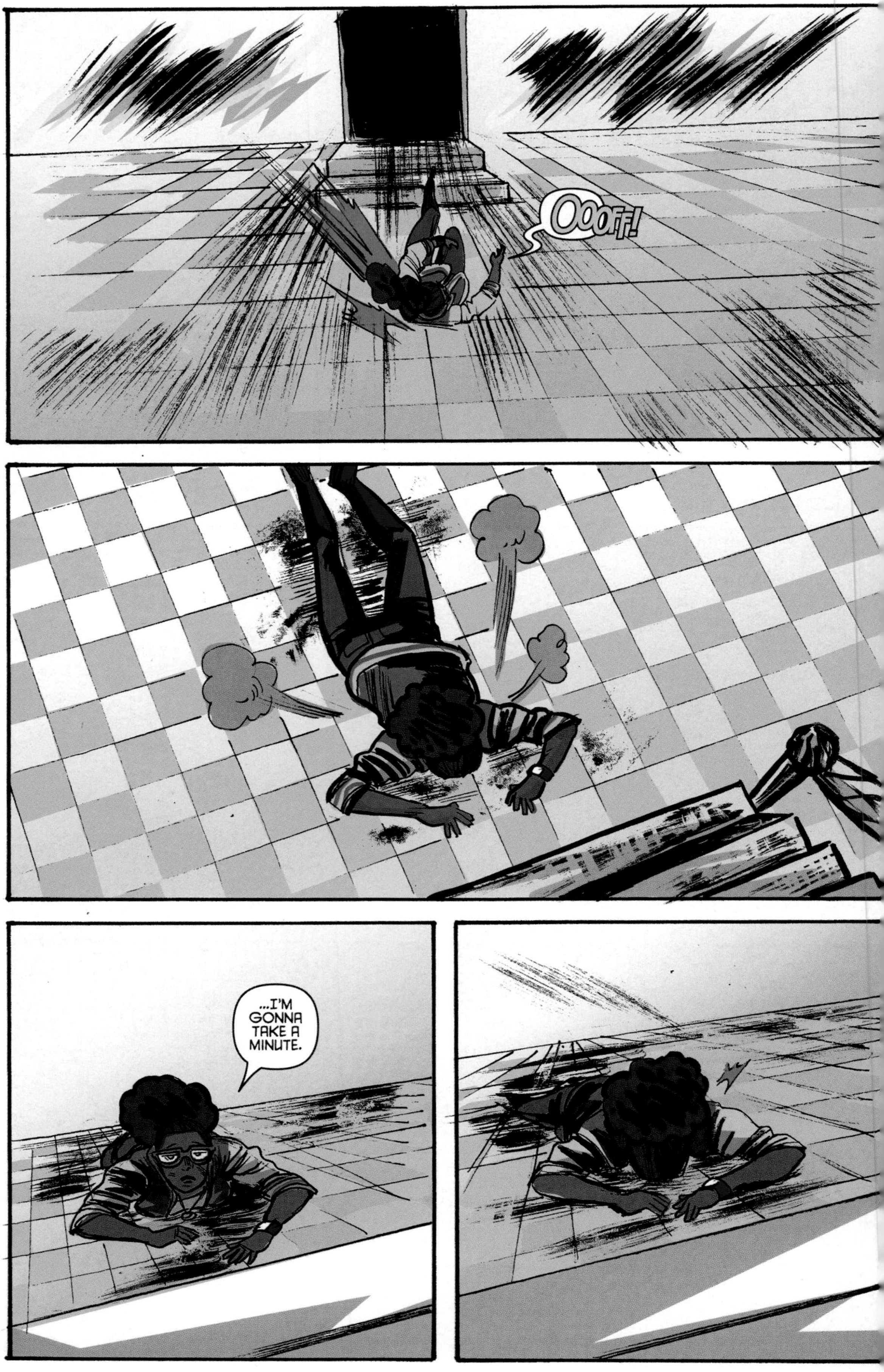
OOOFF!
...I'M GONNA TAKE A MINUTE.

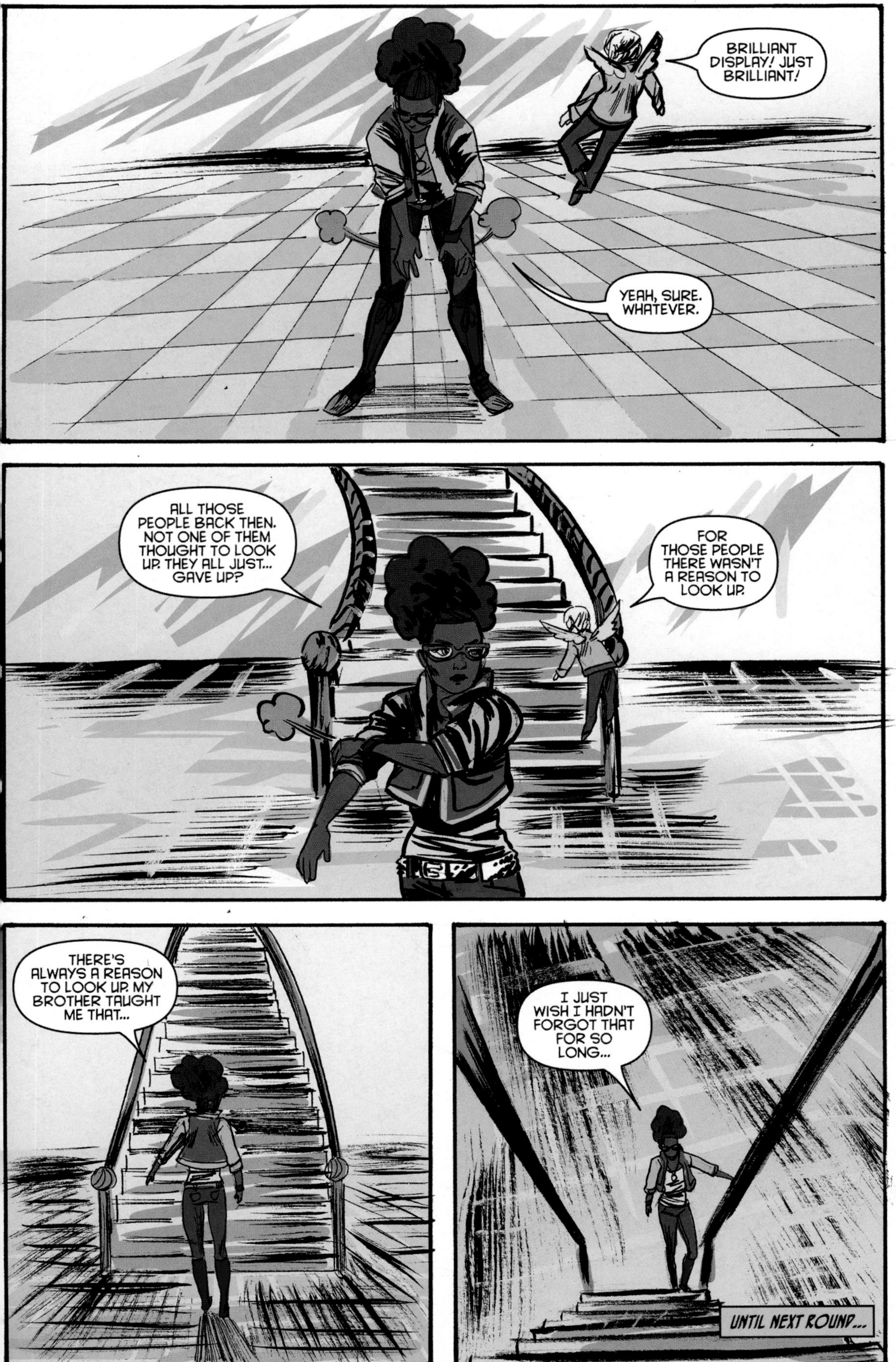
BRILLIANT DISPLAY! JUST BRILLIANT!
YEAH, SURE. WHATEVER.
ALL THOSE PEOPLE BACK THEN. NOT ONE OF THEM THOUGHT TO LOOK UP. THEY ALL JUST... GAVE UP?
FOR THOSE PEOPLE THERE WASN'T A REASON TO LOOK UP.
THERE'S ALWAYS A REASON TO LOOK UP. MY BROTHER TAUGHT ME THAT...
I JUST WISH I HADN'T FORGOT THAT FOR SO LONG...
UNTIL NEXT ROUND...

Bryan Seaton: Publisher - Kevin Freeman: President - Creative Director: Dave Dwonch - Editor In Chief: Shawn Gabborin
Co-Directors of Marketing: Jamal Igle & Kelly Dale - Social Media Director: Jim Dietz - Mad Robot-Scientist: Chad Cicconi - Submissions Editor: Colleen Boyd

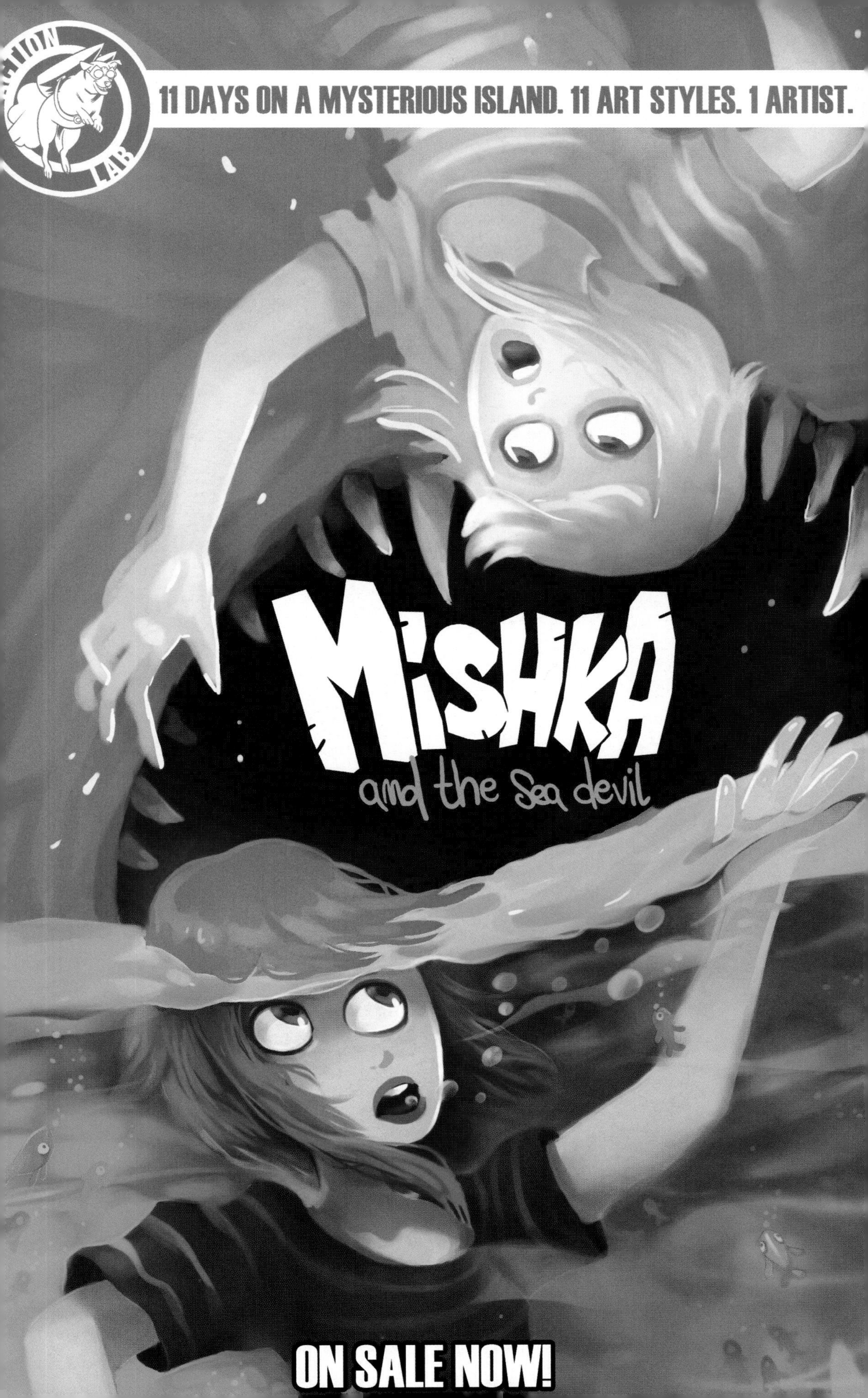

11 DAYS ON A MYSTERIOUS ISLAND. 11 ART STYLES. 1 ARTIST.
MISHKA
and the sea devil
ON SALE NOW!

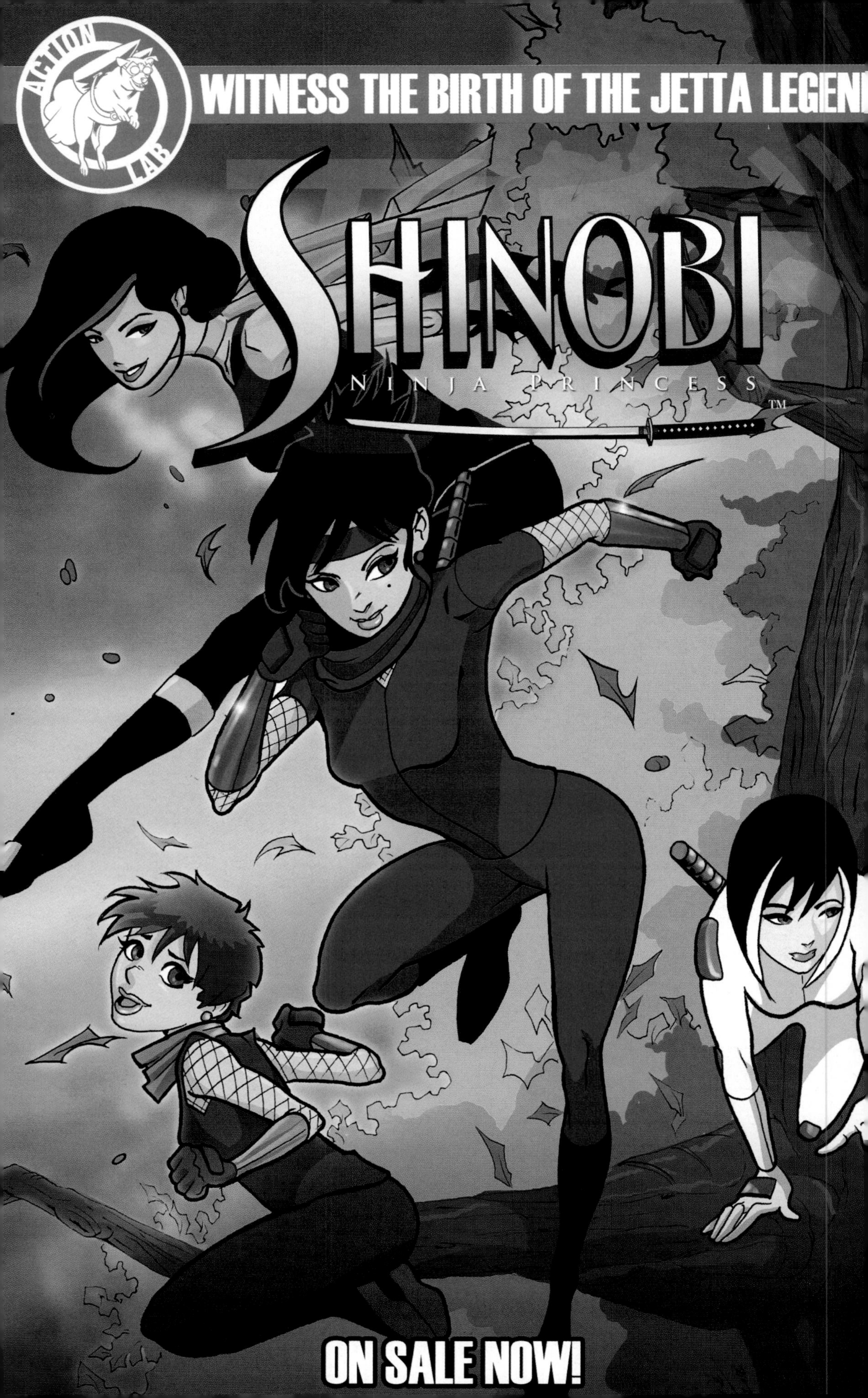
ACTION LAB
WITNESS THE BIRTH OF THE JETTA LEGEN
SHINOBI
NINJA PRINCESS
TM
ON SALE NOW!

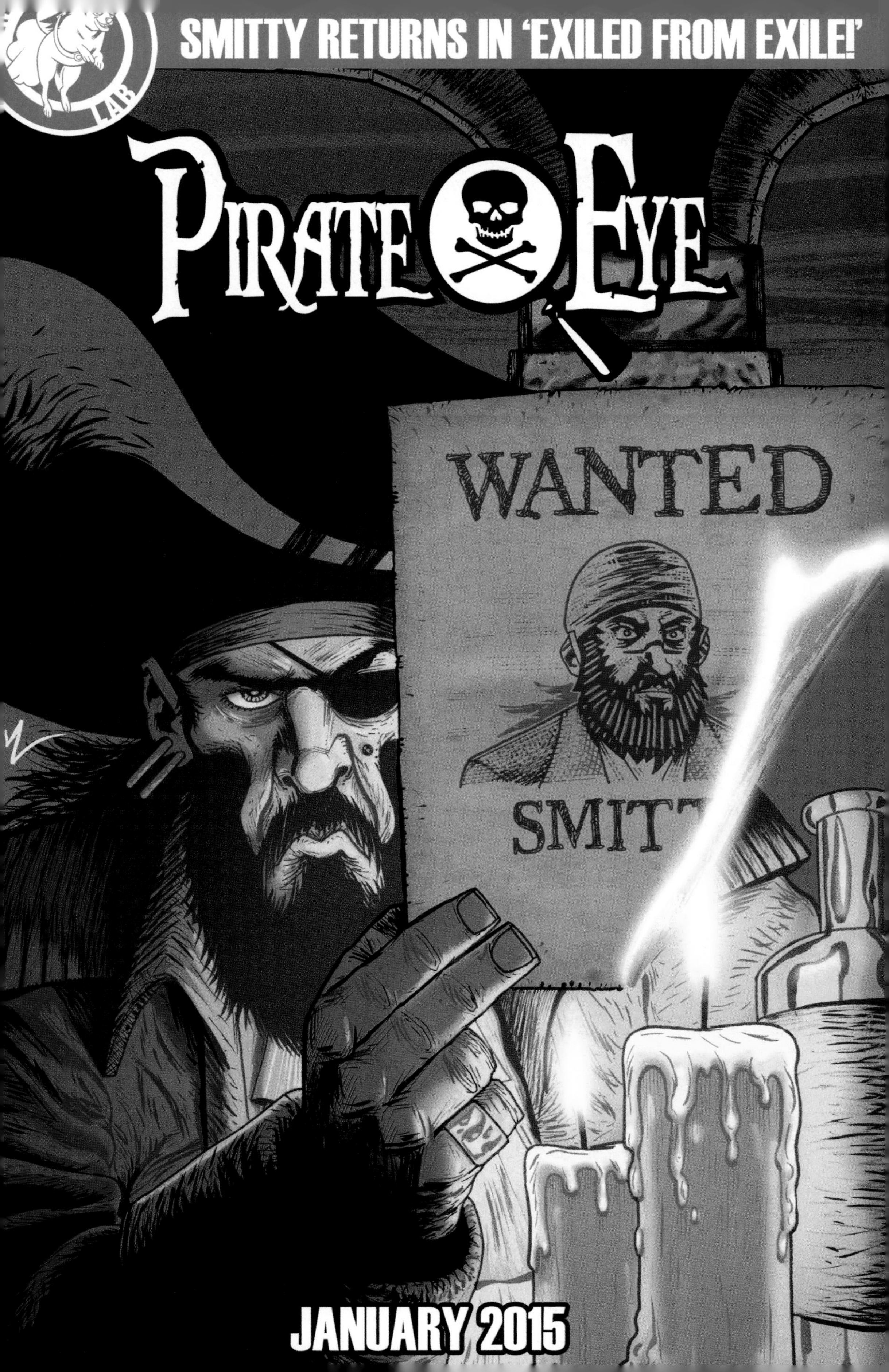
SMITTY RETURNS IN 'EXILED FROM EXILE!'
LAB
PIRATE EYE
WANTED
SMITT
JANUARY 2015

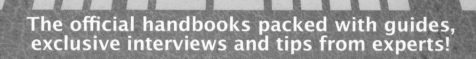
MINECRAFT

The official handbooks packed with guides, exclusive interviews and tips from experts!

COMMUNITY CREATIONS
THE MOST IMPRESSIVE ROYAL HALLS IN THE KINGDOM!

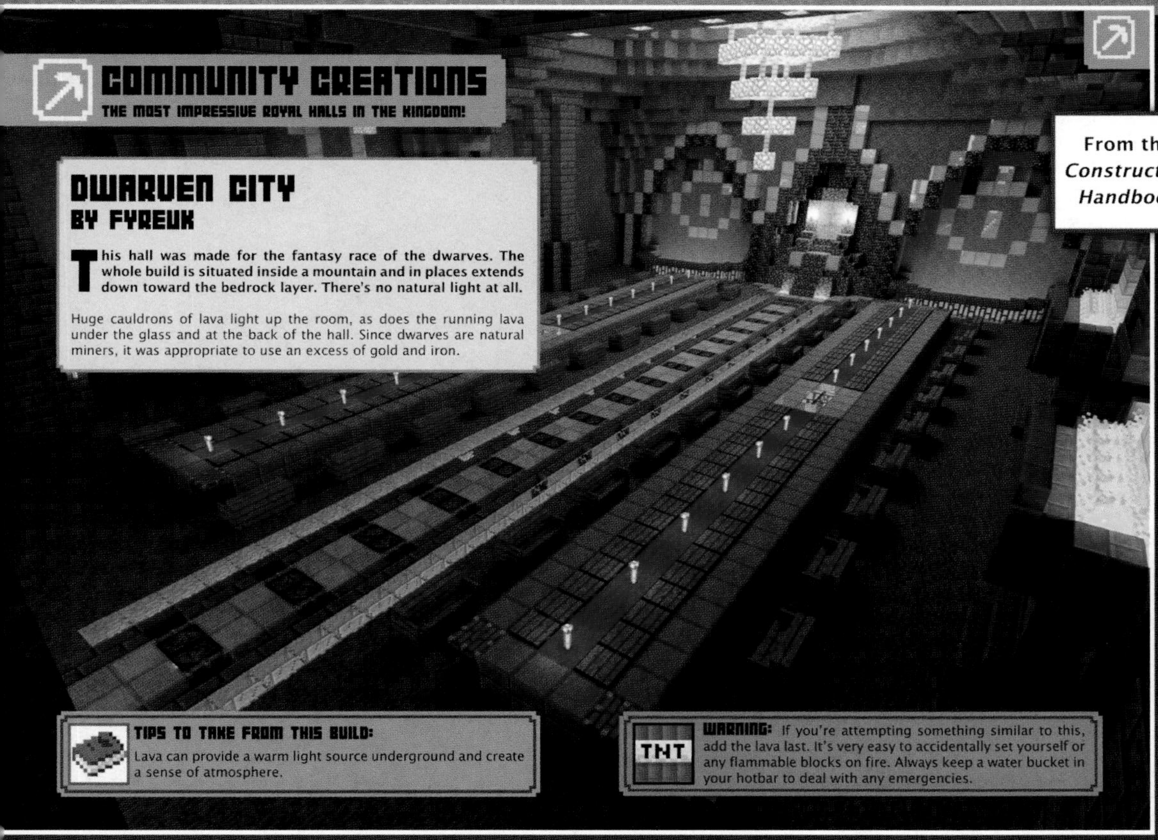

From the
*Construction
Handbook*

DWARVEN CITY
BY FYREUK

This hall was made for the fantasy race of the dwarves. The whole build is situated inside a mountain and in places extends down toward the bedrock layer. There's no natural light at all.

Huge cauldrons of lava light up the room, as does the running lava under the glass and at the back of the hall. Since dwarves are natural miners, it was appropriate to use an excess of gold and iron.

TIPS TO TAKE FROM THIS BUILD:
Lava can provide a warm light source underground and create a sense of atmosphere.

TNT **WARNING:** If you're attempting something similar to this, add the lava last. It's very easy to accidentally set yourself or any flammable blocks on fire. Always keep a water bucket in your hotbar to deal with any emergencies.

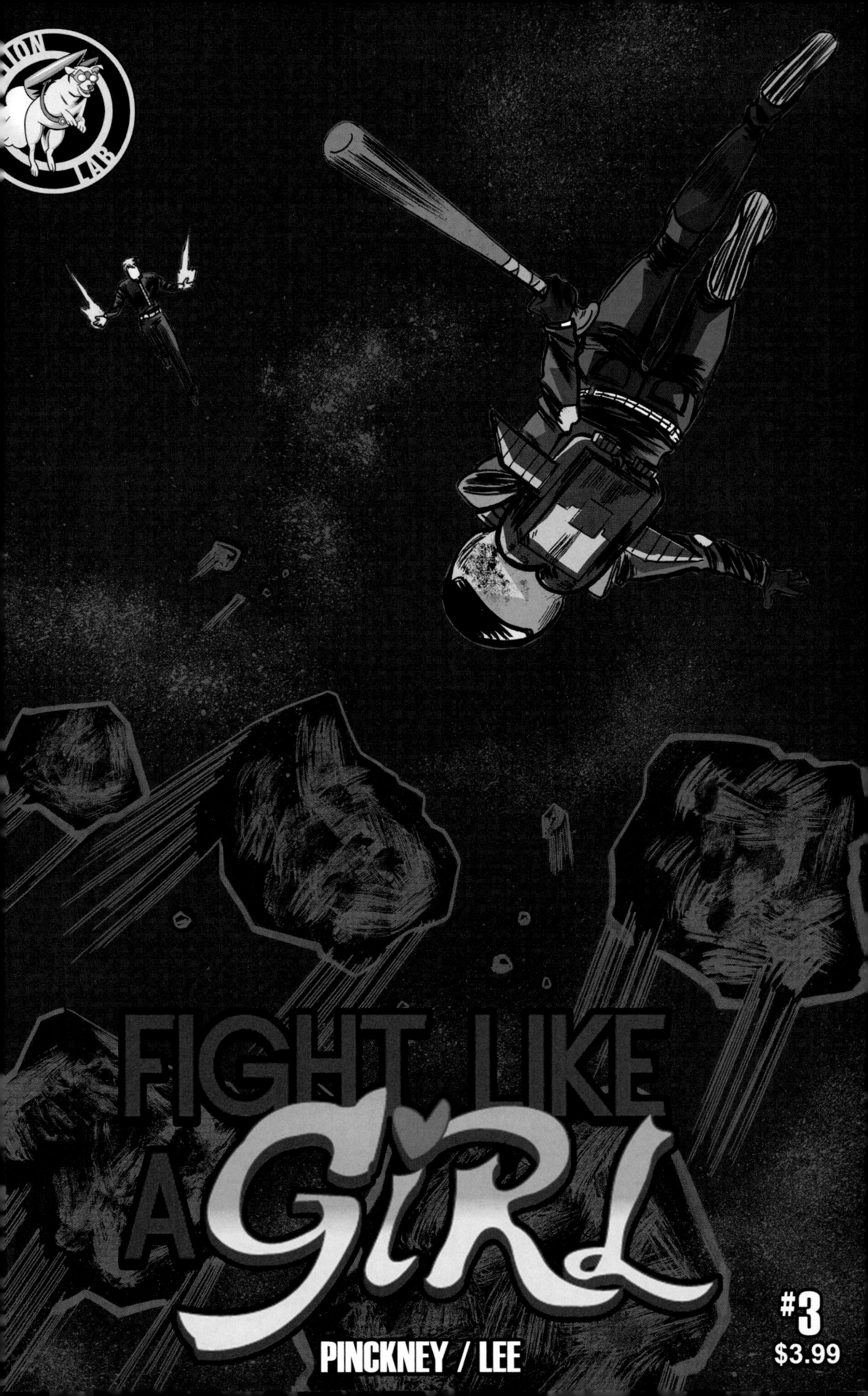
FIGHT LIKE
A GIRL
#3
$3.99
PINCKNEY / LEE

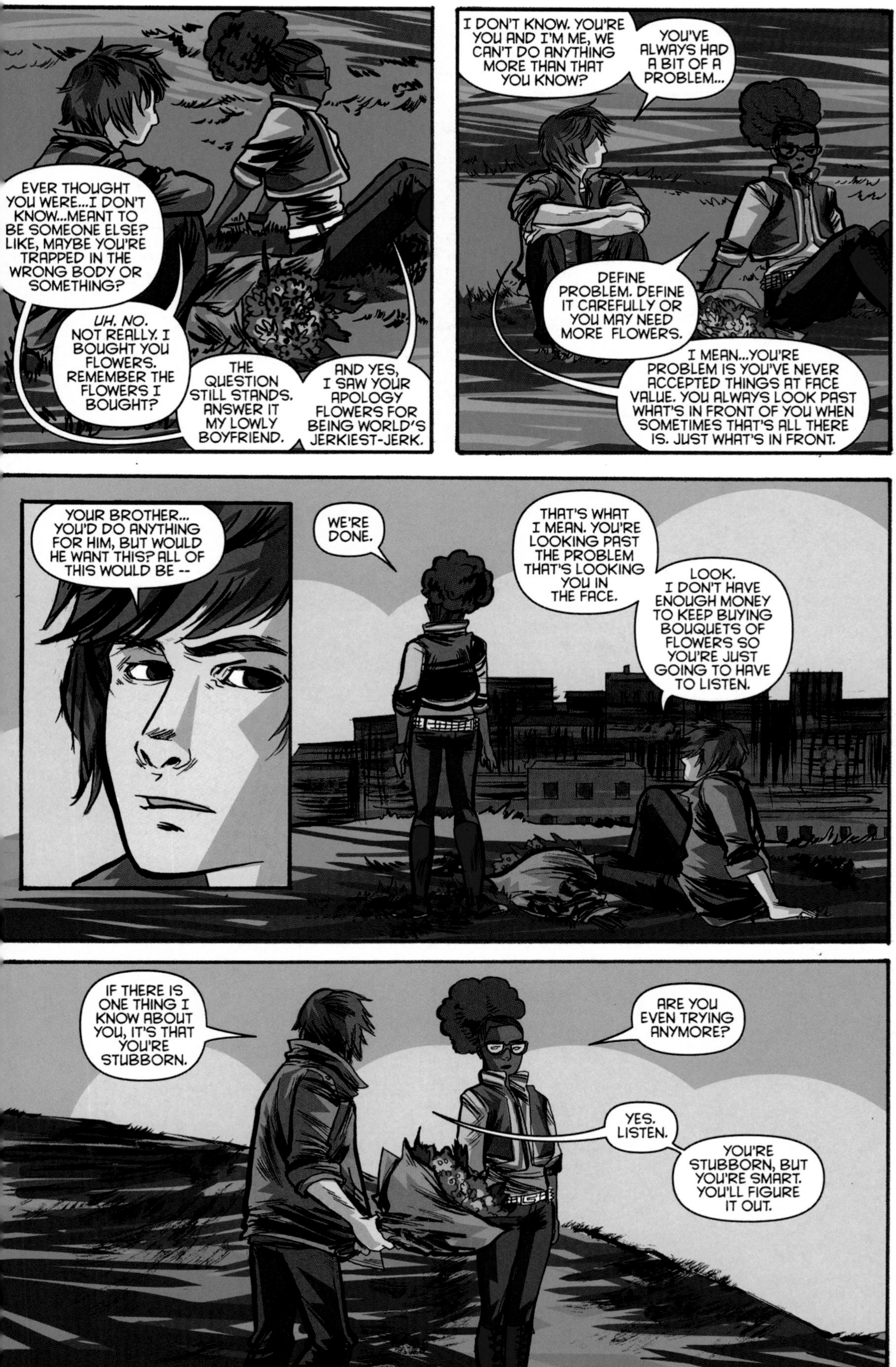
EVER THOUGHT YOU WERE...I DON'T KNOW...MEANT TO BE SOMEONE ELSE? LIKE, MAYBE YOU'RE TRAPPED IN THE WRONG BODY OR SOMETHING?
UH, NO. NOT REALLY. I BOUGHT YOU FLOWERS. REMEMBER THE FLOWERS I BOUGHT?
THE QUESTION STILL STANDS. ANSWER IT MY LOWLY BOYFRIEND.
AND YES, I SAW YOUR APOLOGY FLOWERS FOR BEING WORLD'S JERKIEST-JERK.
I DON'T KNOW. YOU'RE YOU AND I'M ME, WE CAN'T DO ANYTHING MORE THAN THAT YOU KNOW?
YOU'VE ALWAYS HAD A BIT OF A PROBLEM...
DEFINE PROBLEM. DEFINE IT CAREFULLY OR YOU MAY NEED MORE FLOWERS.
I MEAN...YOU'RE PROBLEM IS YOU'VE NEVER ACCEPTED THINGS AT FACE VALUE. YOU ALWAYS LOOK PAST WHAT'S IN FRONT OF YOU WHEN SOMETIMES THAT'S ALL THERE IS. JUST WHAT'S IN FRONT.
YOUR BROTHER... YOU'D DO ANYTHING FOR HIM, BUT WOULD HE WANT THIS? ALL OF THIS WOULD BE --
WE'RE DONE.
THAT'S WHAT I MEAN. YOU'RE LOOKING PAST THE PROBLEM THAT'S LOOKING YOU IN THE FACE.
LOOK. I DON'T HAVE ENOUGH MONEY TO KEEP BUYING BOUQUETS OF FLOWERS SO YOU'RE JUST GOING TO HAVE TO LISTEN.
IF THERE IS ONE THING I KNOW ABOUT YOU, IT'S THAT YOU'RE STUBBORN.
ARE YOU EVEN TRYING ANYMORE?
YES. LISTEN.
YOU'RE STUBBORN, BUT YOU'RE SMART. YOU'LL FIGURE IT OUT.

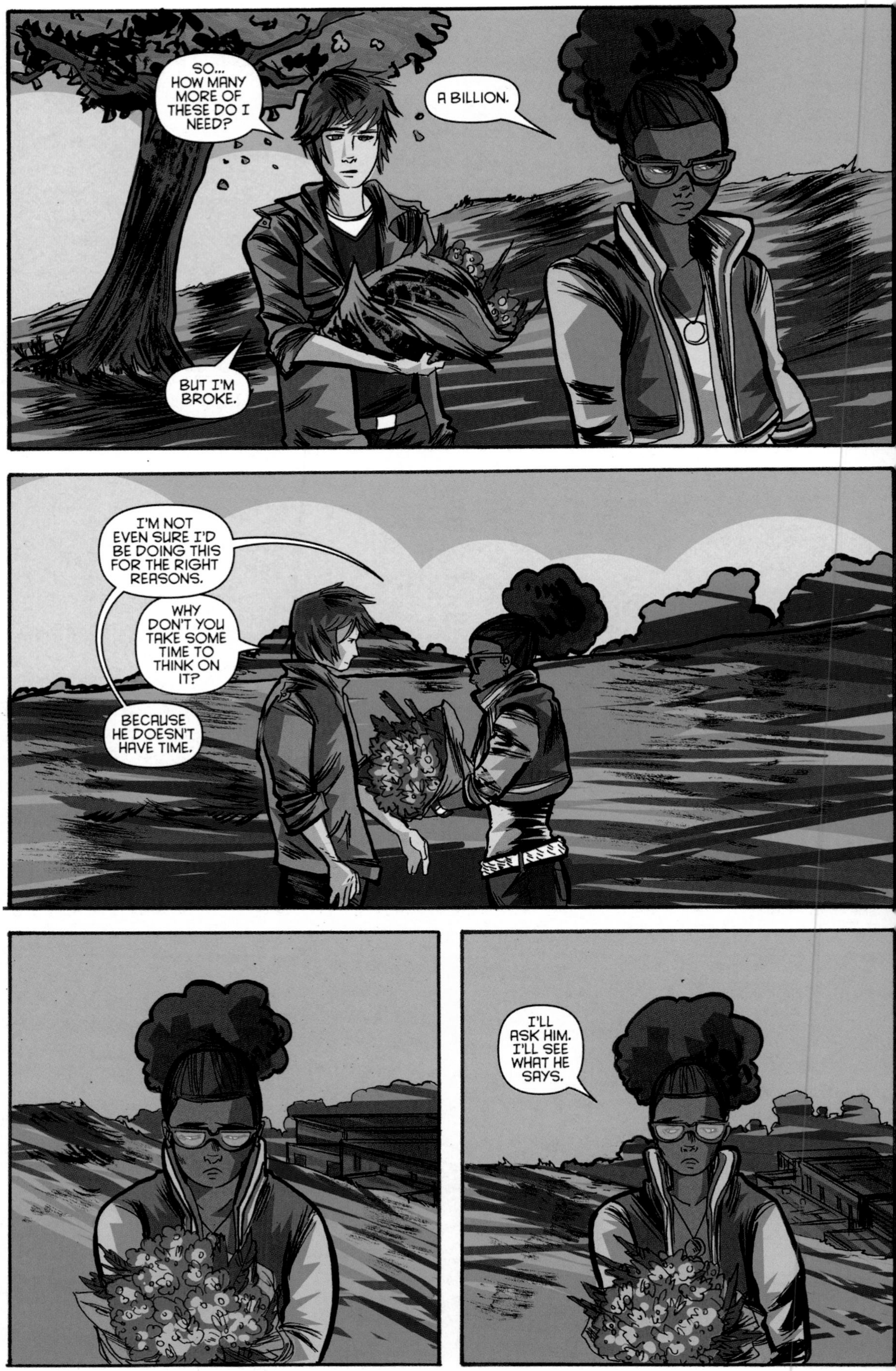
SO... HOW MANY MORE OF THESE DO I NEED?
A BILLION.
BUT I'M BROKE.
I'M NOT EVEN SURE I'D BE DOING THIS FOR THE RIGHT REASONS.
WHY DON'T YOU TAKE SOME TIME TO THINK ON IT?
BECAUSE HE DOESN'T HAVE TIME.
I'LL ASK HIM. I'LL SEE WHAT HE SAYS.

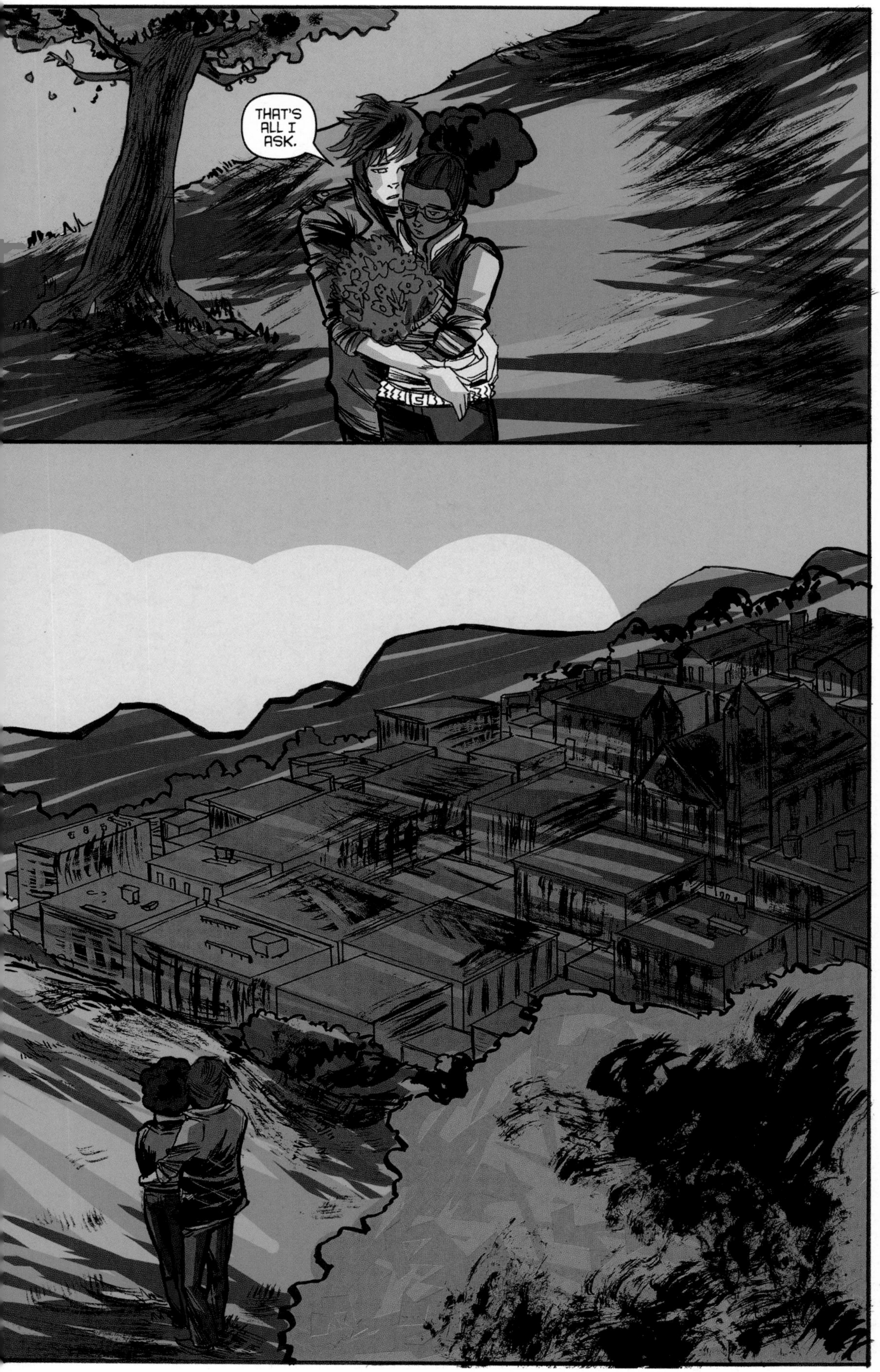
THAT'S ALL I ASK.

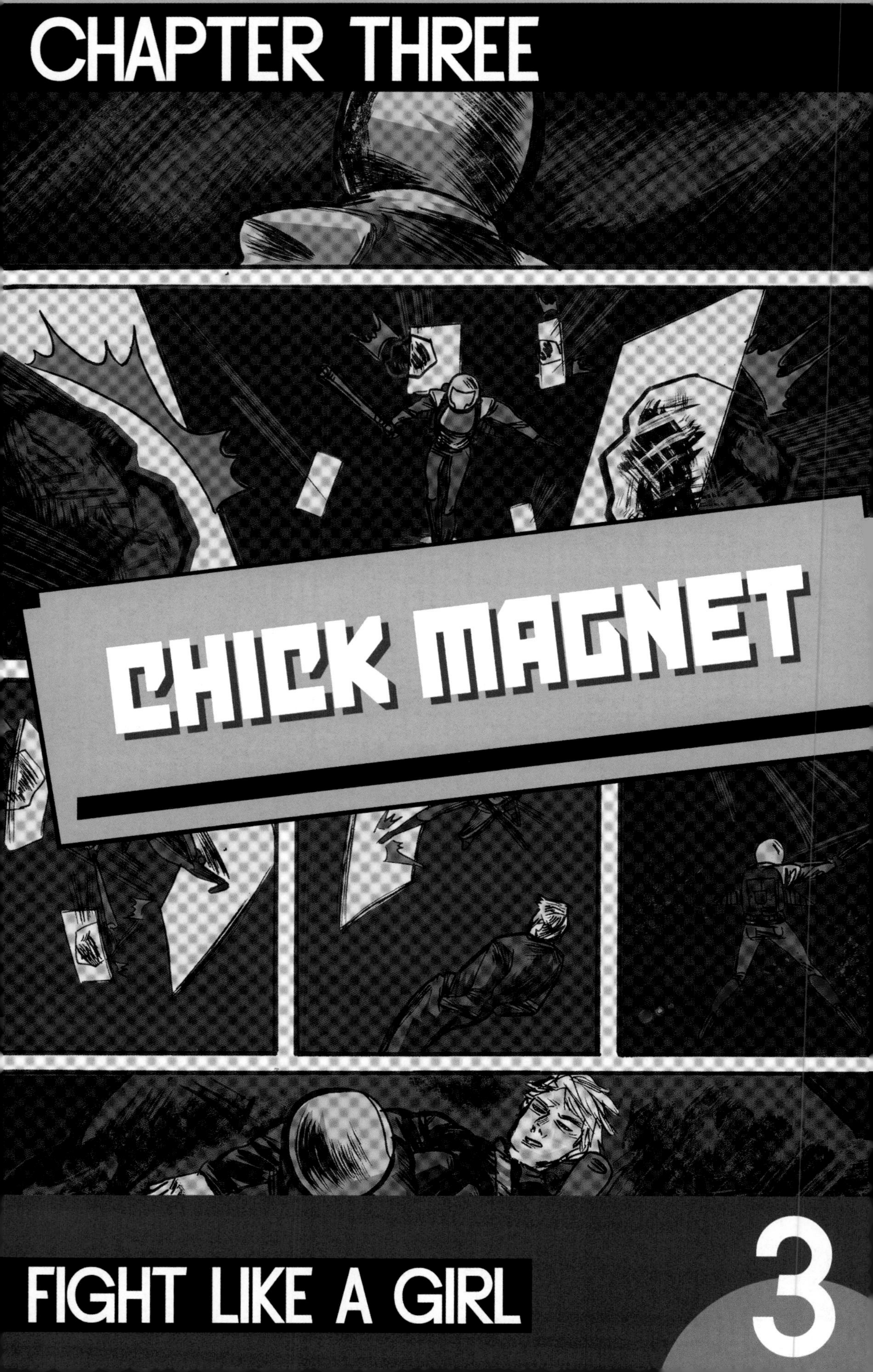
CHAPTER THREE
CHICK MAGNET
FIGHT LIKE A GIRL
3

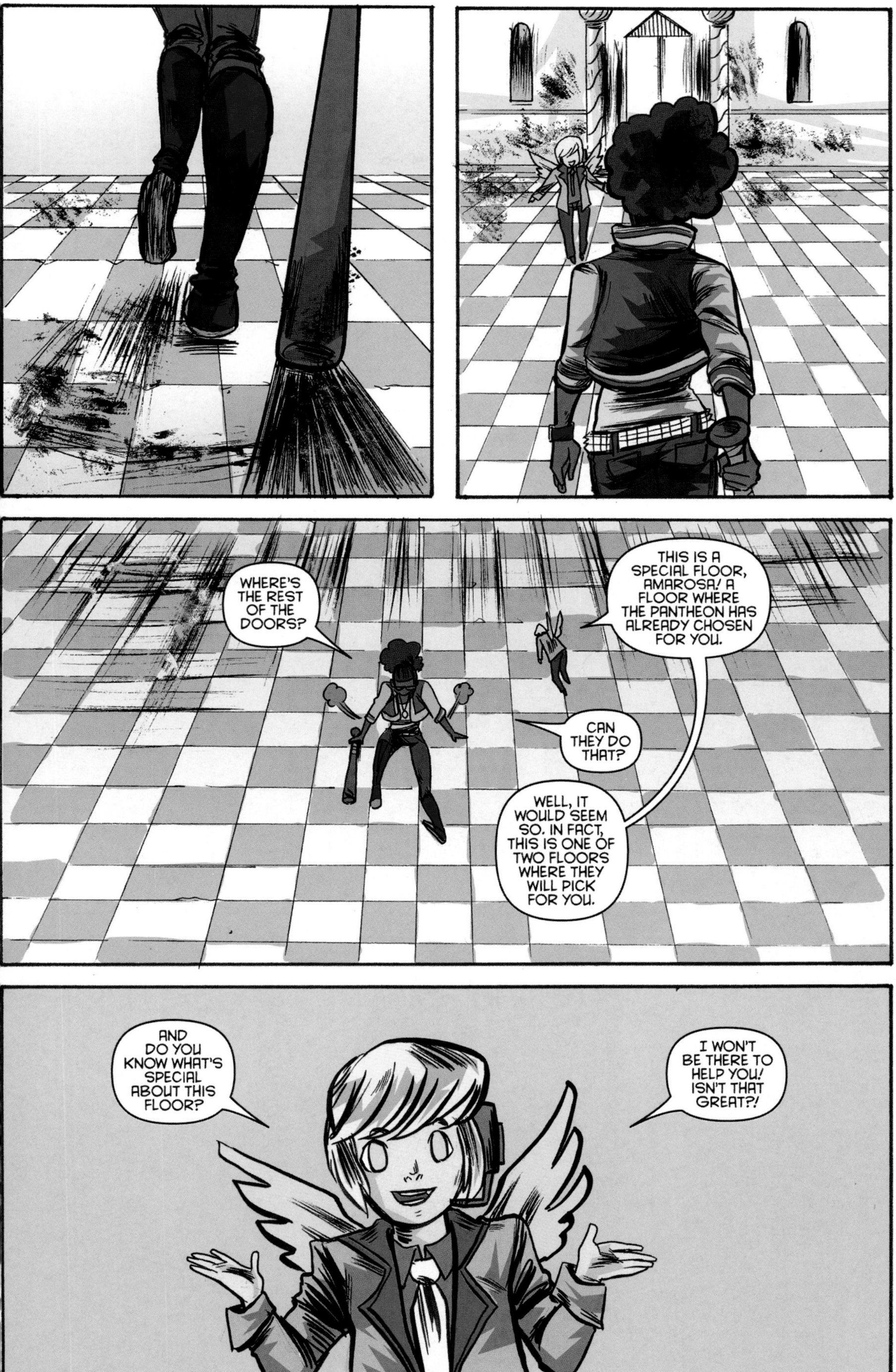
WHERE'S THE REST OF THE DOORS?
THIS IS A SPECIAL FLOOR, AMAROSA! A FLOOR WHERE THE PANTHEON HAS ALREADY CHOSEN FOR YOU.
CAN THEY DO THAT?
WELL, IT WOULD SEEM SO. IN FACT, THIS IS ONE OF TWO FLOORS WHERE THEY WILL PICK FOR YOU.
AND DO YOU KNOW WHAT'S SPECIAL ABOUT THIS FLOOR?
I WON'T BE THERE TO HELP YOU! ISN'T THAT GREAT?!

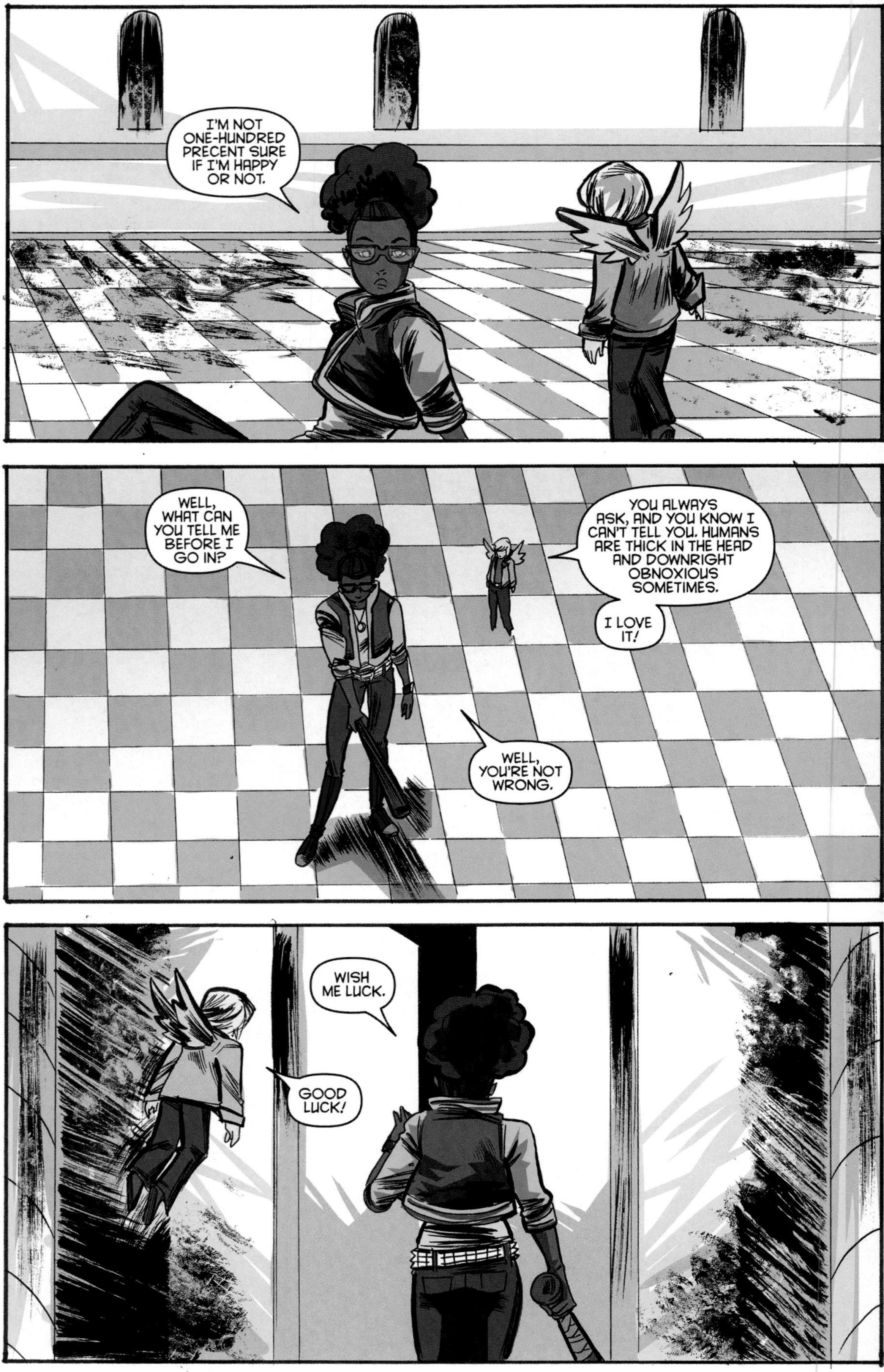
I'M NOT ONE-HUNDRED PRECENT SURE IF I'M HAPPY OR NOT.
WELL, WHAT CAN YOU TELL ME BEFORE I GO IN?
YOU ALWAYS ASK, AND YOU KNOW I CAN'T TELL YOU. HUMANS ARE THICK IN THE HEAD AND DOWNRIGHT OBNOXIOUS SOMETIMES.
I LOVE IT!
WELL, YOU'RE NOT WRONG.
WISH ME LUCK.
GOOD LUCK!

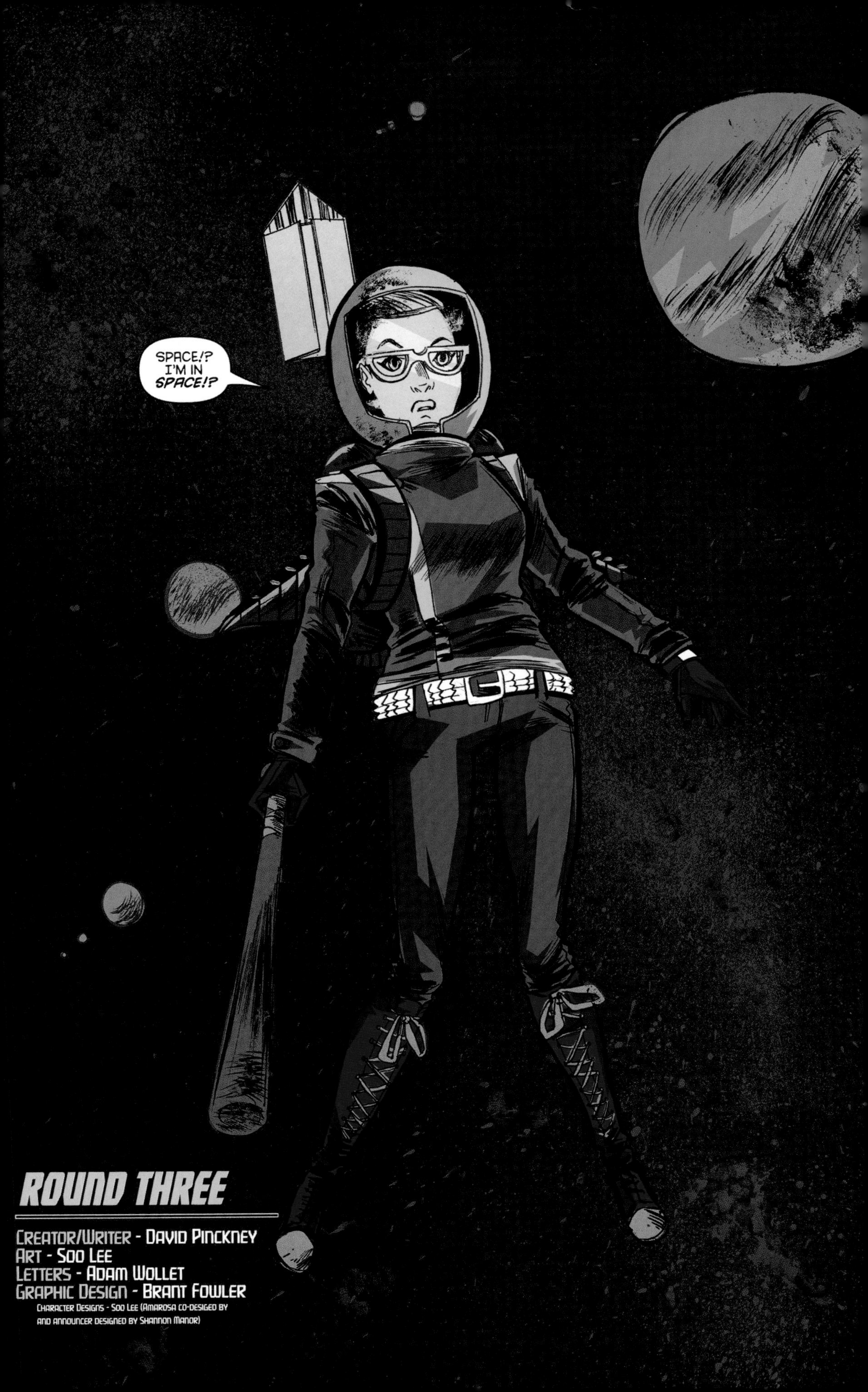
SPACE!? I'M IN SPACE!?

ROUND THREE

Creator/Writer - David Pinckney
Art - Soo Lee
Letters - Adam Wollet
Graphic Design - Brant Fowler

Character Designs - Soo Lee (Amarosa co-desiged by and announcer designed by Shannon Manor)

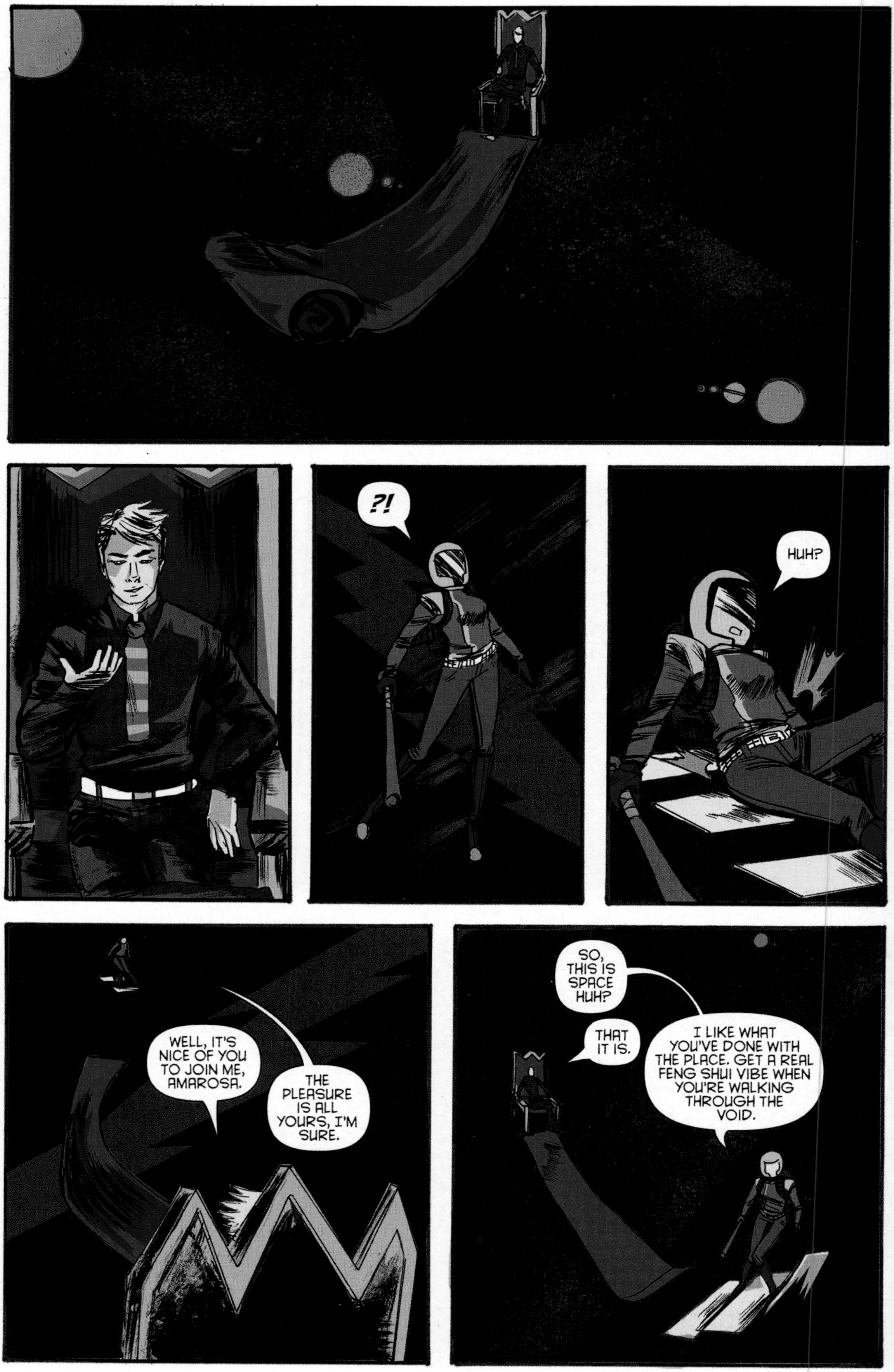
?!
HUH?
WELL, IT'S NICE OF YOU TO JOIN ME, AMAROSA.
THE PLEASURE IS ALL YOURS, I'M SURE.
SO, THIS IS SPACE HUH?
THAT IT IS.
I LIKE WHAT YOU'VE DONE WITH THE PLACE. GET A REAL FENG SHUI VIBE WHEN YOU'RE WALKING THROUGH THE VOID.

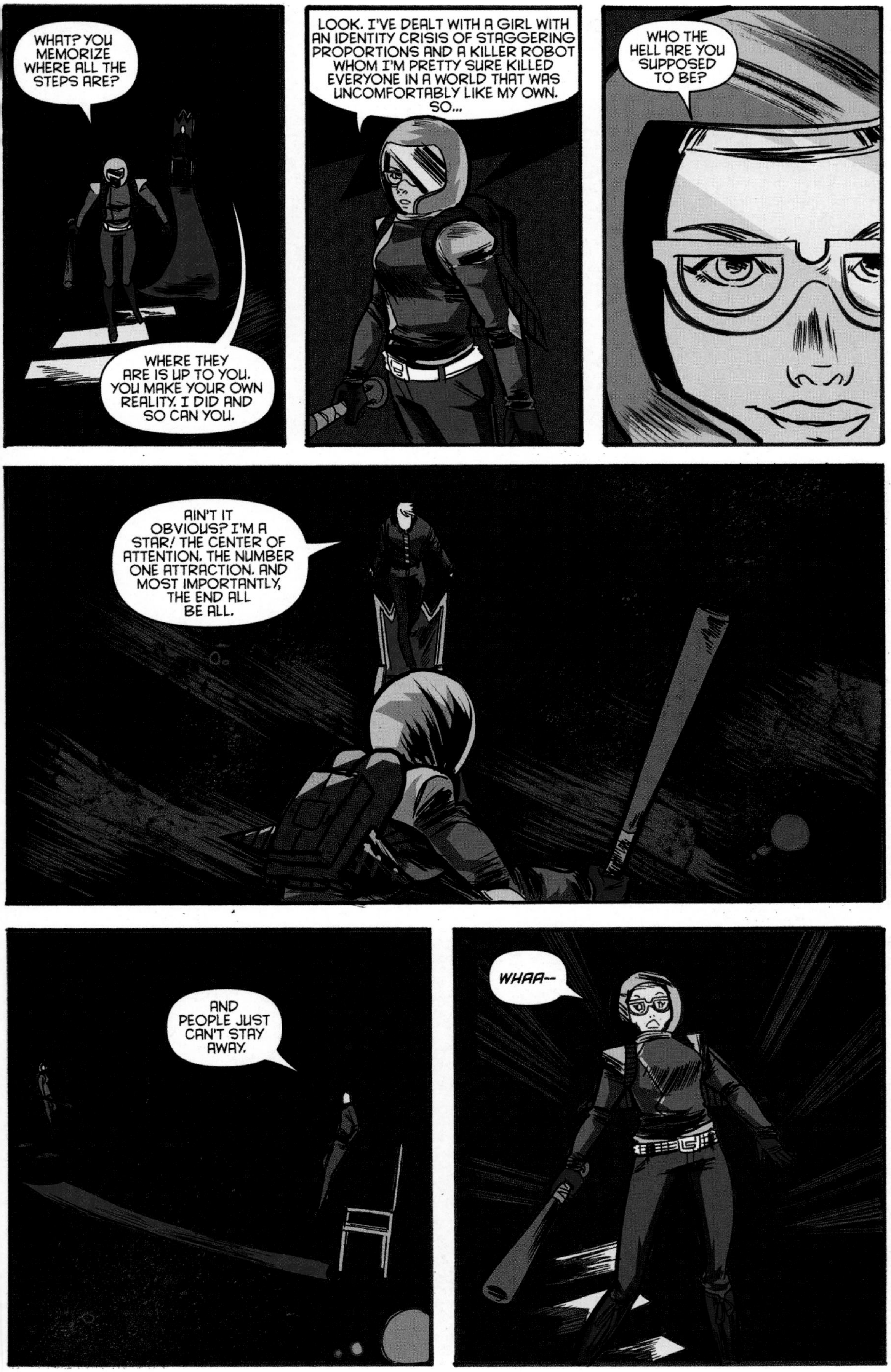
WHAT? YOU MEMORIZE WHERE ALL THE STEPS ARE?
WHERE THEY ARE IS UP TO YOU. YOU MAKE YOUR OWN REALITY. I DID AND SO CAN YOU.
LOOK. I'VE DEALT WITH A GIRL WITH AN IDENTITY CRISIS OF STAGGERING PROPORTIONS AND A KILLER ROBOT WHOM I'M PRETTY SURE KILLED EVERYONE IN A WORLD THAT WAS UNCOMFORTABLY LIKE MY OWN. SO...
WHO THE HELL ARE YOU SUPPOSED TO BE?
AIN'T IT OBVIOUS? I'M A STAR! THE CENTER OF ATTENTION. THE NUMBER ONE ATTRACTION. AND MOST IMPORTANTLY, THE END ALL BE ALL.
AND PEOPLE JUST CAN'T STAY AWAY.
WHAA--

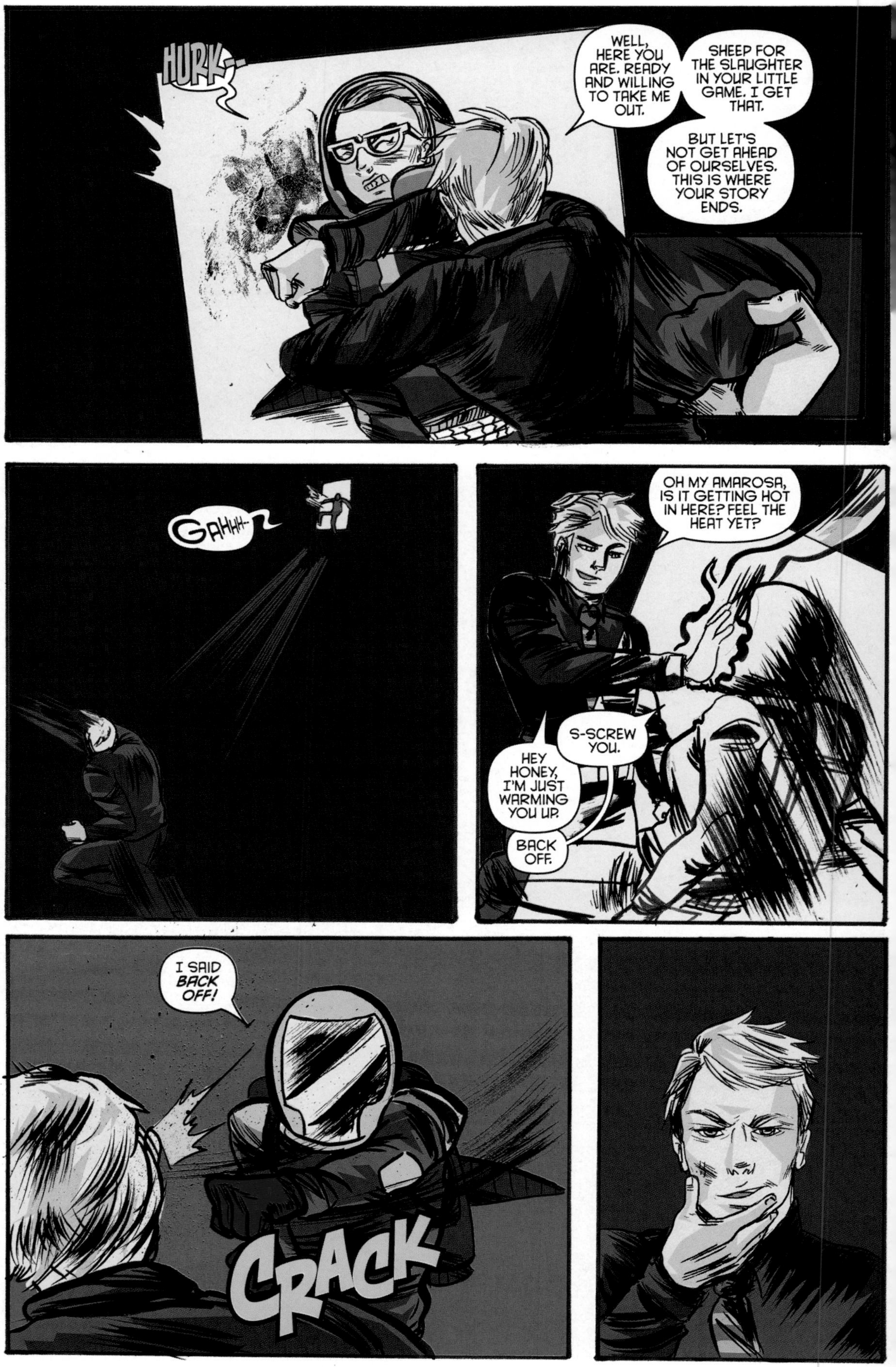
HURK--
WELL, HERE YOU ARE. READY AND WILLING TO TAKE ME OUT.
SHEEP FOR THE SLAUGHTER IN YOUR LITTLE GAME. I GET THAT.
BUT LET'S NOT GET AHEAD OF OURSELVES. THIS IS WHERE YOUR STORY ENDS.
GAHHH--
OH MY AMAROSA, IS IT GETTING HOT IN HERE? FEEL THE HEAT YET?
S-SCREW YOU.
HEY HONEY, I'M JUST WARMING YOU UP.
BACK OFF.
I SAID BACK OFF!
CRACK

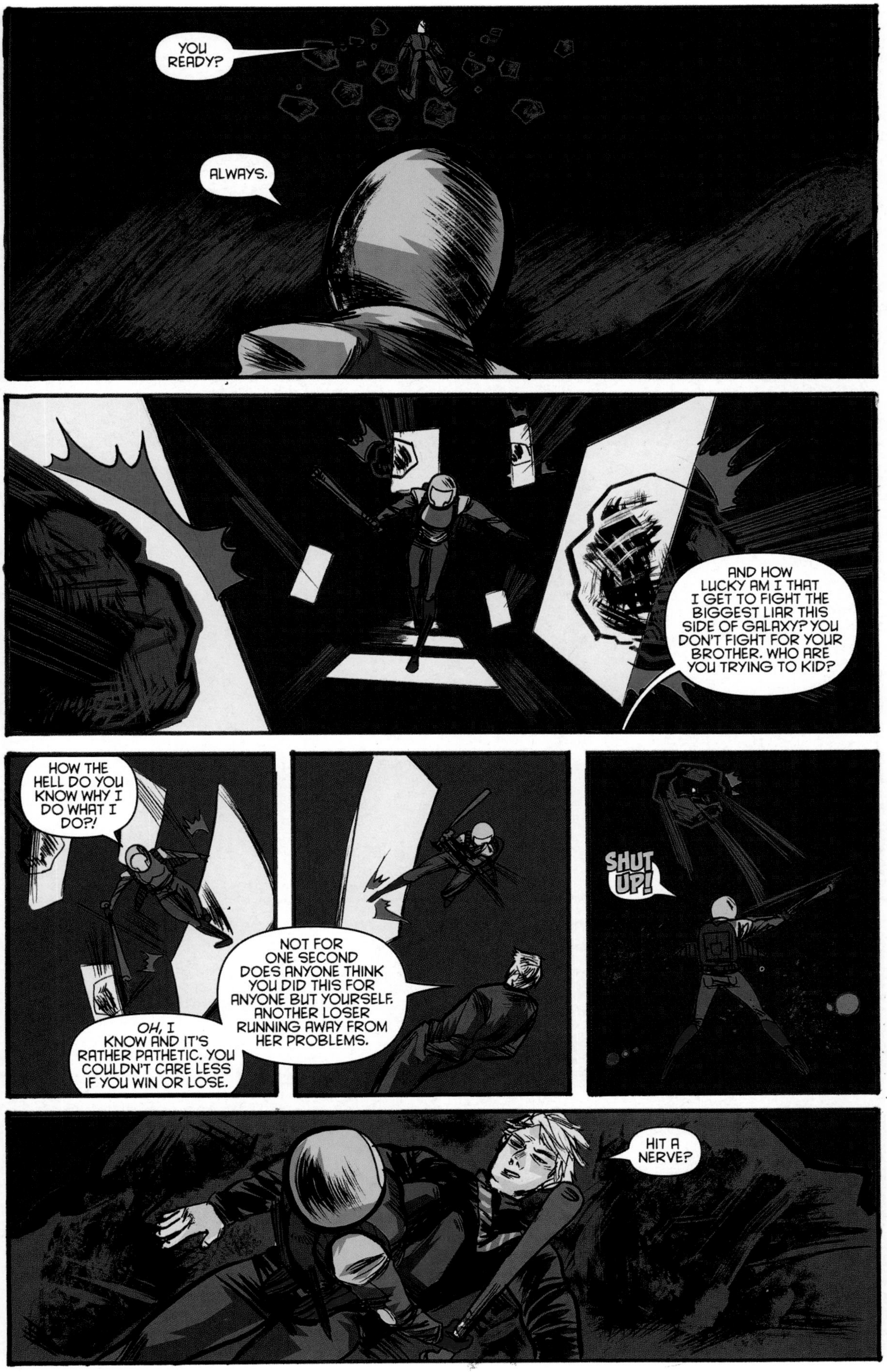
YOU READY?
ALWAYS.
AND HOW LUCKY AM I THAT I GET TO FIGHT THE BIGGEST LIAR THIS SIDE OF GALAXY? YOU DON'T FIGHT FOR YOUR BROTHER. WHO ARE YOU TRYING TO KID?
HOW THE HELL DO YOU KNOW WHY I DO WHAT I DO?!
OH, I KNOW AND IT'S RATHER PATHETIC. YOU COULDN'T CARE LESS IF YOU WIN OR LOSE.
NOT FOR ONE SECOND DOES ANYONE THINK YOU DID THIS FOR ANYONE BUT YOURSELF. ANOTHER LOSER RUNNING AWAY FROM HER PROBLEMS.
SHUT UP!
HIT A NERVE?

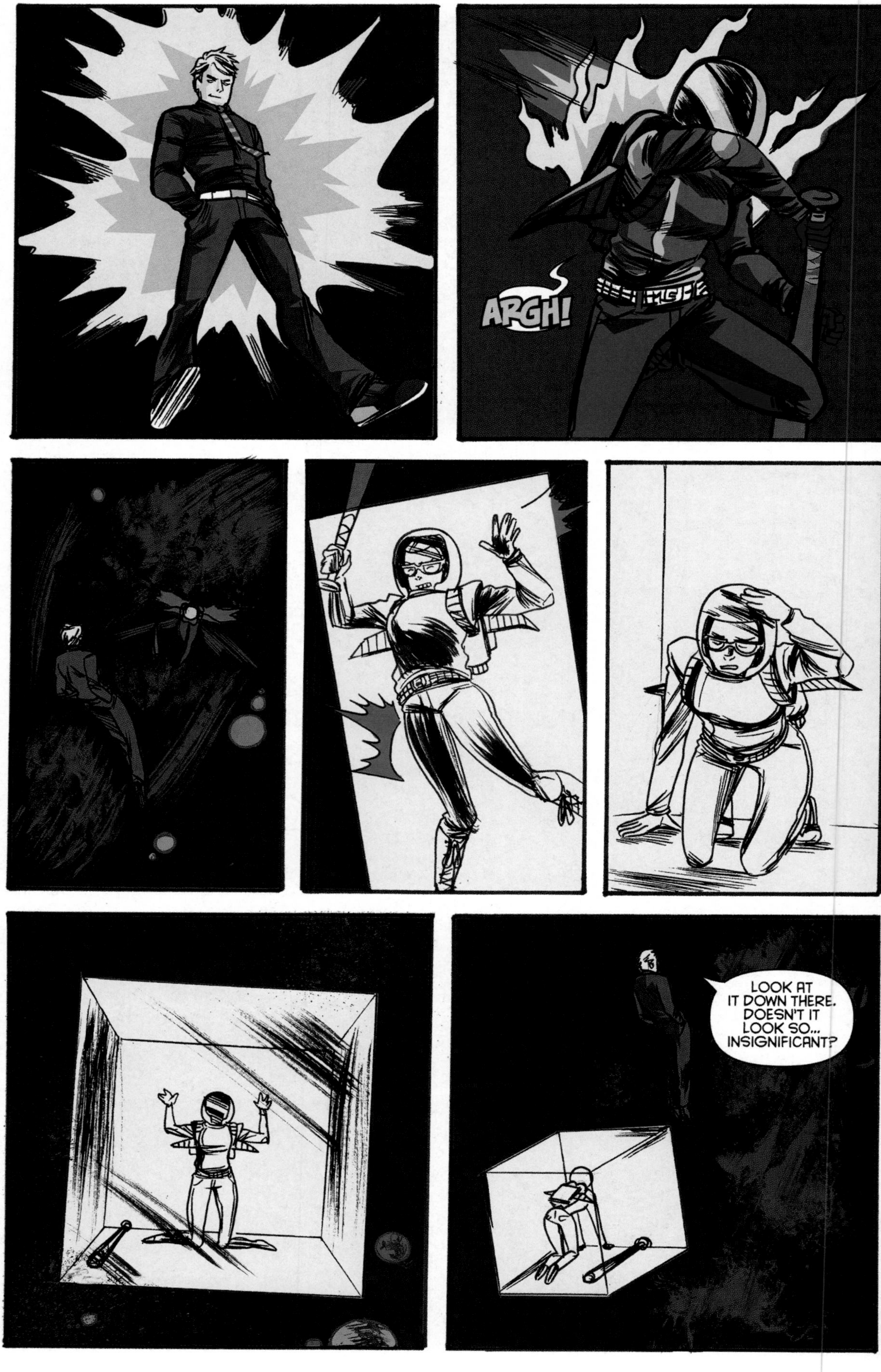
ARGH!
LOOK AT IT DOWN THERE. DOESN'T IT LOOK SO... INSIGNIFICANT?

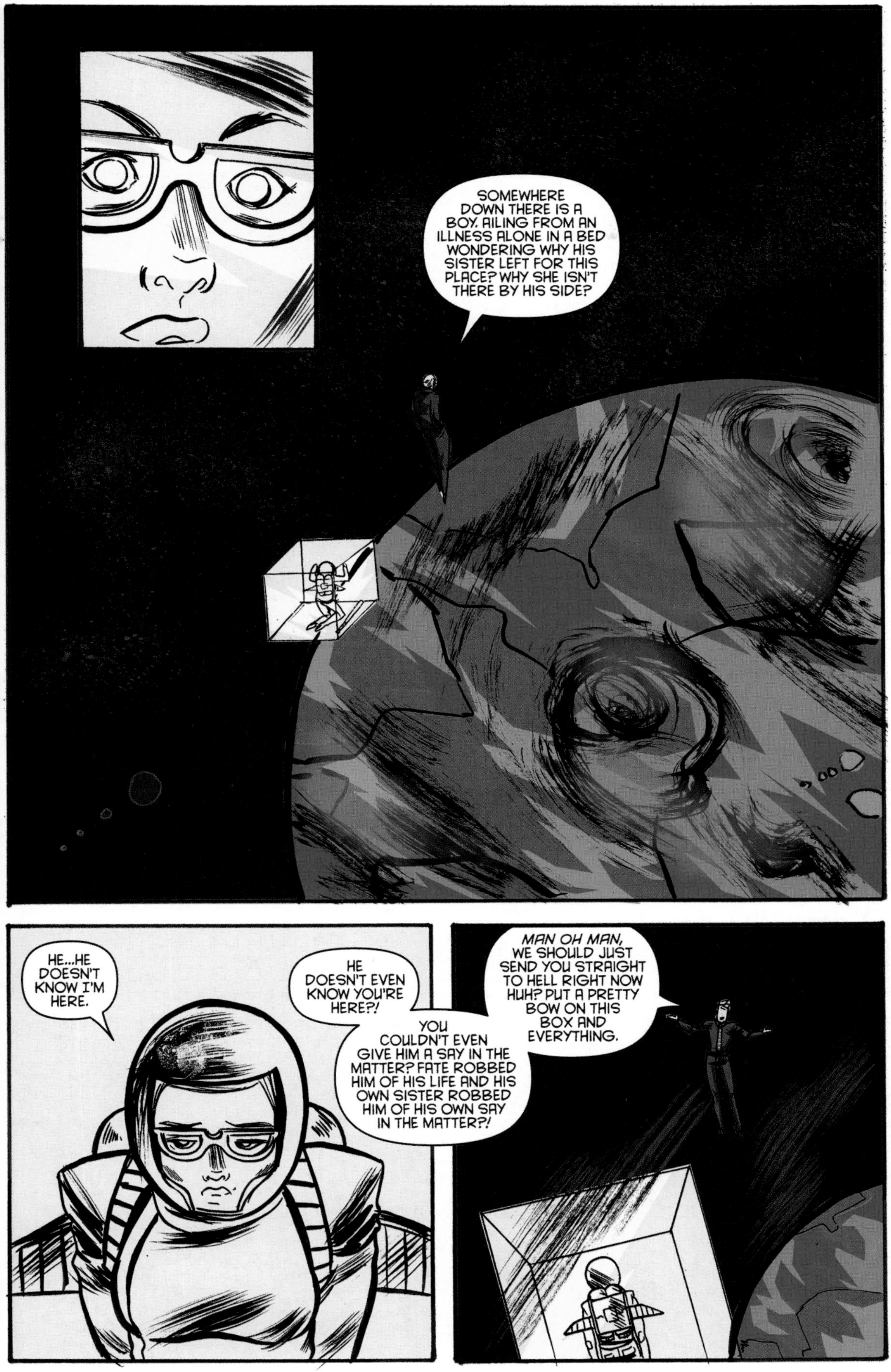
SOMEWHERE DOWN THERE IS A BOY. AILING FROM AN ILLNESS ALONE IN A BED WONDERING WHY HIS SISTER LEFT FOR THIS PLACE? WHY SHE ISN'T THERE BY HIS SIDE?
HE...HE DOESN'T KNOW I'M HERE.
HE DOESN'T EVEN KNOW YOU'RE HERE?!
YOU COULDN'T EVEN GIVE HIM A SAY IN THE MATTER? FATE ROBBED HIM OF HIS LIFE AND HIS OWN SISTER ROBBED HIM OF HIS OWN SAY IN THE MATTER?!
MAN OH MAN, WE SHOULD JUST SEND YOU STRAIGHT TO HELL RIGHT NOW HUH? PUT A PRETTY BOW ON THIS BOX AND EVERYTHING.

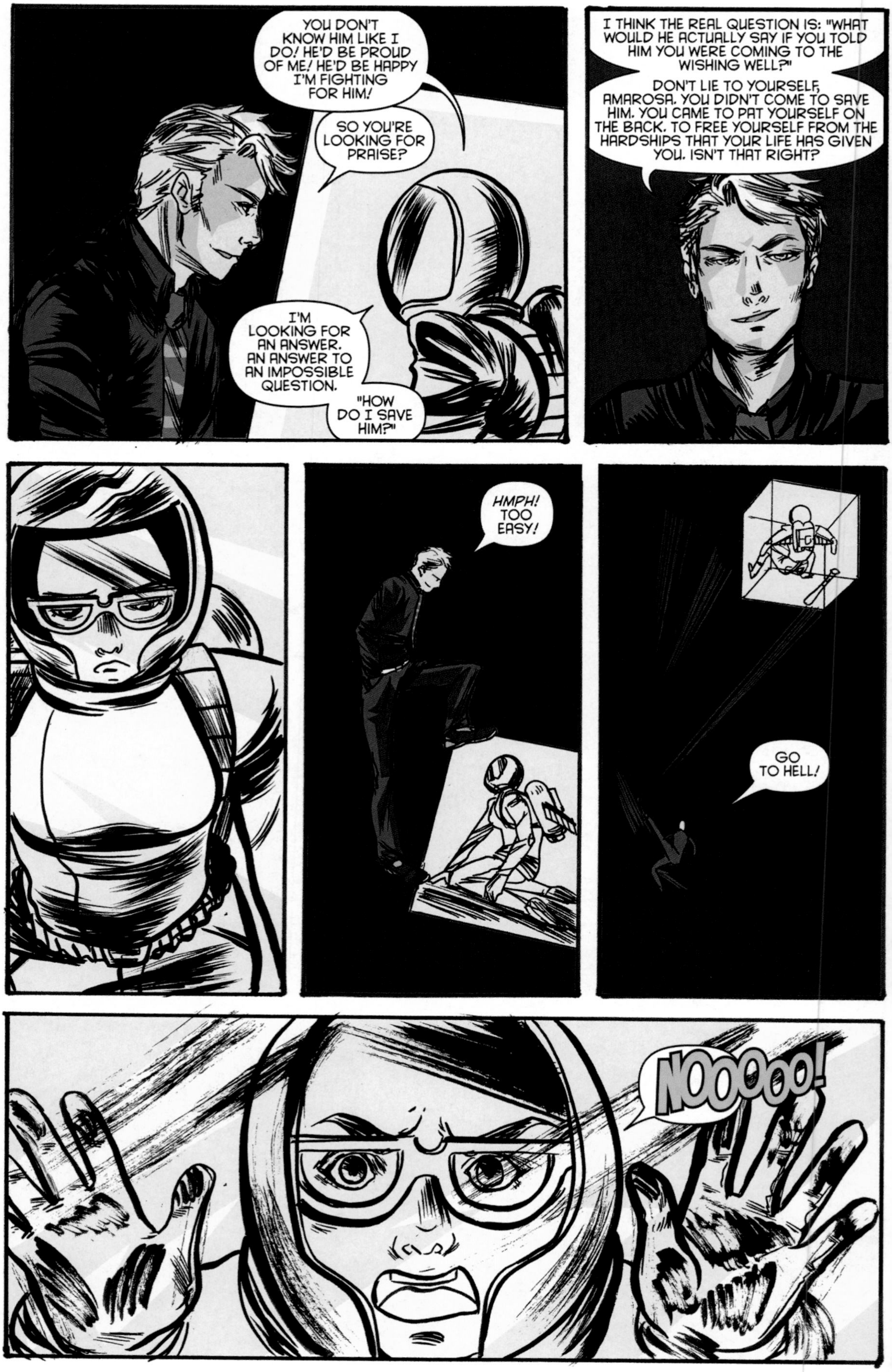
YOU DON'T KNOW HIM LIKE I DO! HE'D BE PROUD OF ME! HE'D BE HAPPY I'M FIGHTING FOR HIM!
SO YOU'RE LOOKING FOR PRAISE?
I'M LOOKING FOR AN ANSWER. AN ANSWER TO AN IMPOSSIBLE QUESTION.
"HOW DO I SAVE HIM?"
I THINK THE REAL QUESTION IS: "WHAT WOULD HE ACTUALLY SAY IF YOU TOLD HIM YOU WERE COMING TO THE WISHING WELL?"
DON'T LIE TO YOURSELF, AMAROSA. YOU DIDN'T COME TO SAVE HIM. YOU CAME TO PAT YOURSELF ON THE BACK. TO FREE YOURSELF FROM THE HARDSHIPS THAT YOUR LIFE HAS GIVEN YOU. ISN'T THAT RIGHT?
HMPH! TOO EASY!
GO TO HELL!
NOOOOO!

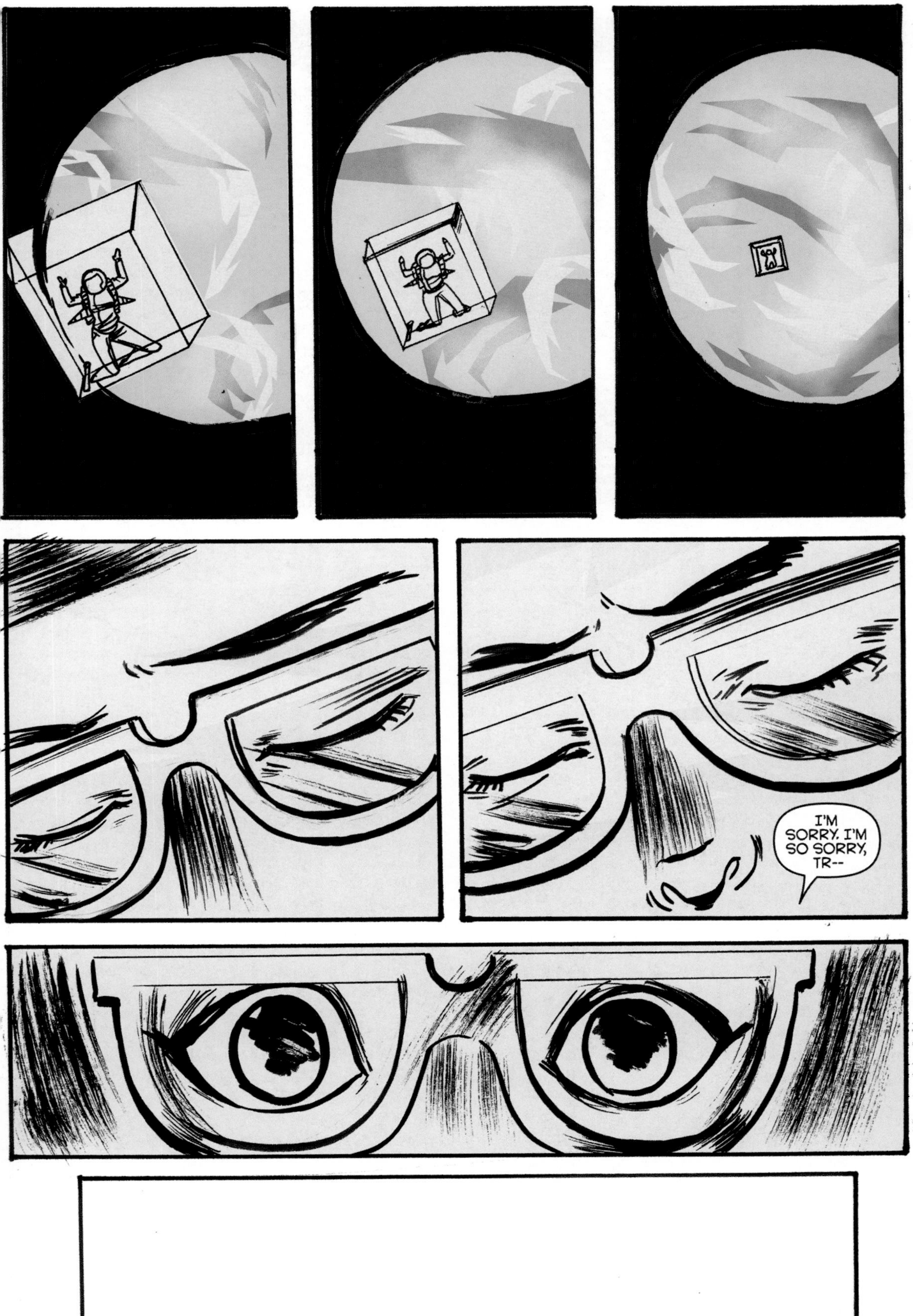
I'M SORRY. I'M SO SORRY, TR--

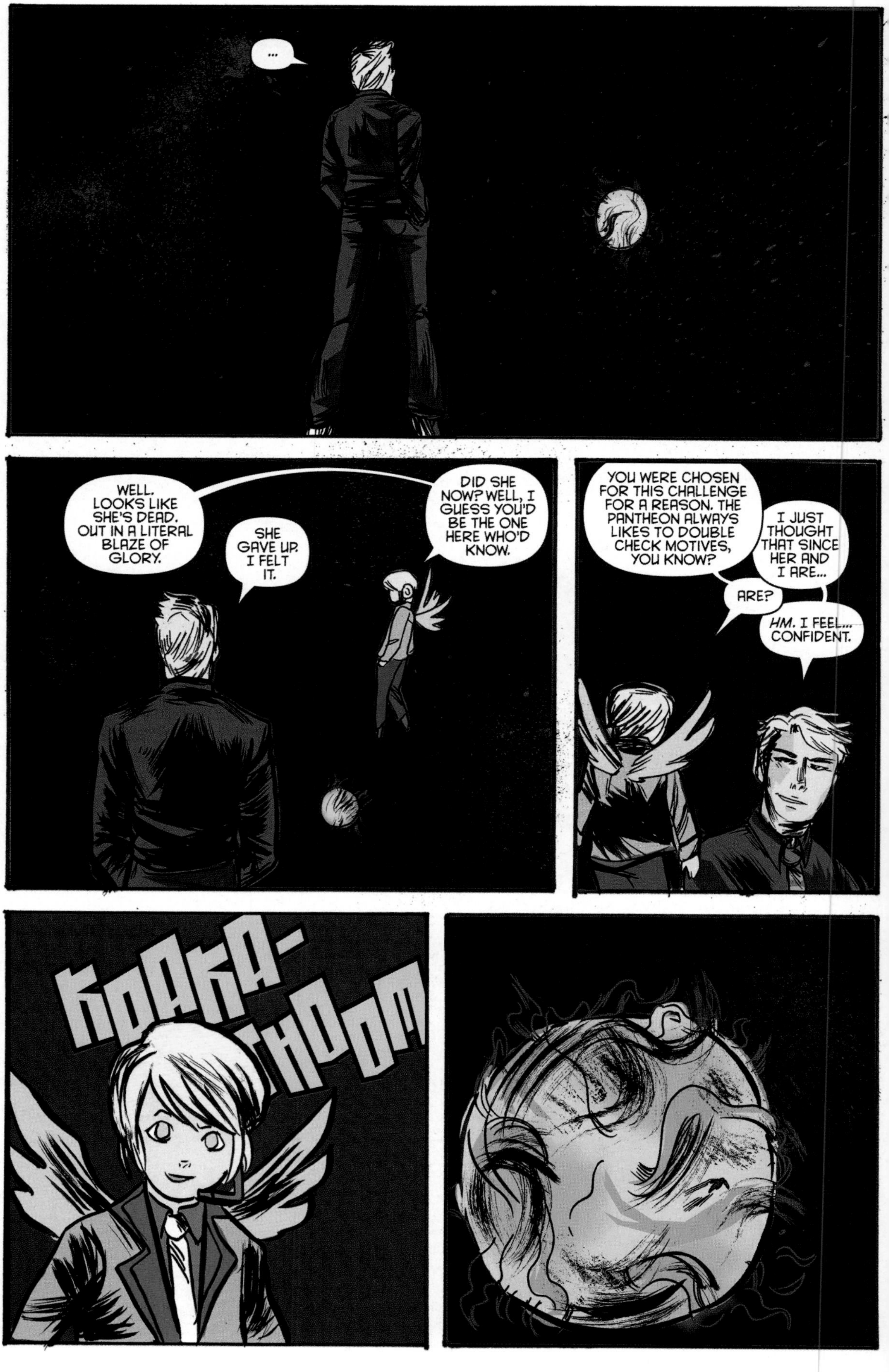
...
WELL. LOOKS LIKE SHE'S DEAD. OUT IN A LITERAL BLAZE OF GLORY.
SHE GAVE UP. I FELT IT.
DID SHE NOW? WELL, I GUESS YOU'D BE THE ONE HERE WHO'D KNOW.
YOU WERE CHOSEN FOR THIS CHALLENGE FOR A REASON. THE PANTHEON ALWAYS LIKES TO DOUBLE CHECK MOTIVES, YOU KNOW?
I JUST THOUGHT THAT SINCE HER AND I ARE...
ARE?
HM. I FEEL... CONFIDENT.
KRAKA-THOOM

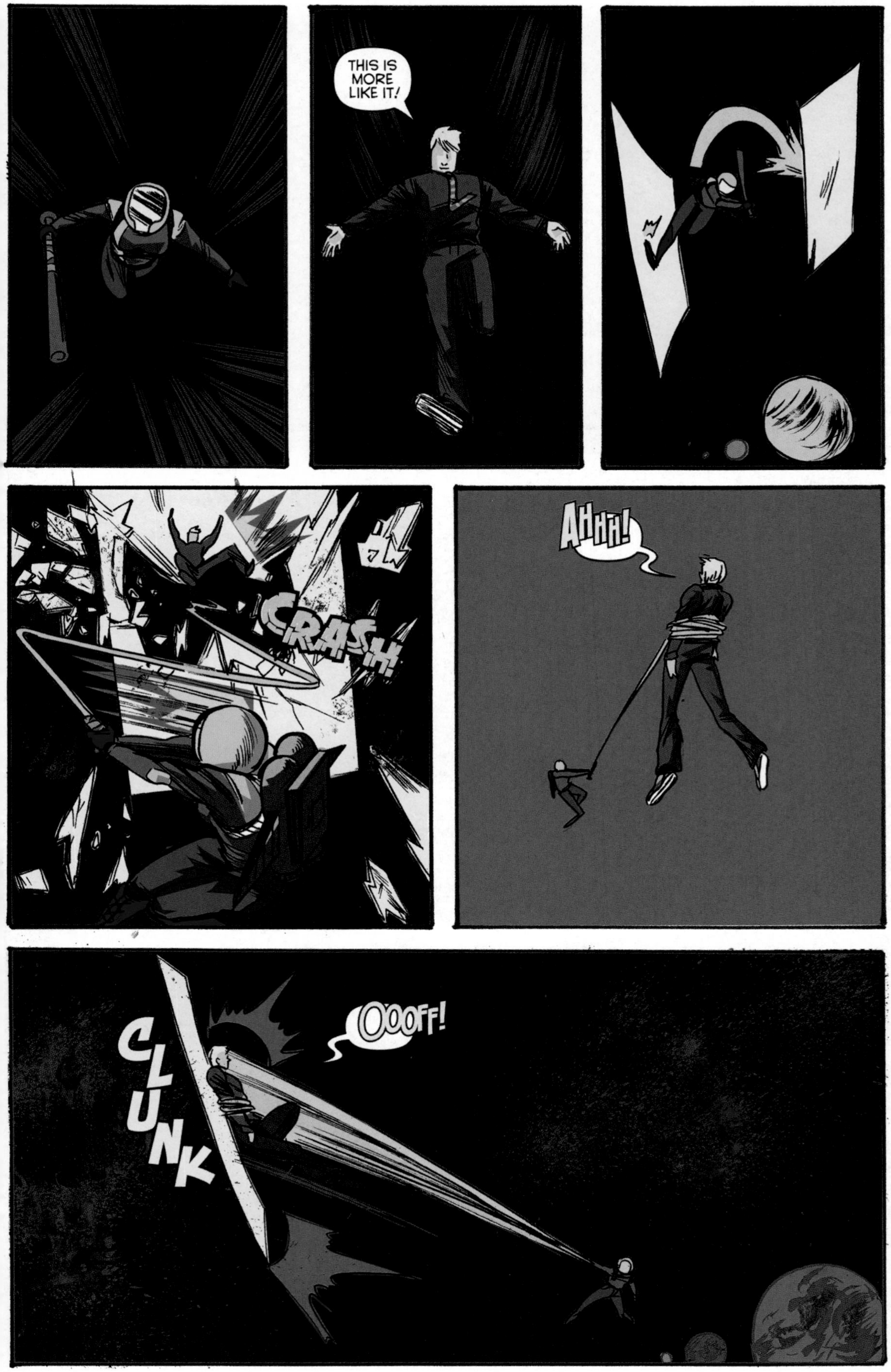
THIS IS MORE LIKE IT!
CRASH!
AHHH!
CLUNK
OOOFF!

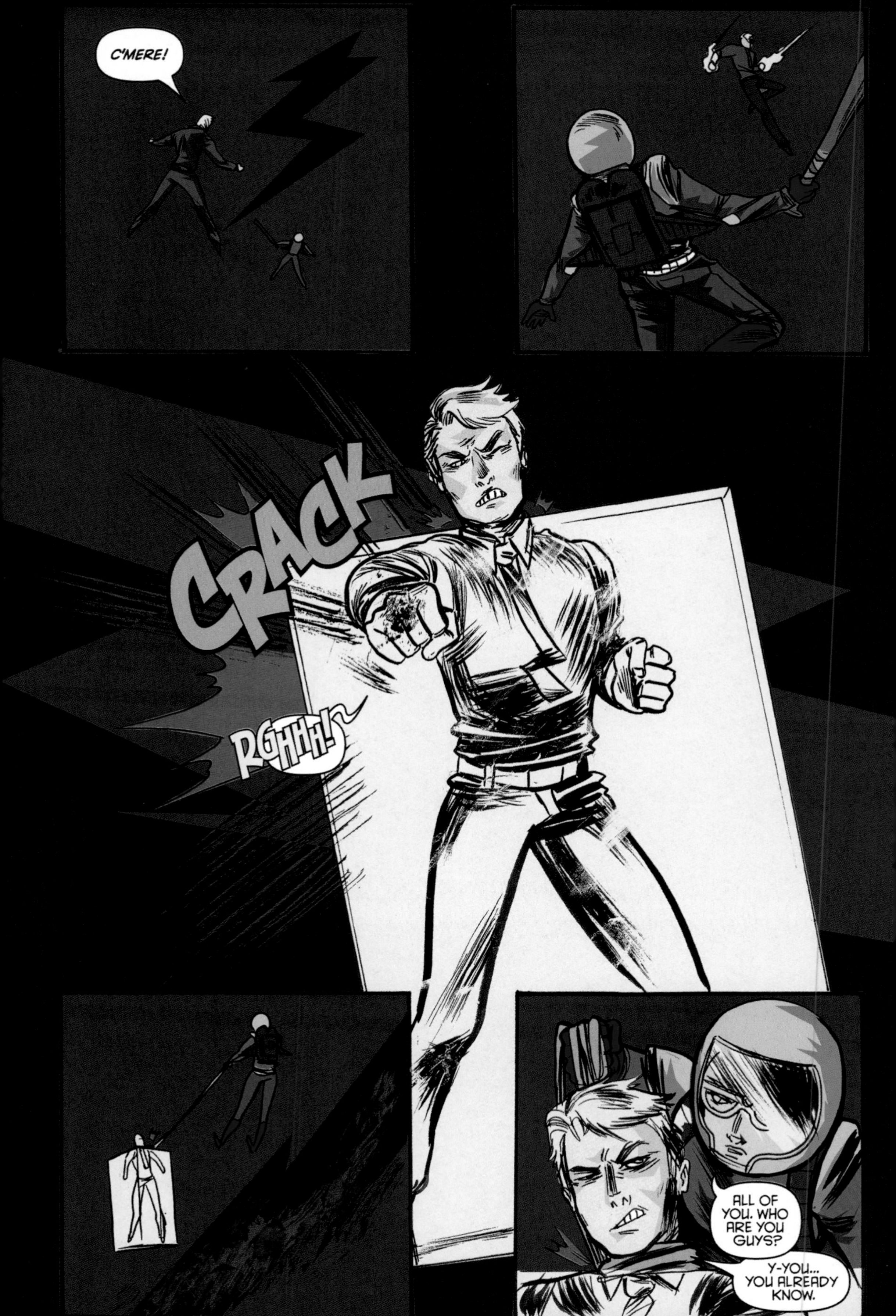
C'MERE!
CRACK
RGHHH!
ALL OF YOU. WHO ARE YOU GUYS?
Y-YOU... YOU ALREADY KNOW.

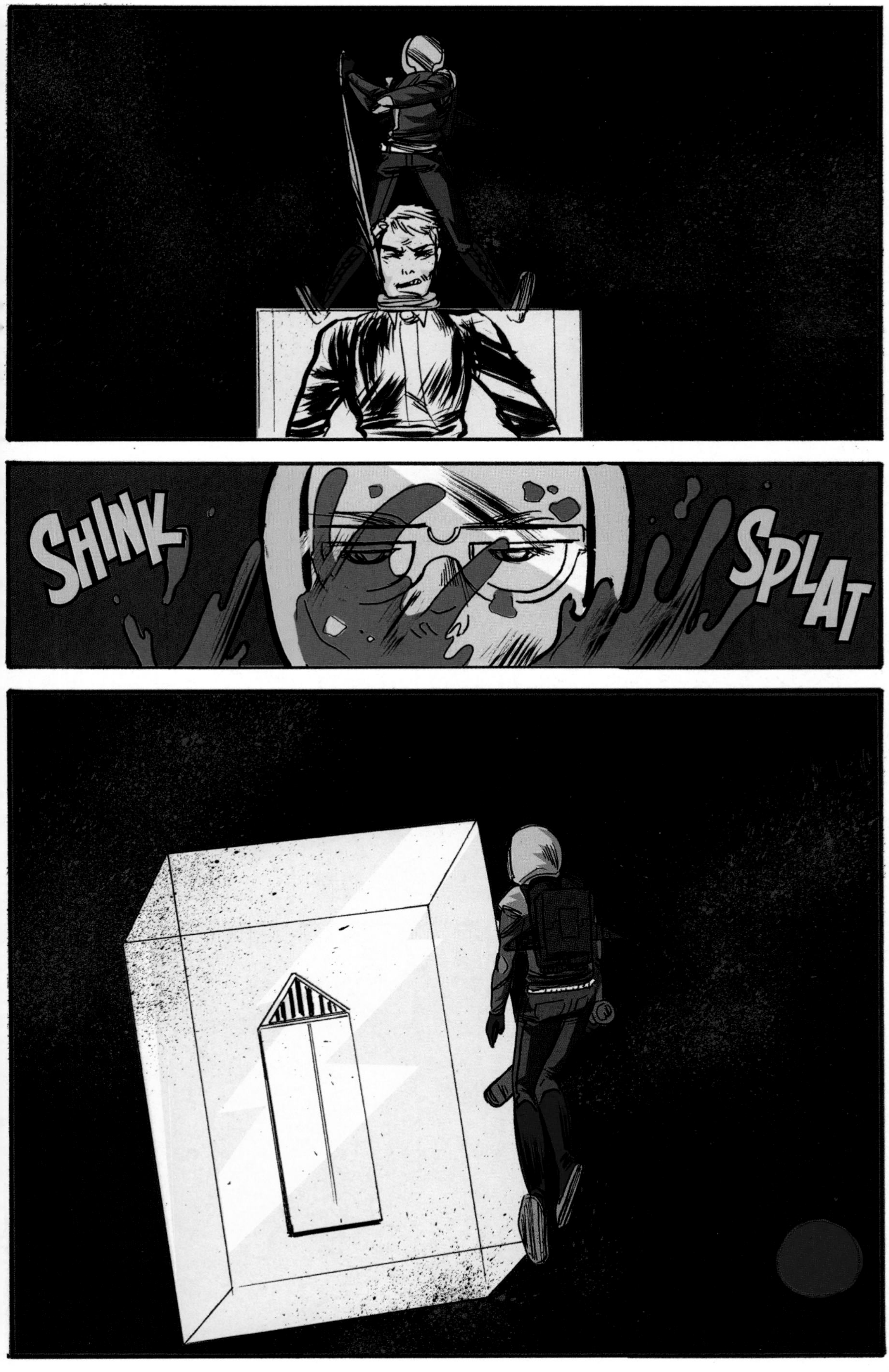
SHINK
SPLAT

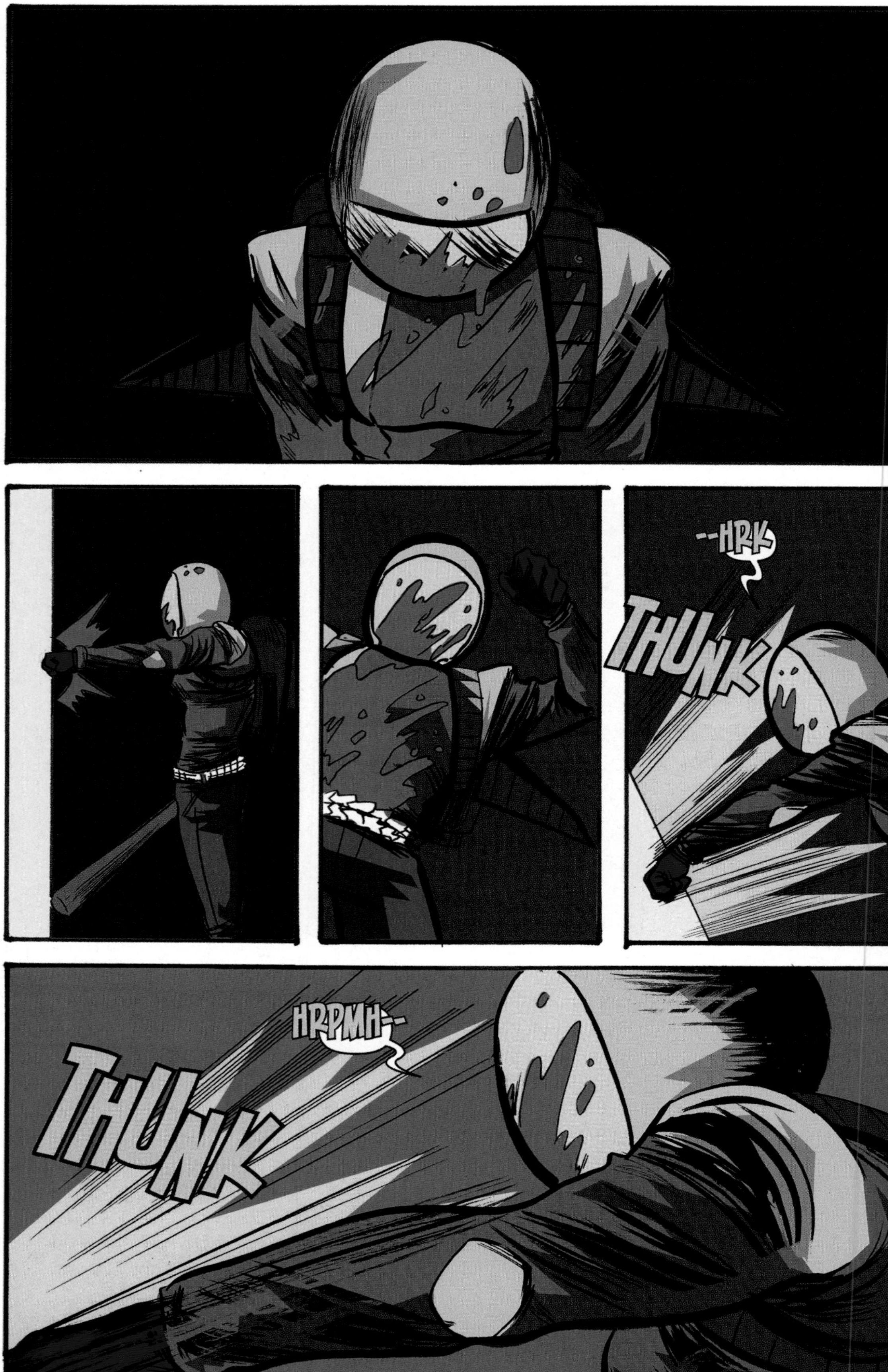
--HRK
THUNK
HRPMH--
THUNK

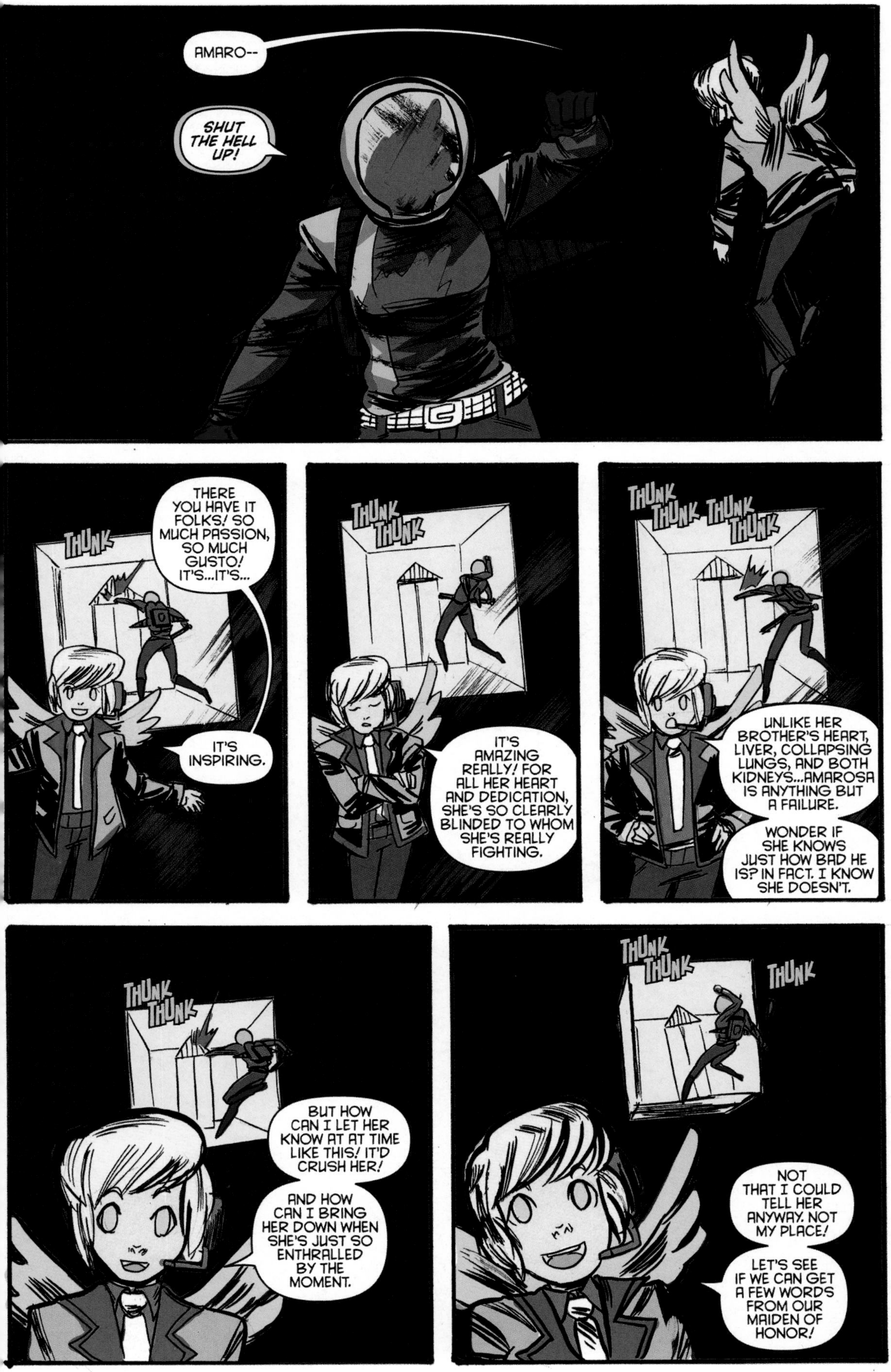

AMARO--
SHUT THE HELL UP!
THUNK
THERE YOU HAVE IT FOLKS! SO MUCH PASSION, SO MUCH GUSTO! IT'S...IT'S...
IT'S INSPIRING.
THUNK THUNK
IT'S AMAZING REALLY! FOR ALL HER HEART AND DEDICATION, SHE'S SO CLEARLY BLINDED TO WHOM SHE'S REALLY FIGHTING.
THUNK THUNK THUNK THUNK
UNLIKE HER BROTHER'S HEART, LIVER, COLLAPSING LUNGS, AND BOTH KIDNEYS...AMAROSA IS ANYTHING BUT A FAILURE.
WONDER IF SHE KNOWS JUST HOW BAD HE IS? IN FACT. I KNOW SHE DOESN'T.
THUNK THUNK
BUT HOW CAN I LET HER KNOW AT AT TIME LIKE THIS! IT'D CRUSH HER!
AND HOW CAN I BRING HER DOWN WHEN SHE'S JUST SO ENTHRALLED BY THE MOMENT.
THUNK THUNK
THUNK
NOT THAT I COULD TELL HER ANYWAY. NOT MY PLACE!
LET'S SEE IF WE CAN GET A FEW WORDS FROM OUR MAIDEN OF HONOR!

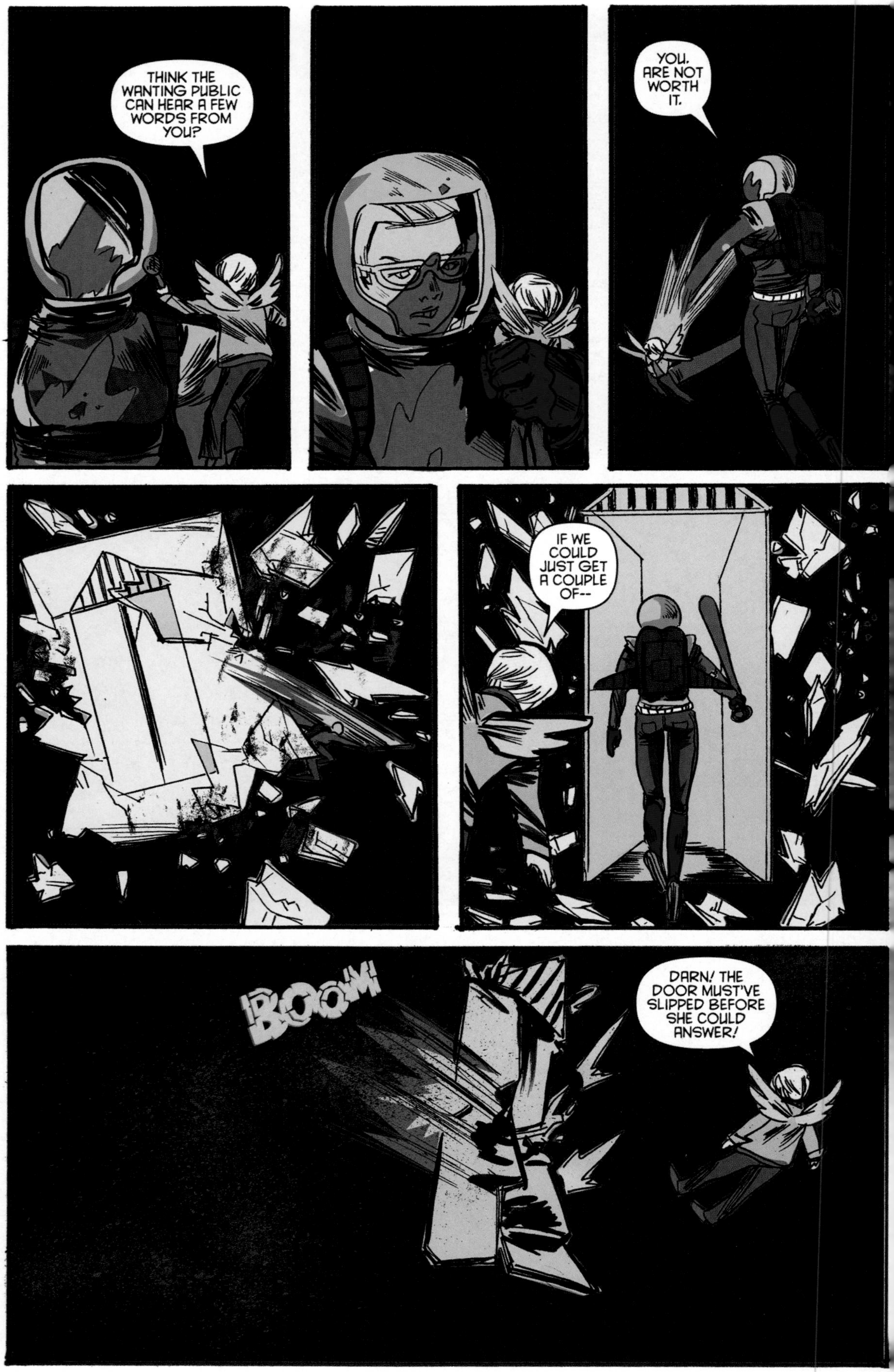
THINK THE WANTING PUBLIC CAN HEAR A FEW WORDS FROM YOU?
YOU. ARE NOT WORTH IT.
IF WE COULD JUST GET A COUPLE OF--
BOOM!
DARN! THE DOOR MUST'VE SLIPPED BEFORE SHE COULD ANSWER!

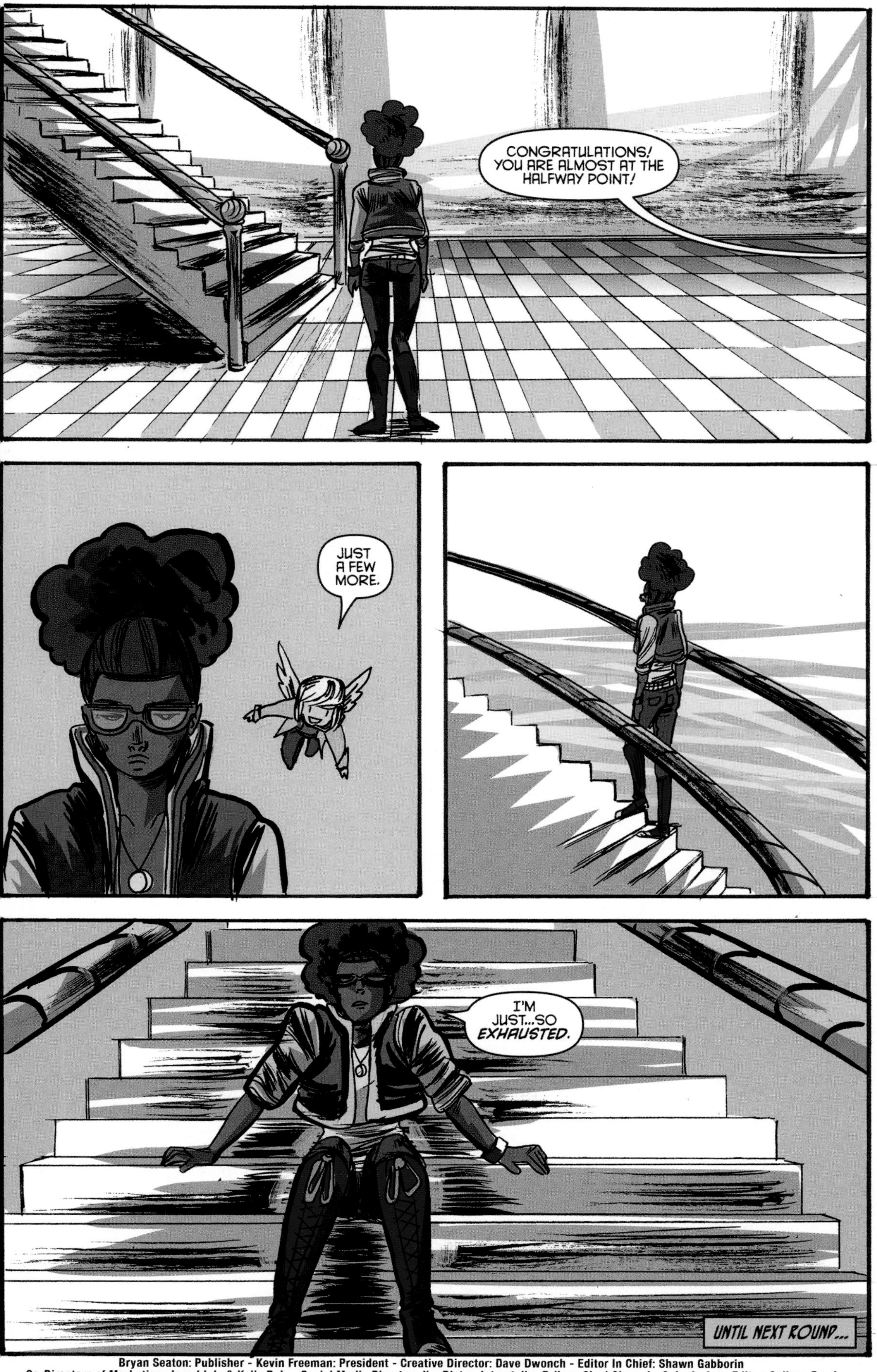
CONGRATULATIONS! YOU ARE ALMOST AT THE HALFWAY POINT!
JUST A FEW MORE.
I'M JUST...SO EXHAUSTED.
UNTIL NEXT ROUND...

Bryan Seaton: Publisher - Kevin Freeman: President - Creative Director: Dave Dwonch - Editor In Chief: Shawn Gabborin
Co-Directors of Marketing: Jamal Igle & Kelly Dale - Social Media Director: Jim Dietz - Interstellar Fellow: Chad Cicconi - Submissions Editor: Colleen Boyd

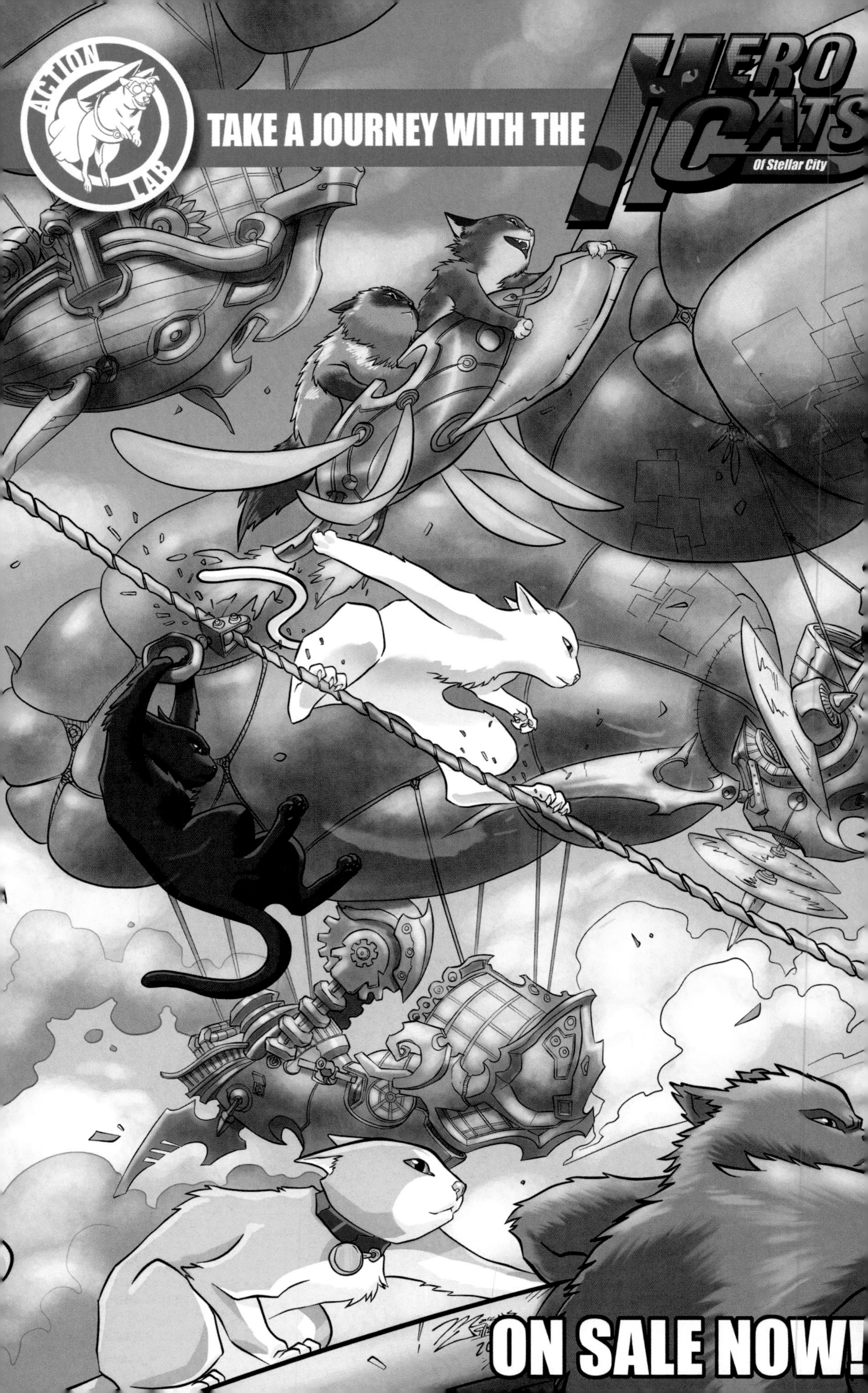
ACTION LAB
TAKE A JOURNEY WITH THE
HERO CATS
Of Stellar City
ON SALE NOW!

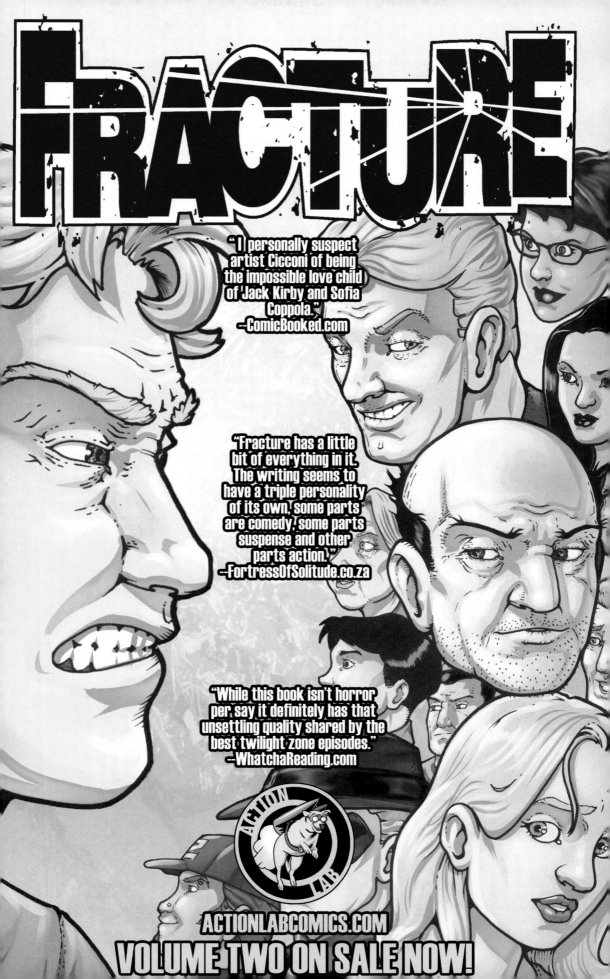

FRACTURE

"I personally suspect artist Cicconi of being the impossible love child of Jack Kirby and Sofia Coppola."
--ComicBooked.com

"Fracture has a little bit of everything in it. The writing seems to have a triple personality of its own, some parts are comedy, some parts suspense and other parts action."
--FortressOfSolitude.co.za

"While this book isn't horror per say it definitely has that unsettling quality shared by the best twilight zone episodes."
--WhatchaReading.com

ACTIONLABCOMICS.COM
VOLUME TWO ON SALE NOW!

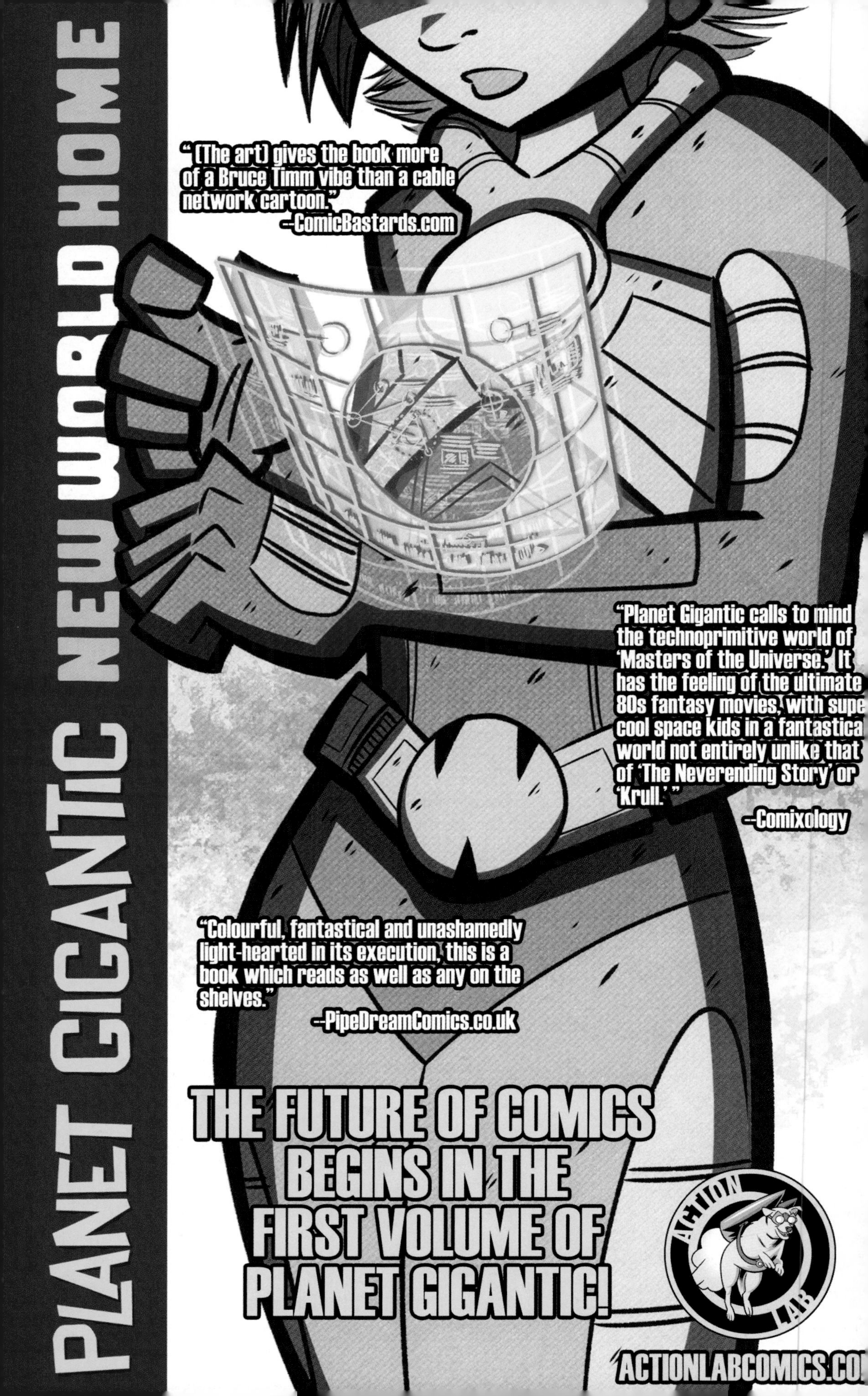
PLANET GIGANTIC NEW WORLD HOME
“(The art) gives the book more of a Bruce Timm vibe than a cable network cartoon.” --ComicBastards.com
“Planet Gigantic calls to mind the technoprimitive world of ‘Masters of the Universe.’ It has the feeling of the ultimate 80s fantasy movies, with supe cool space kids in a fantastica world not entirely unlike that of ‘The Neverending Story’ or ‘Krull.’ ” --Comixology
“Colourful, fantastical and unashamedly light-hearted in its execution, this is a book which reads as well as any on the shelves.” --PipeDreamComics.co.uk
THE FUTURE OF COMICS BEGINS IN THE FIRST VOLUME OF PLANET GIGANTIC!
ACTION LAB
ACTIONLABCOMICS.CO

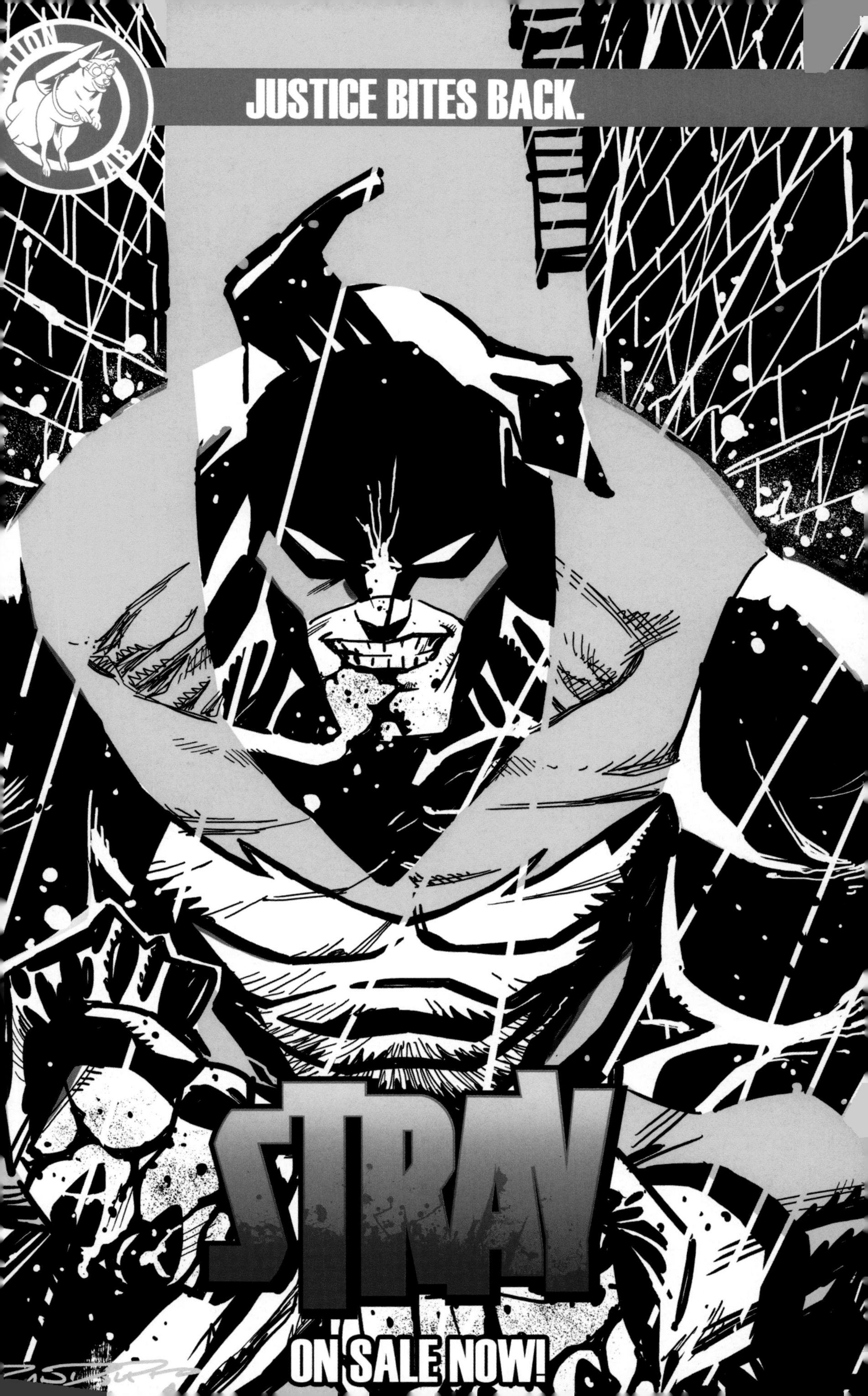
JUSTICE BITES BACK.
STRAY
ON SALE NOW!

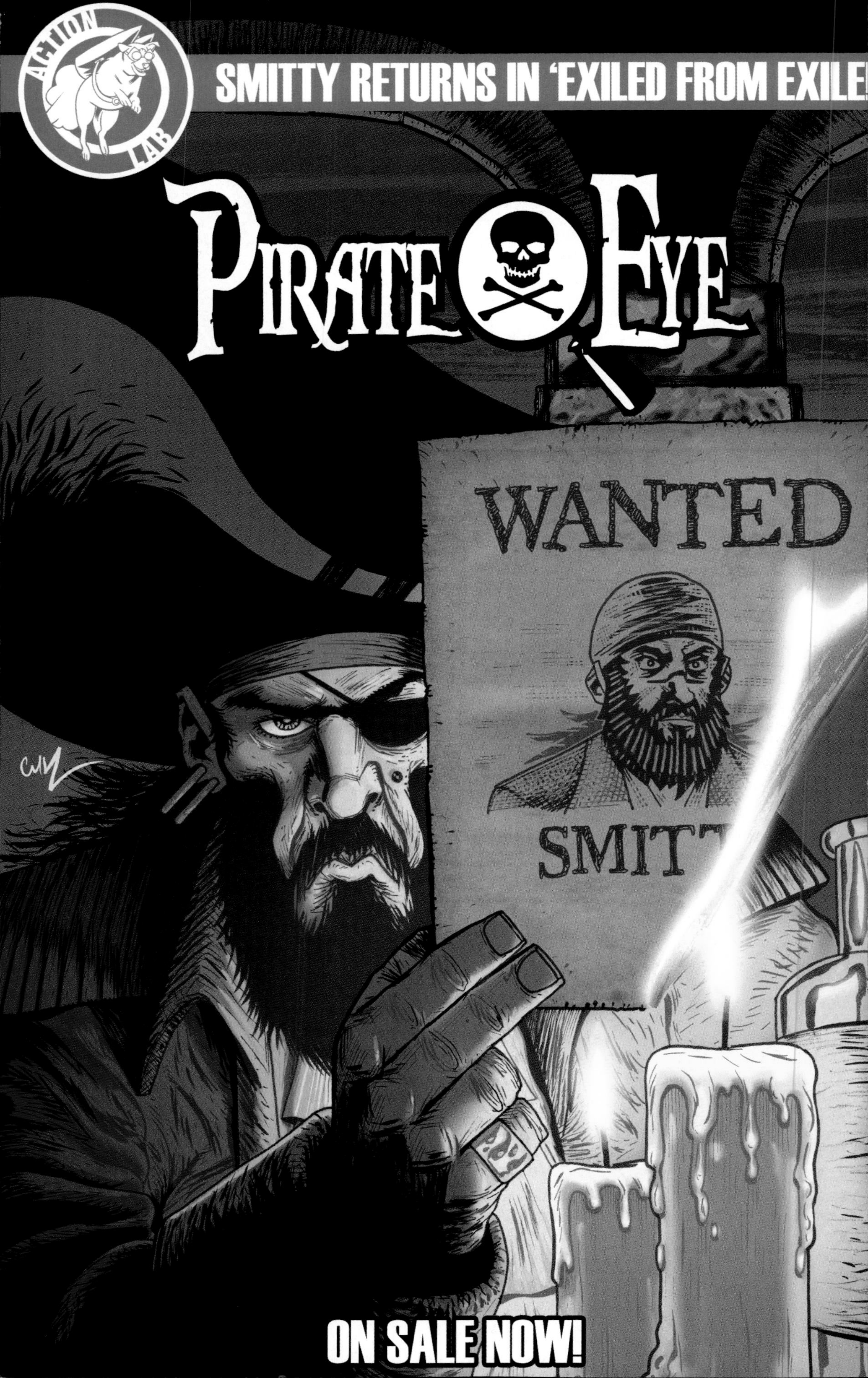
ACTION LAB
SMITTY RETURNS IN 'EXILED FROM EXILE!
PIRATE EYE
WANTED
SMITT
ON SALE NOW!

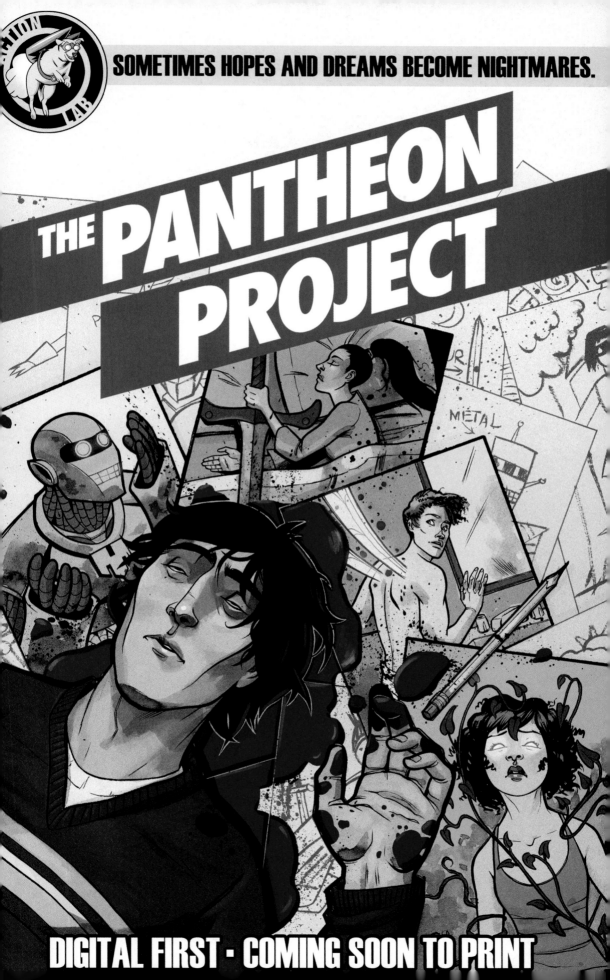

READ MORE NOW

Fight Like A Girl - Action Lab
www.actionlabcomics.com

00311

7 00465 77248 0

ACTIONLABCOMICS.COM

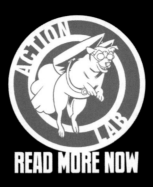

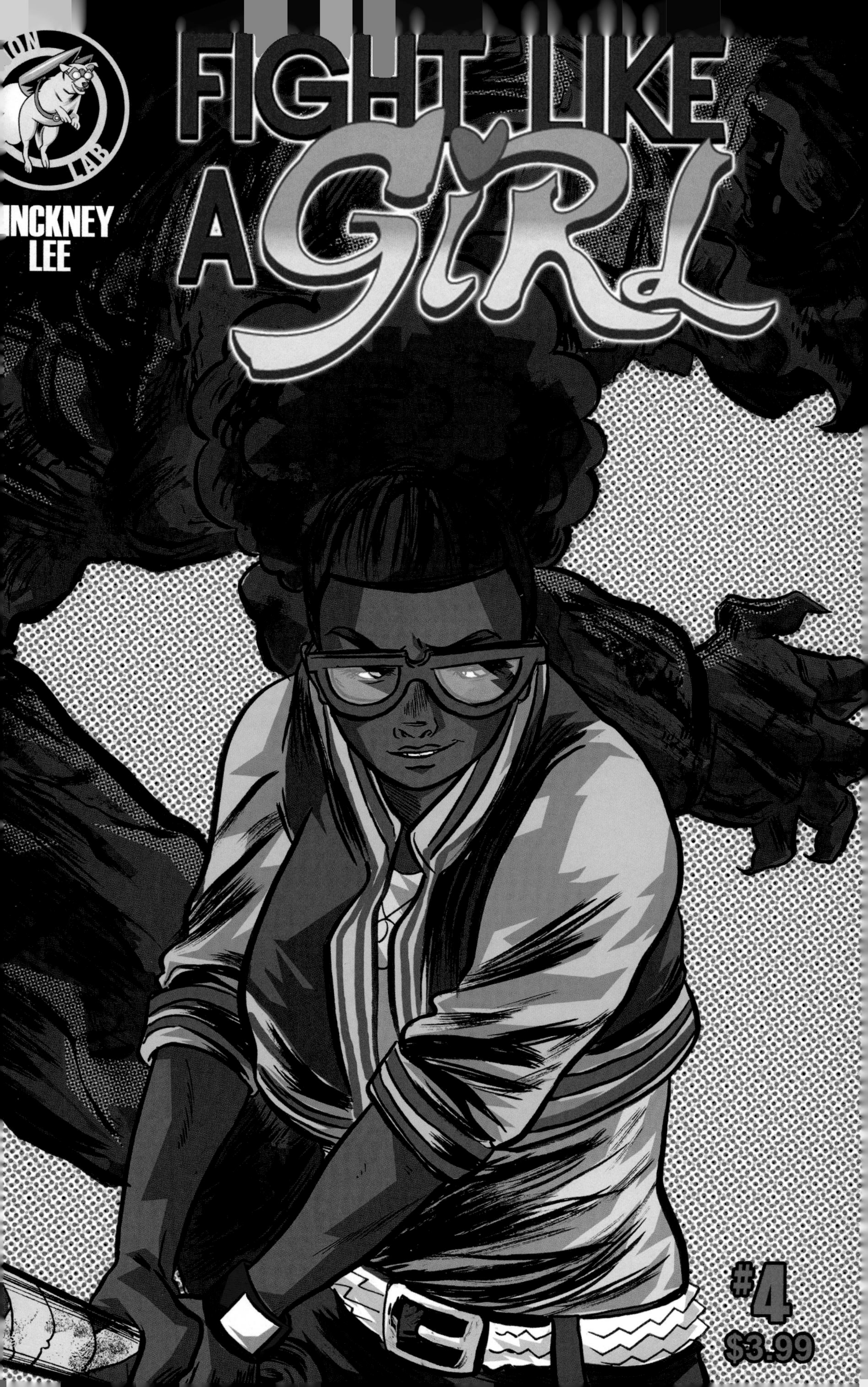
FIGHT LIKE A GIRL
INCKNEY
LEE
LAB
#4
$3.99

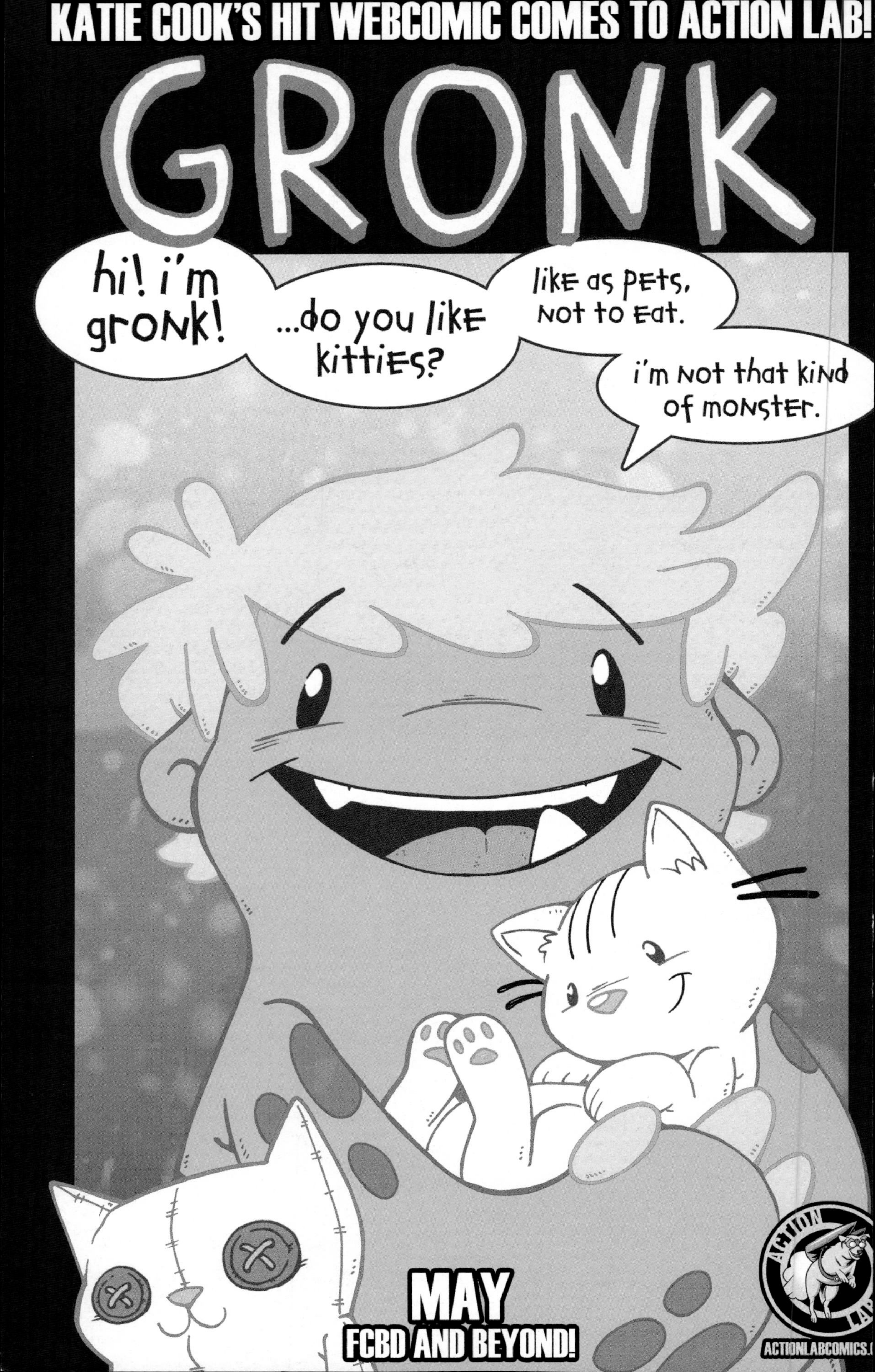

KATIE COOK'S HIT WEBCOMIC COMES TO ACTION LAB!
GRONK
hi! i'm gronk!
...do you like kitties?
like as pets, not to eat.
i'm not that kind of monster.
ACTION LAB
MAY
FCBD AND BEYOND!
ACTIONLABCOMICS.

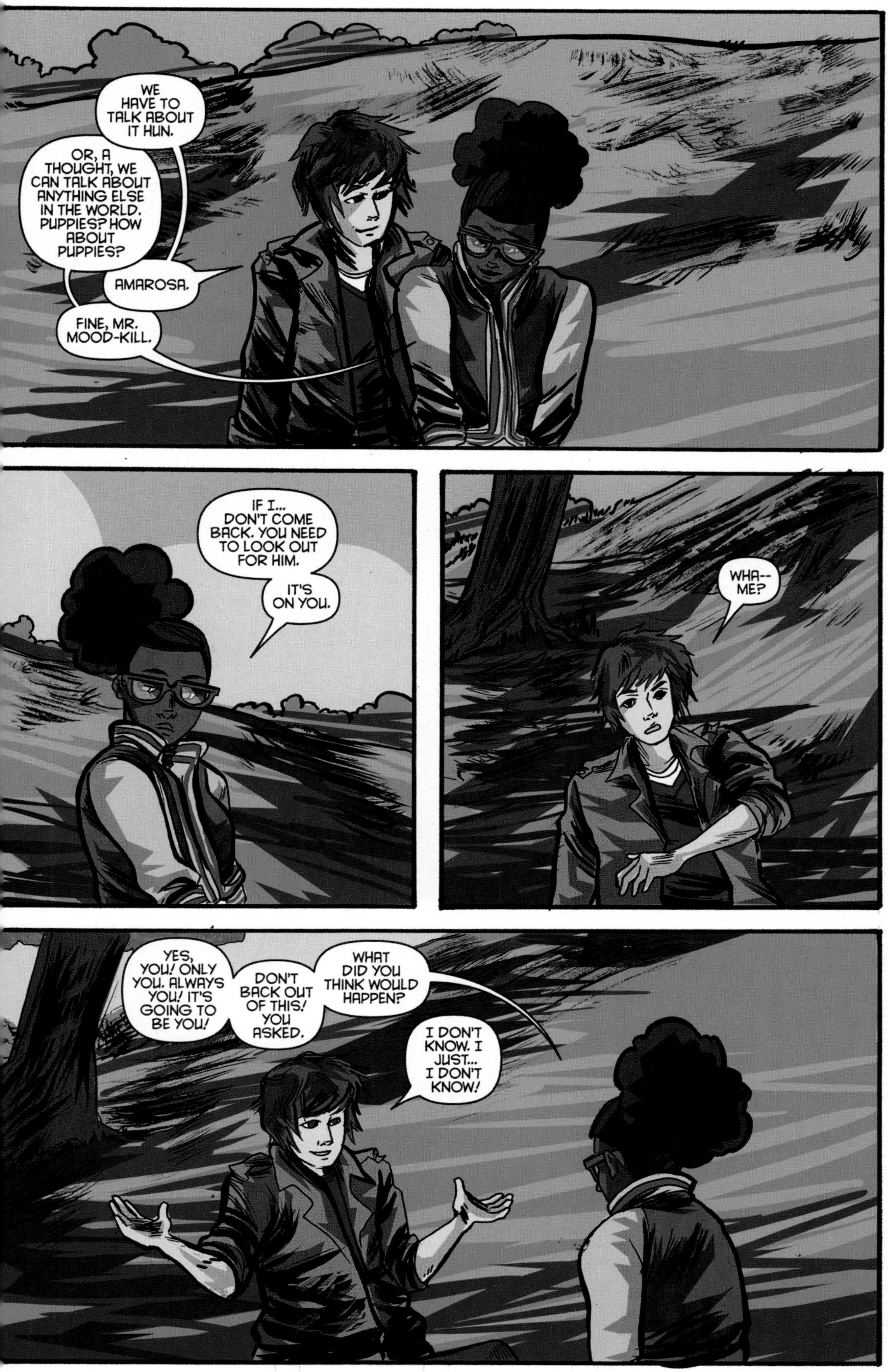
WE HAVE TO TALK ABOUT IT HUN.
OR, A THOUGHT, WE CAN TALK ABOUT ANYTHING ELSE IN THE WORLD. PUPPIES? HOW ABOUT PUPPIES?
AMAROSA.
FINE, MR. MOOD-KILL.
IF I... DON'T COME BACK. YOU NEED TO LOOK OUT FOR HIM.
IT'S ON YOU.
WHA-- ME?
YES, YOU! ONLY YOU. ALWAYS YOU! IT'S GOING TO BE YOU!
DON'T BACK OUT OF THIS! YOU ASKED.
WHAT DID YOU THINK WOULD HAPPEN?
I DON'T KNOW. I JUST... I DON'T KNOW!

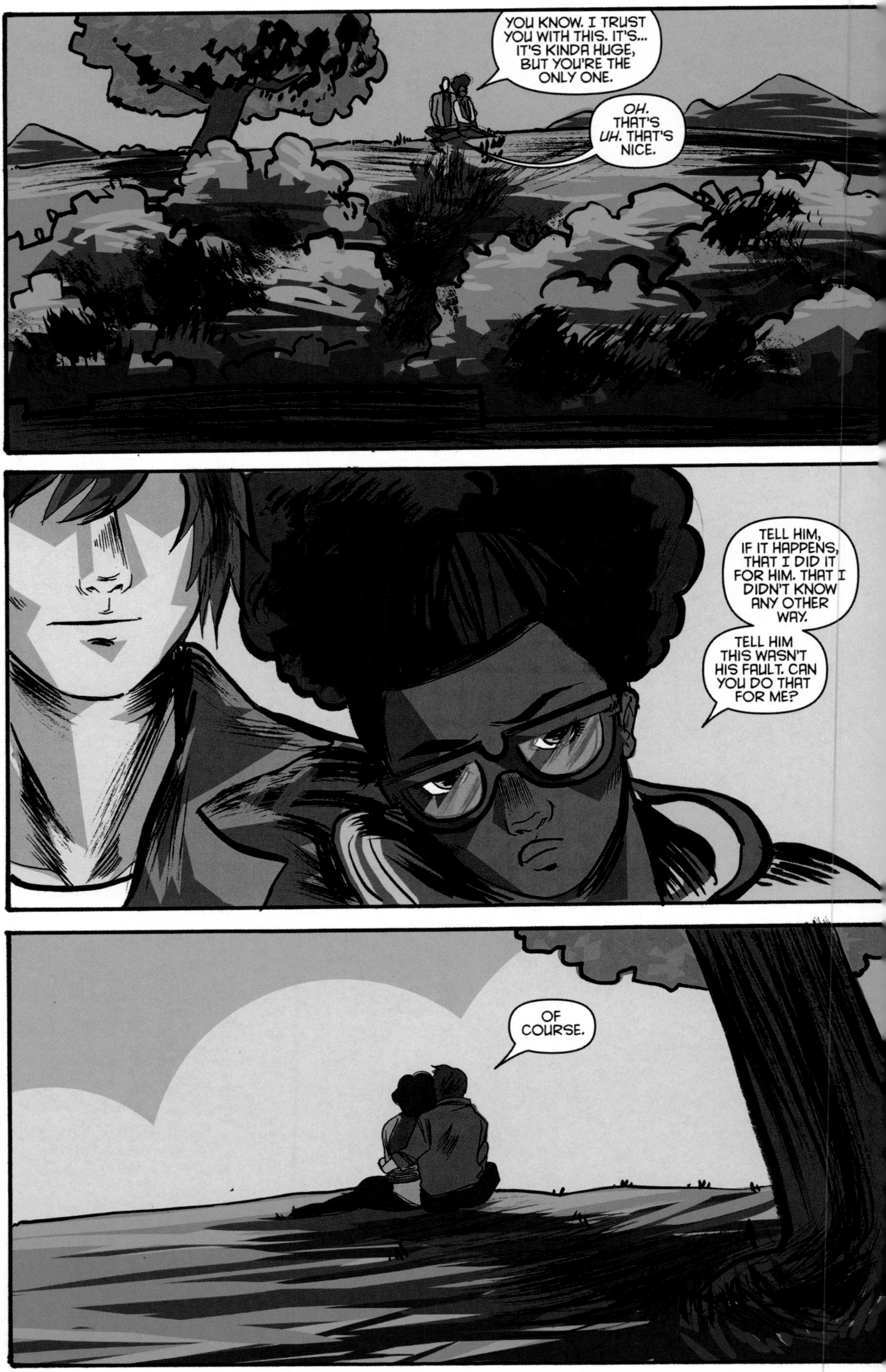
YOU KNOW. I TRUST YOU WITH THIS. IT'S... IT'S KINDA HUGE, BUT YOU'RE THE ONLY ONE.
OH. THAT'S UH. THAT'S NICE.
TELL HIM, IF IT HAPPENS, THAT I DID IT FOR HIM. THAT I DIDN'T KNOW ANY OTHER WAY.
TELL HIM THIS WASN'T HIS FAULT. CAN YOU DO THAT FOR ME?
OF COURSE.

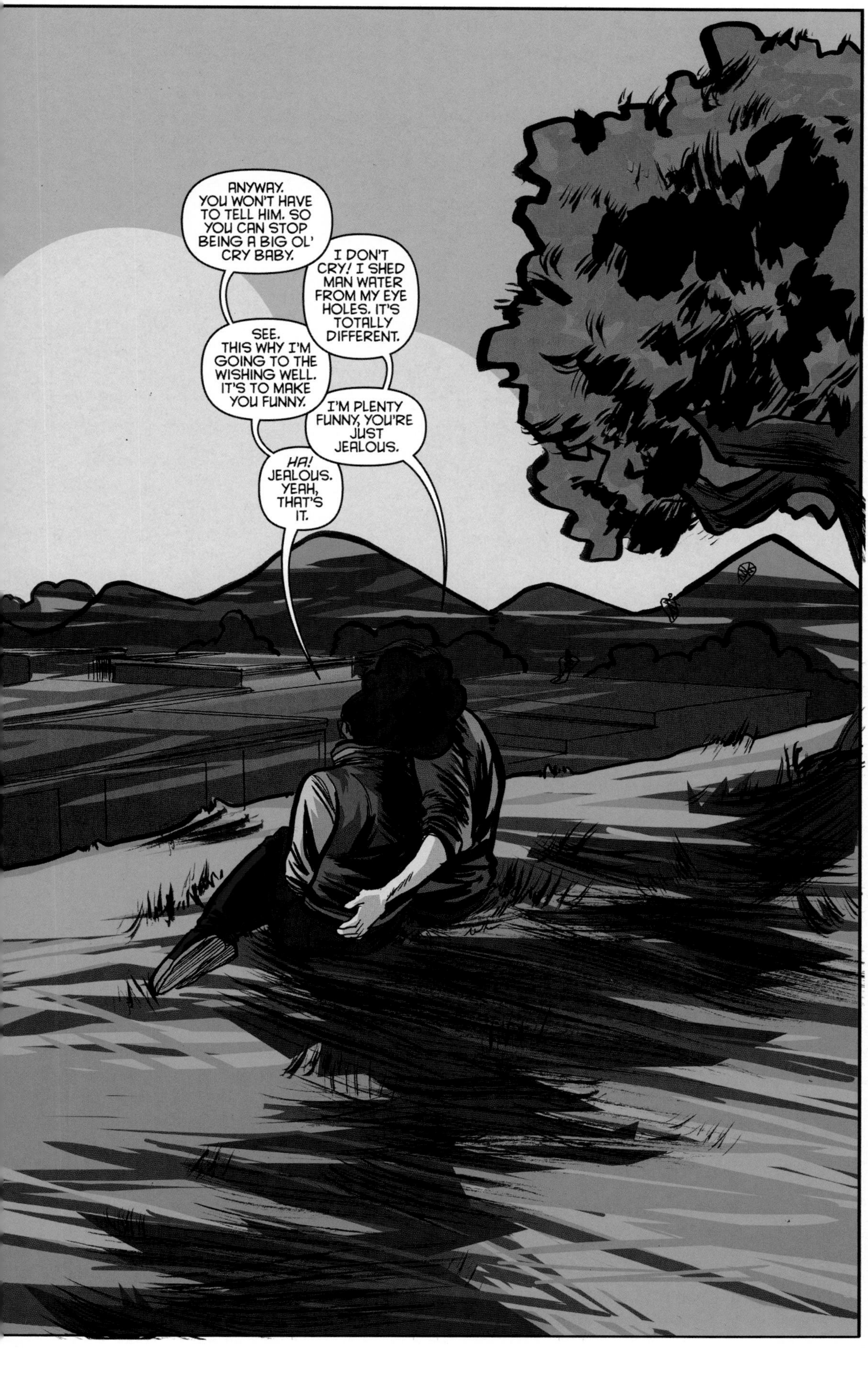
ANYWAY. YOU WON'T HAVE TO TELL HIM. SO YOU CAN STOP BEING A BIG OL' CRY BABY.
I DON'T CRY! I SHED MAN WATER FROM MY EYE HOLES. IT'S TOTALLY DIFFERENT.
SEE. THIS WHY I'M GOING TO THE WISHING WELL. IT'S TO MAKE YOU FUNNY.
I'M PLENTY FUNNY, YOU'RE JUST JEALOUS.
HA! JEALOUS. YEAH, THAT'S IT.

CHAPTER FOUR

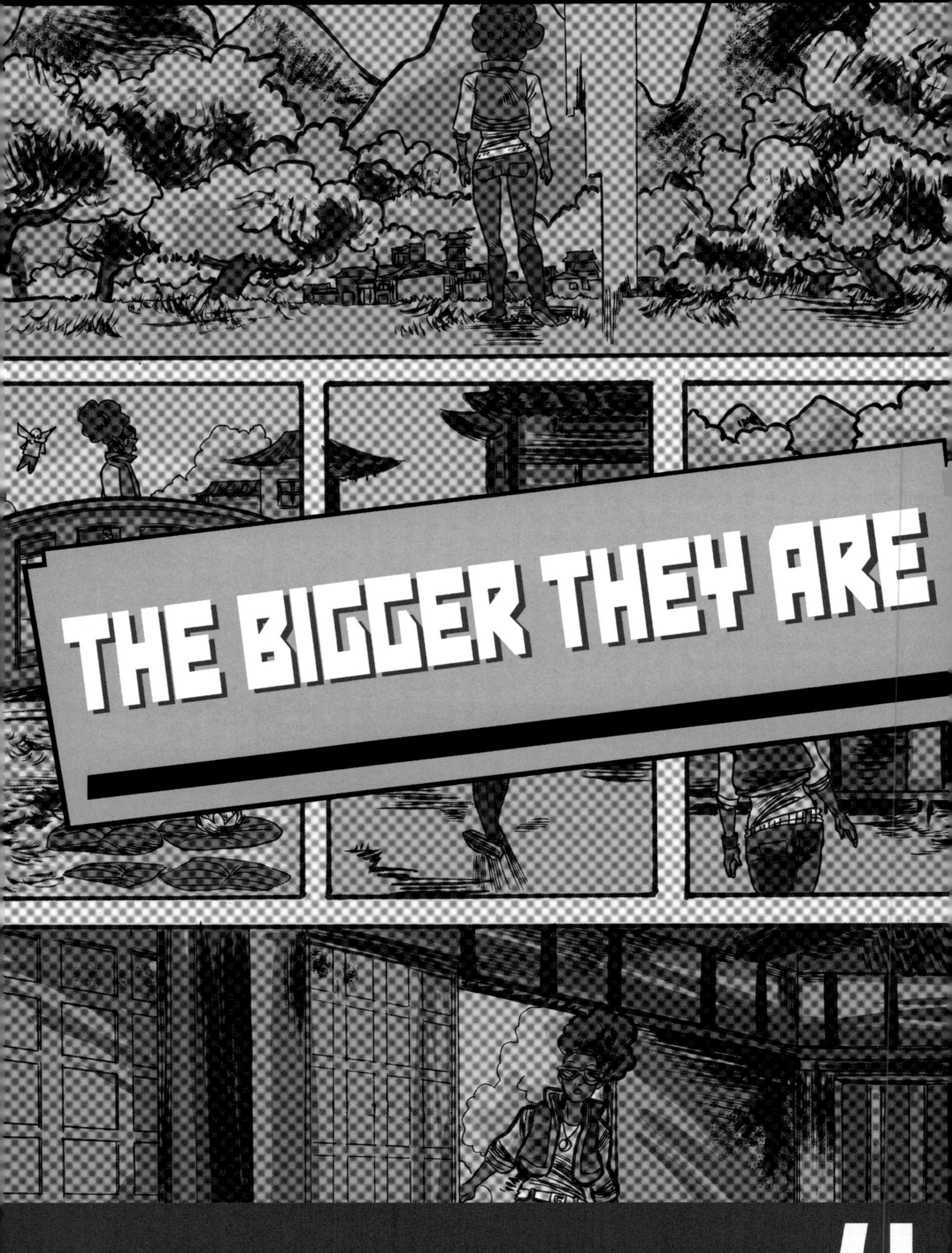

THE BIGGER THEY ARE

FIGHT LIKE A GIRL

4

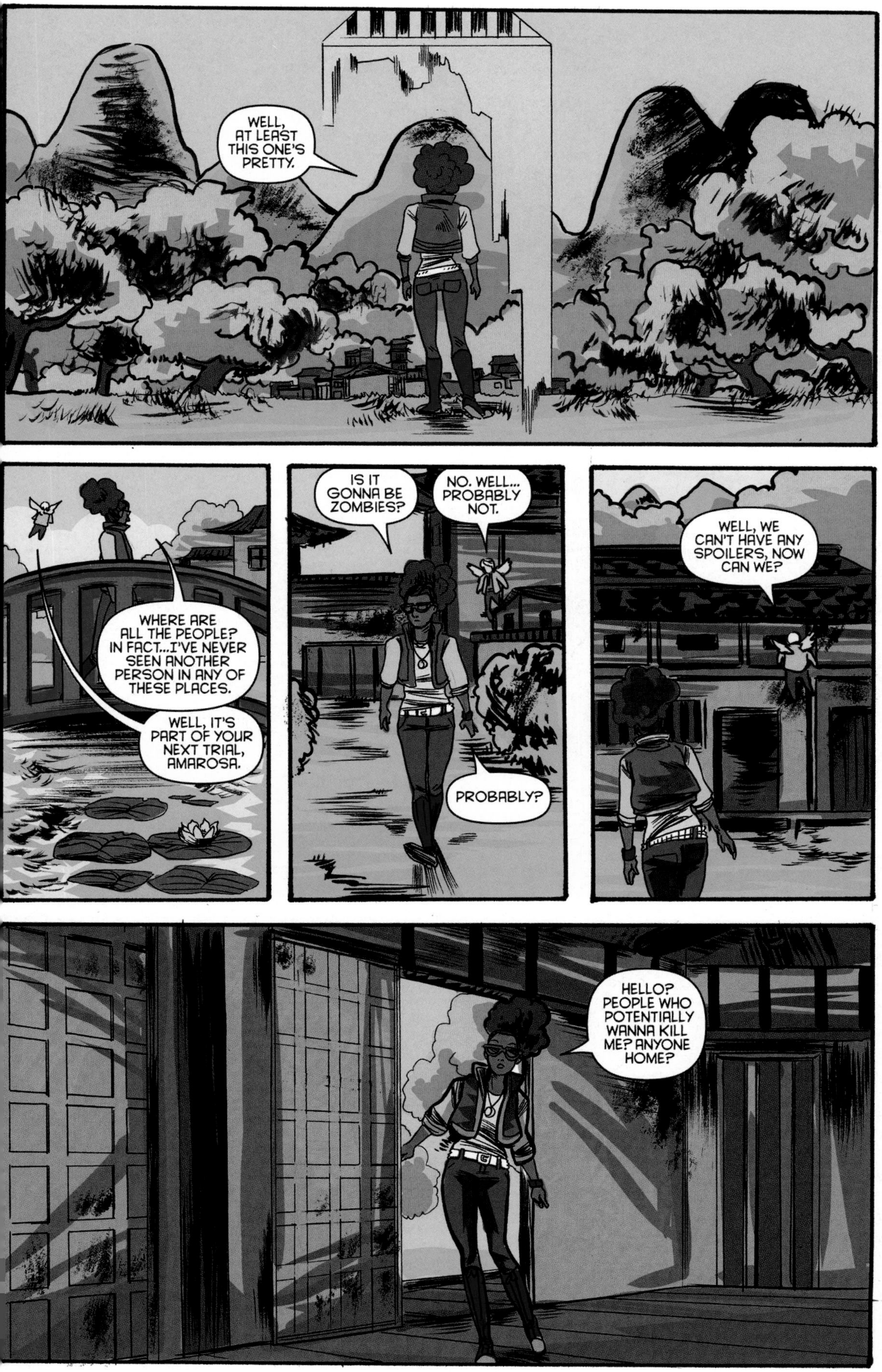
WELL, AT LEAST THIS ONE'S PRETTY.
WHERE ARE ALL THE PEOPLE? IN FACT...I'VE NEVER SEEN ANOTHER PERSON IN ANY OF THESE PLACES.
WELL, IT'S PART OF YOUR NEXT TRIAL, AMAROSA.
IS IT GONNA BE ZOMBIES?
NO. WELL... PROBABLY NOT.
PROBABLY?
WELL, WE CAN'T HAVE ANY SPOILERS, NOW CAN WE?
HELLO? PEOPLE WHO POTENTIALLY WANNA KILL ME? ANYONE HOME?

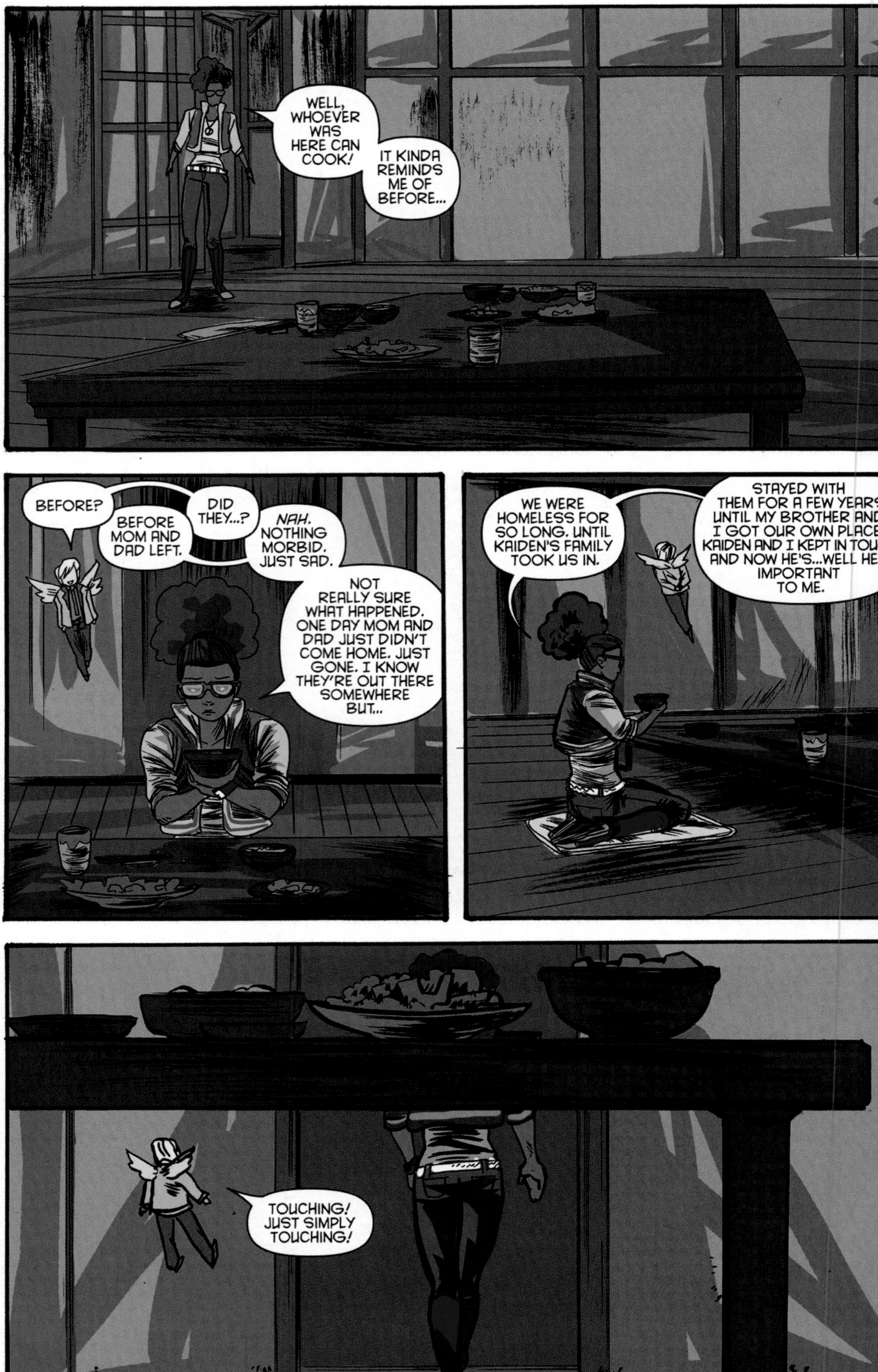
WELL, WHOEVER WAS HERE CAN COOK!
IT KINDA REMINDS ME OF BEFORE...
BEFORE?
BEFORE MOM AND DAD LEFT.
DID THEY...?
NAH. NOTHING MORBID. JUST SAD.
NOT REALLY SURE WHAT HAPPENED. ONE DAY MOM AND DAD JUST DIDN'T COME HOME. JUST GONE. I KNOW THEY'RE OUT THERE SOMEWHERE BUT...
WE WERE HOMELESS FOR SO LONG. UNTIL KAIDEN'S FAMILY TOOK US IN.
STAYED WITH THEM FOR A FEW YEARS UNTIL MY BROTHER AND I GOT OUR OWN PLACE. KAIDEN AND I KEPT IN TOUCH AND NOW HE'S...WELL HE'S IMPORTANT TO ME.
TOUCHING! JUST SIMPLY TOUCHING!

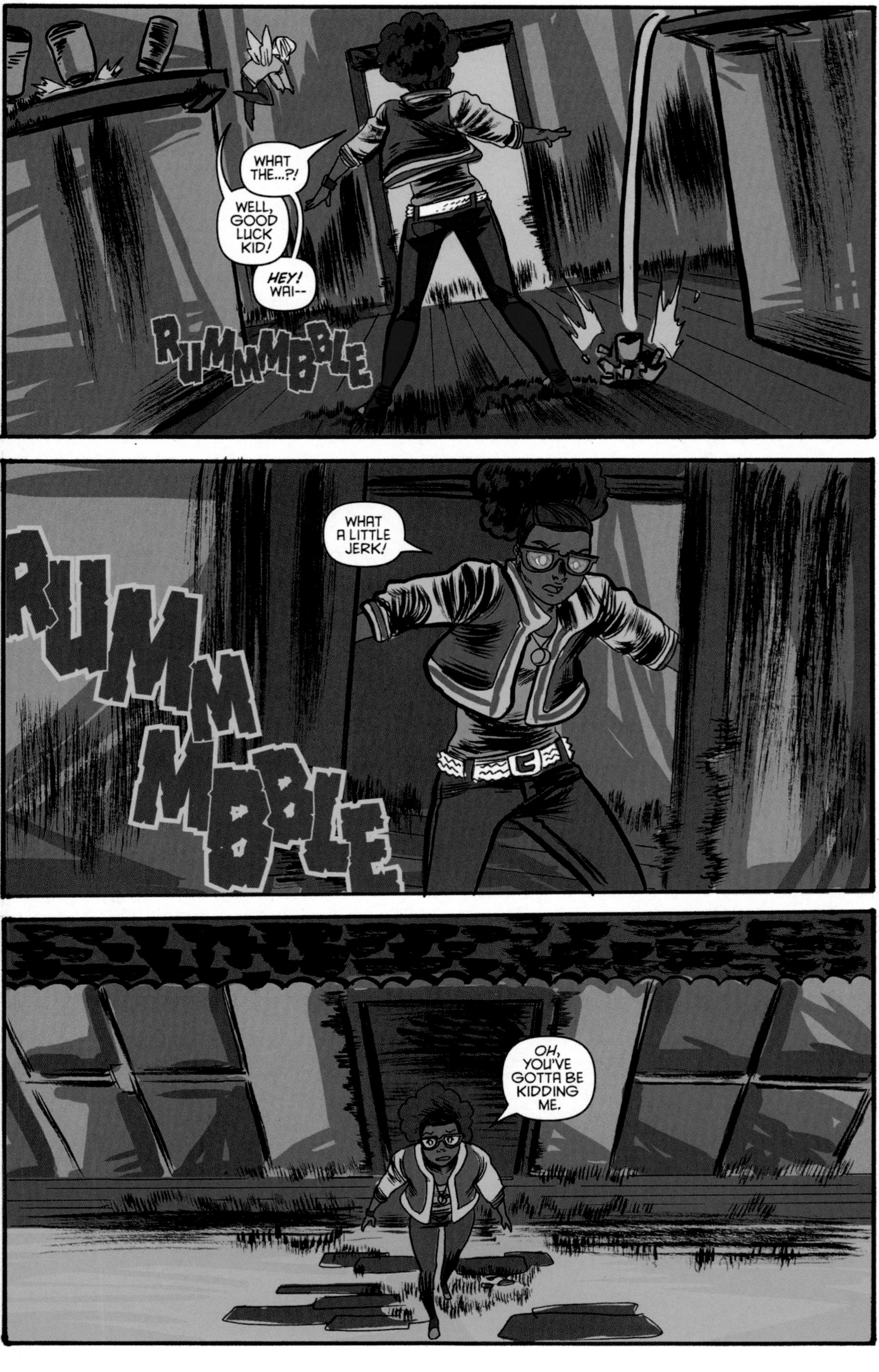

WHAT THE...?!
WELL, GOOD LUCK KID!
HEY! WAI--
RUMMMBBLE
WHAT A LITTLE JERK!
RUMMMBBLE
OH, YOU'VE GOTTA BE KIDDING ME.

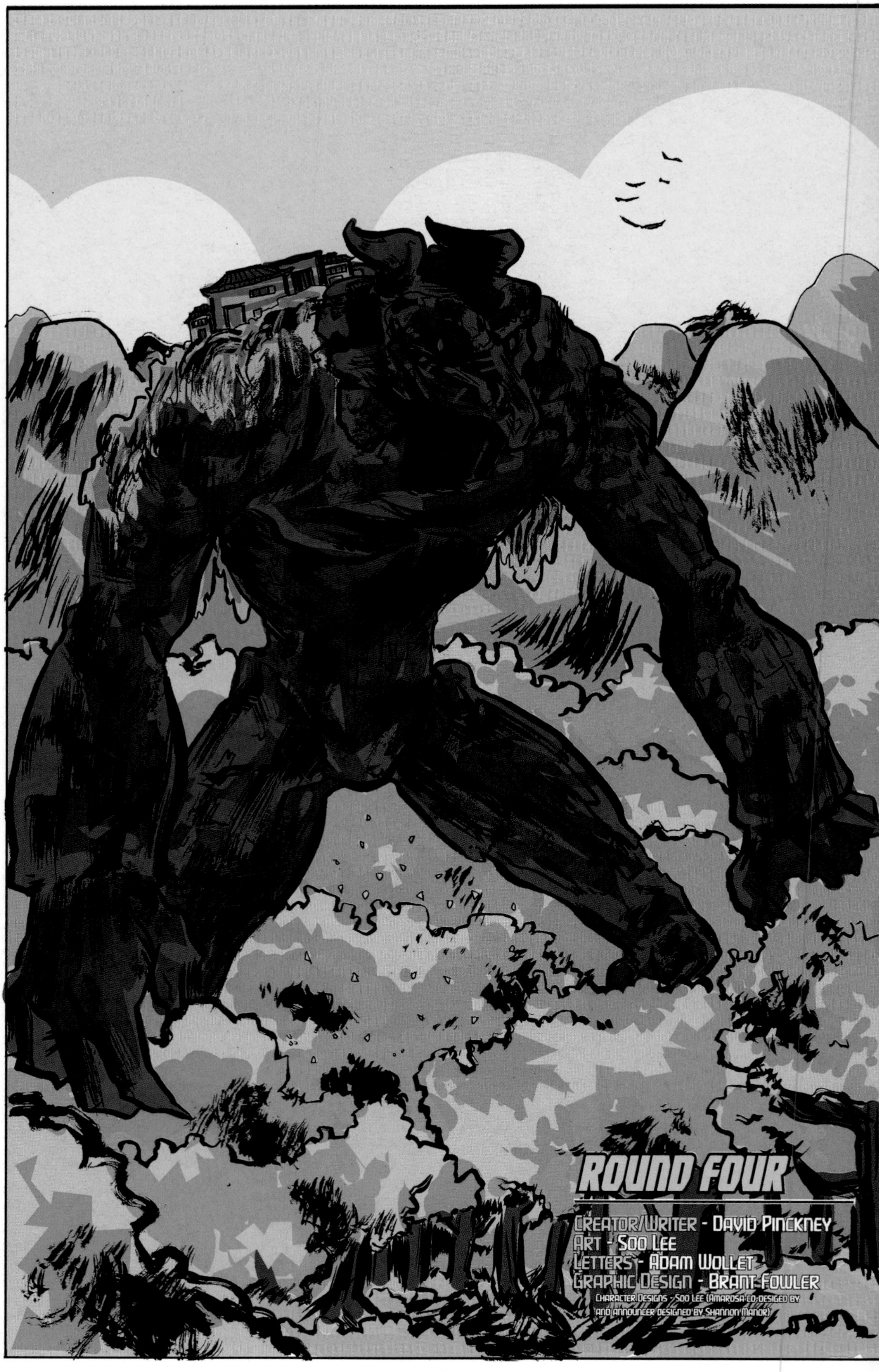
ROUND FOUR
CREATOR/WRITER - DAVID PINCKNEY
ART - SOO LEE
LETTERS - ADAM WOLLET
GRAPHIC DESIGN - BRANT FOWLER
CHARACTER DESIGNS - SOO LEE (AMAROSA CO-DESIGED BY
AND ANNOUNCER DESIGNED BY SHANNON MANOR)

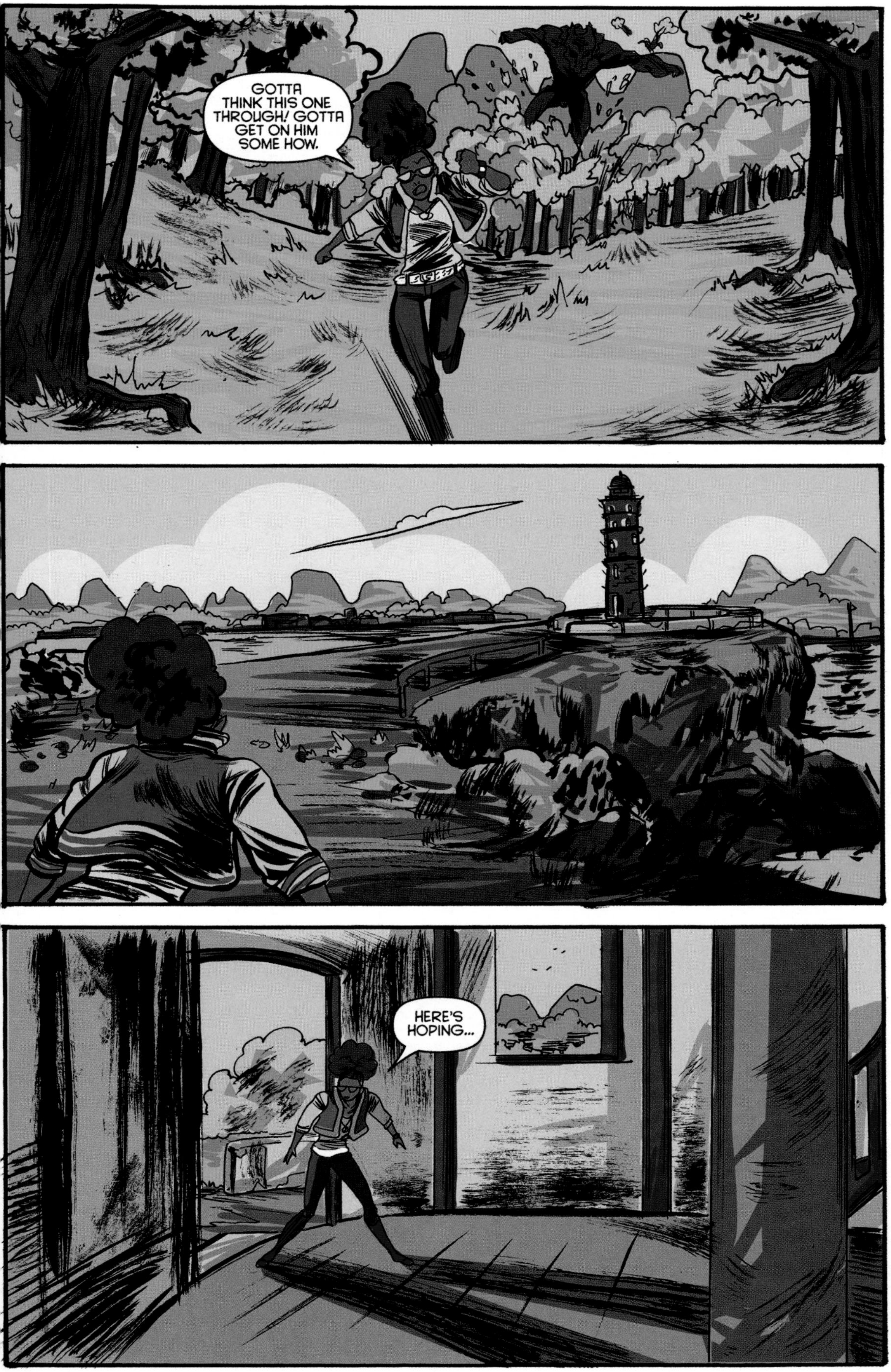
GOTTA THINK THIS ONE THROUGH! GOTTA GET ON HIM SOME HOW.
HERE'S HOPING...

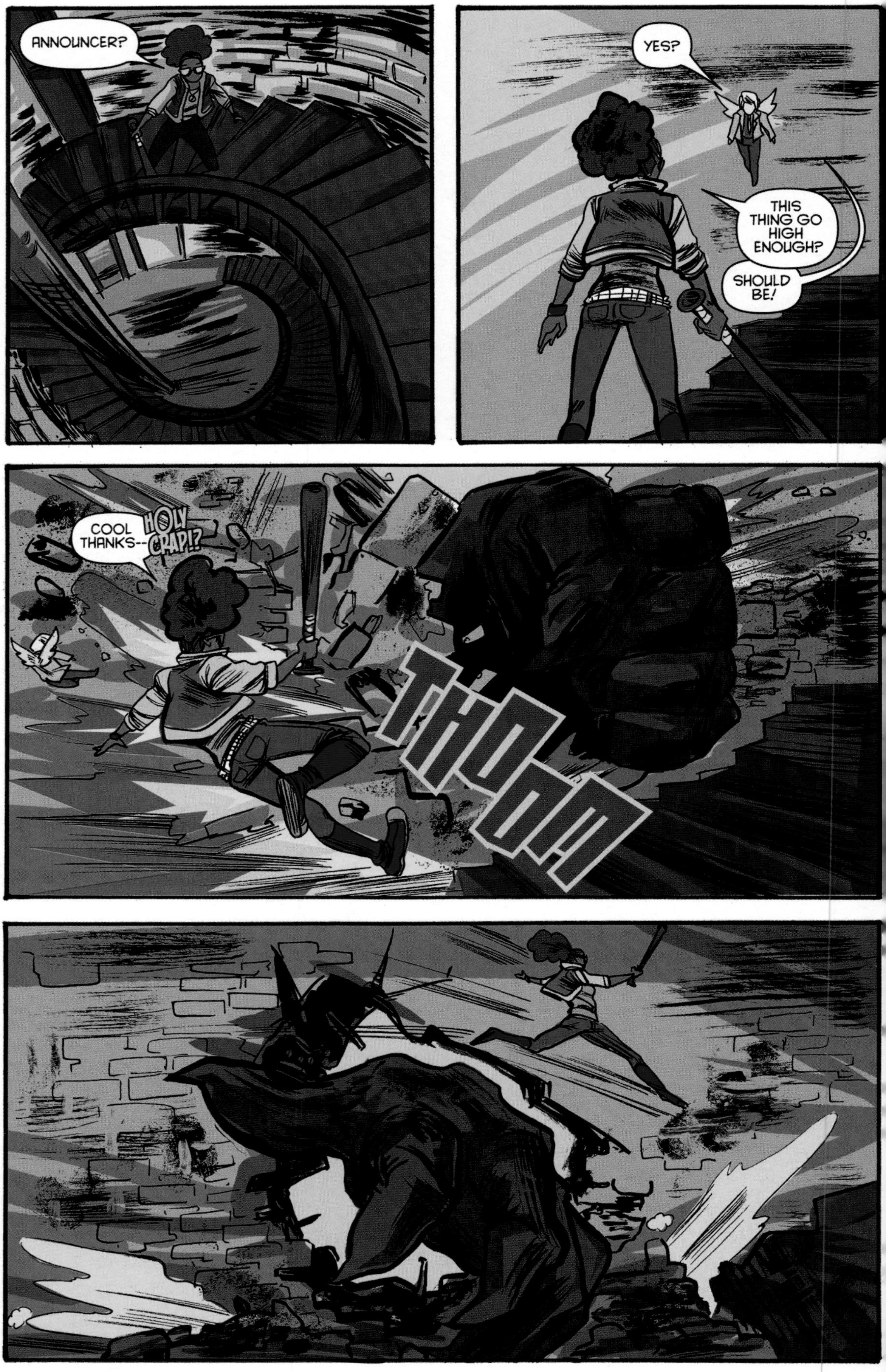
ANNOUNCER?
YES?
THIS THING GO HIGH ENOUGH?
SHOULD BE!
COOL THANKS--
HOLY CRAP!?
THOOM

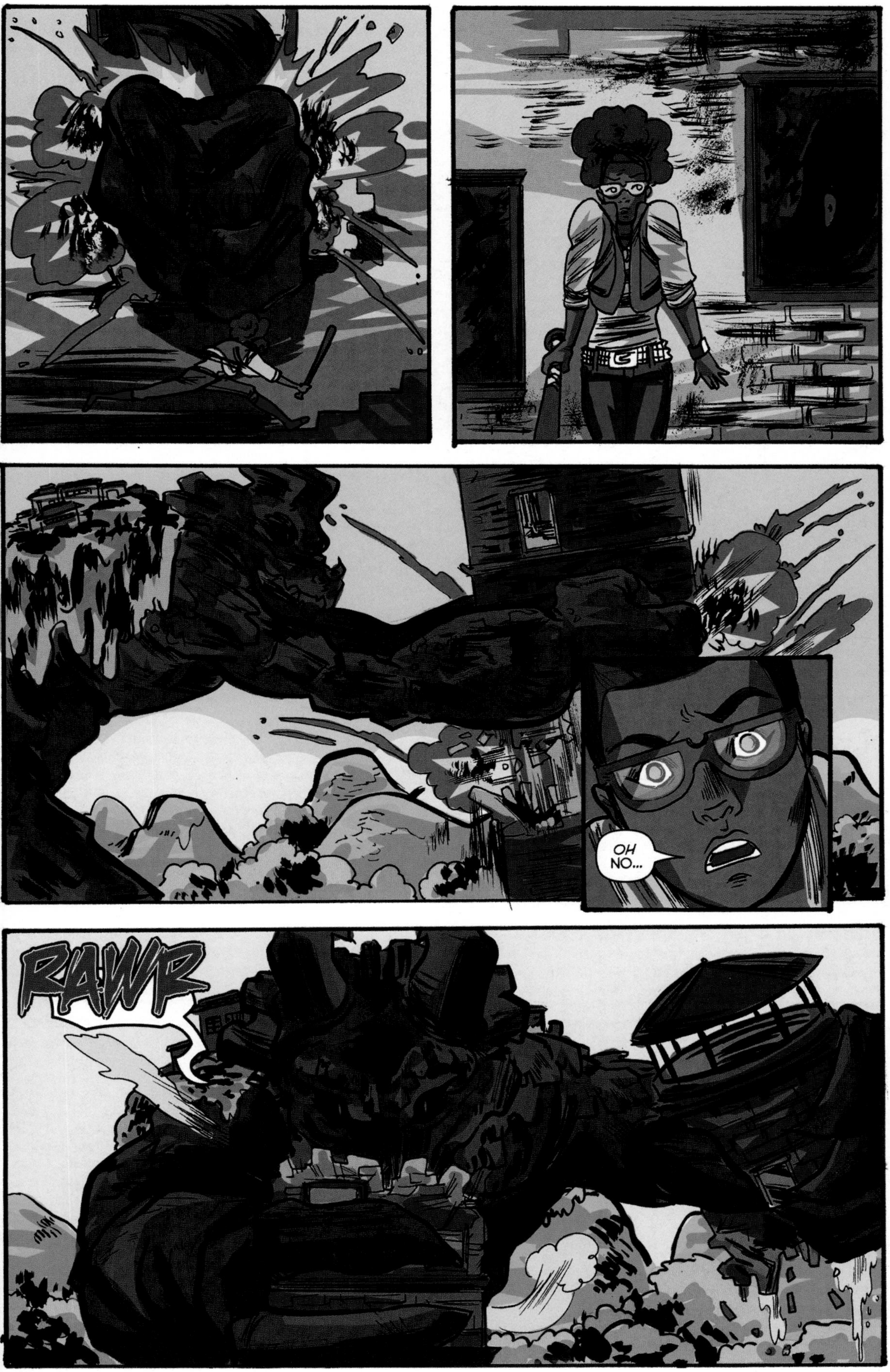
OH NO...
RAWR

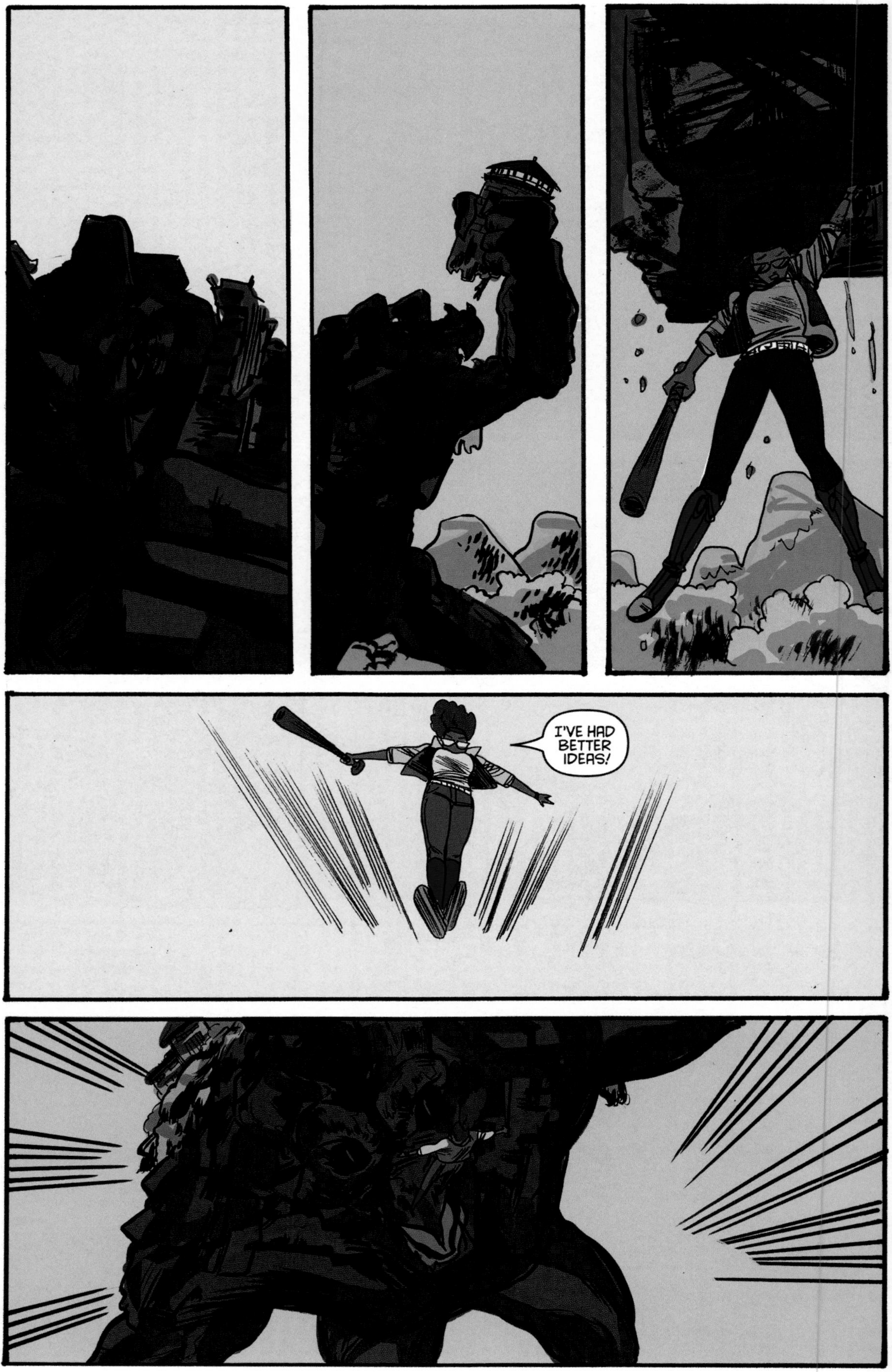
I'VE HAD BETTER IDEAS!

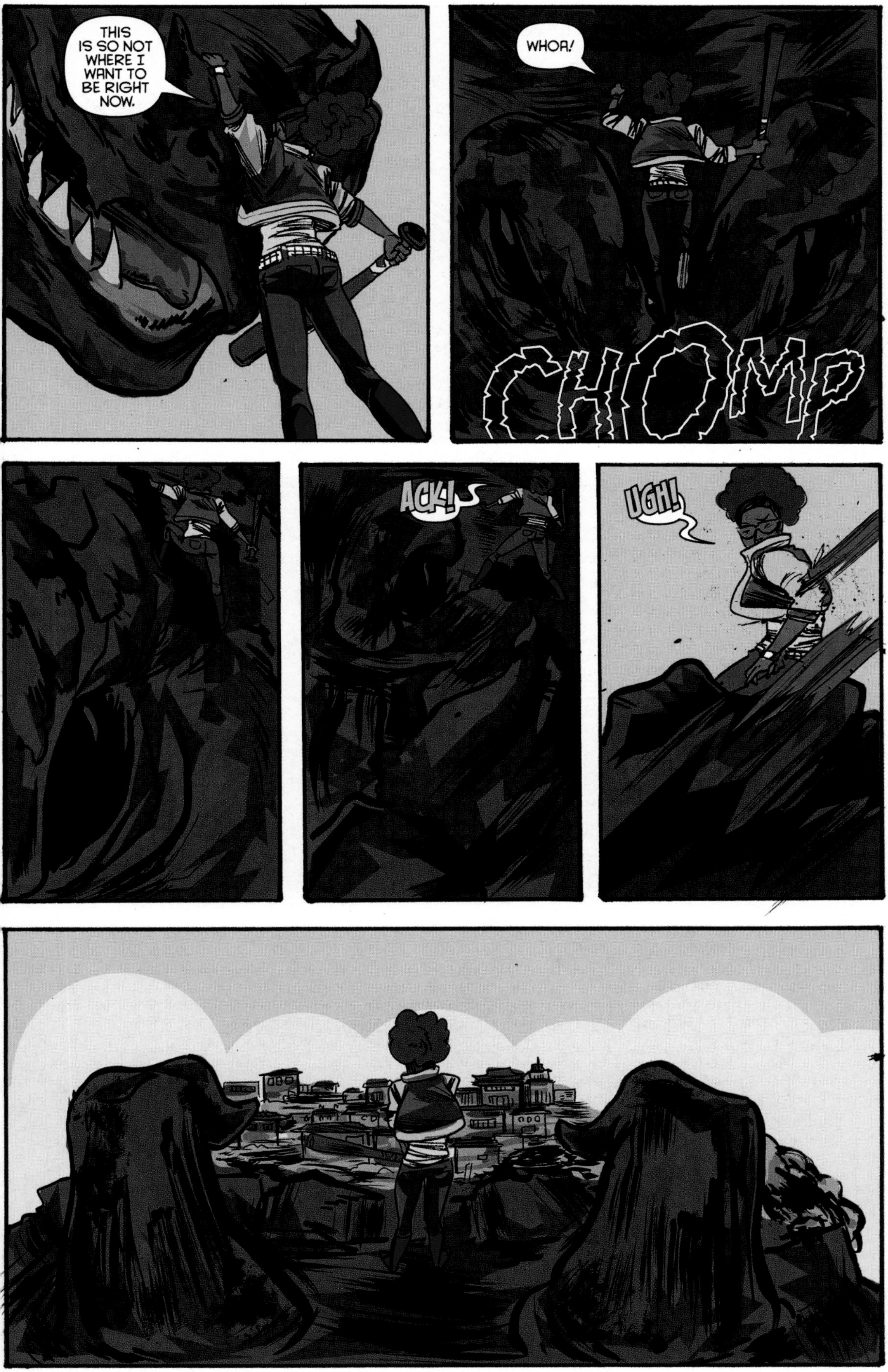
THIS IS SO NOT WHERE I WANT TO BE RIGHT NOW.
WHOA!
CHOMP
ACK!
UGH!

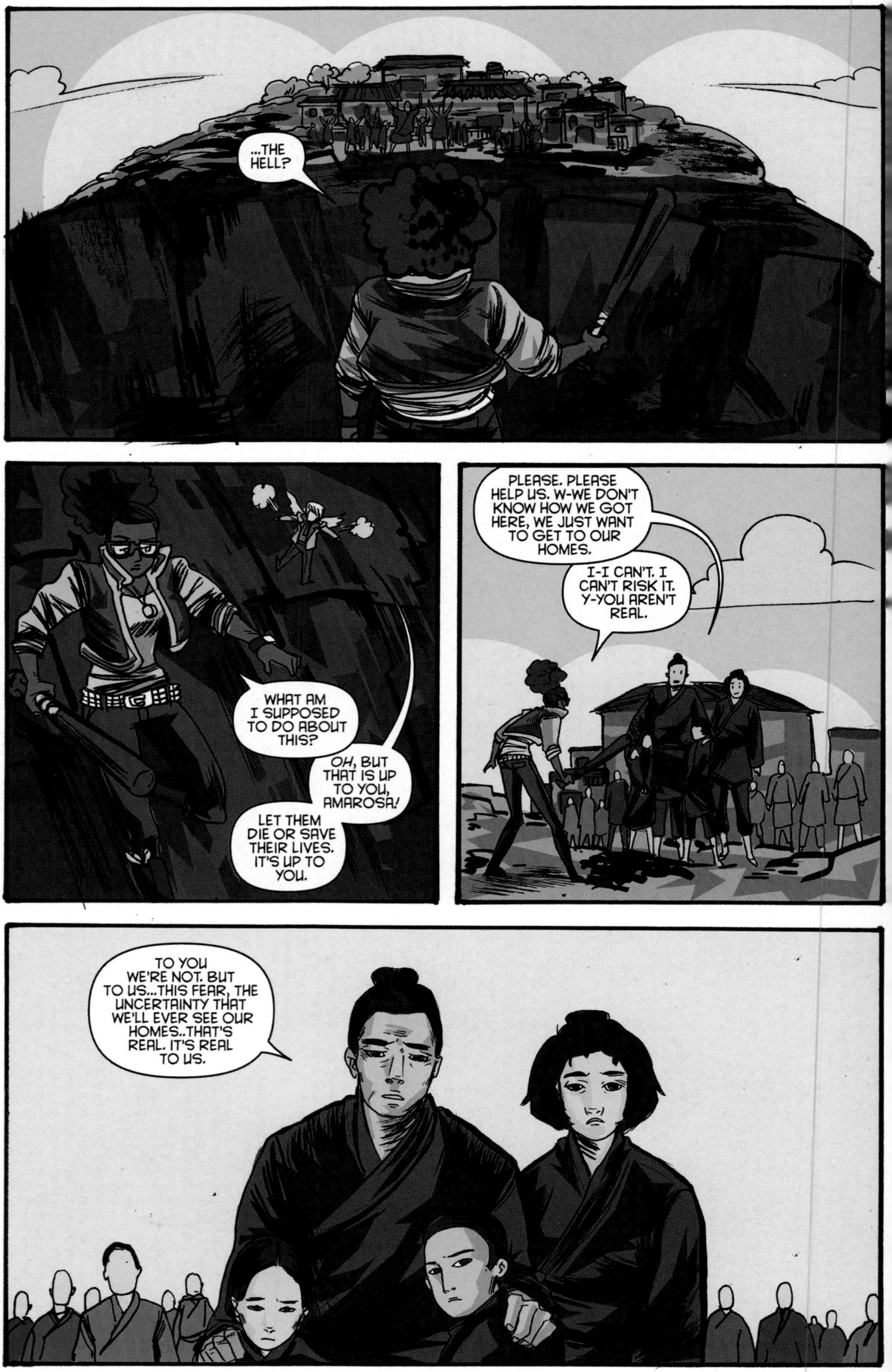
...THE HELL?
WHAT AM I SUPPOSED TO DO ABOUT THIS?
OH, BUT THAT IS UP TO YOU, AMAROSA!
LET THEM DIE OR SAVE THEIR LIVES. IT'S UP TO YOU.
PLEASE. PLEASE HELP US. W-WE DON'T KNOW HOW WE GOT HERE, WE JUST WANT TO GET TO OUR HOMES.
I-I CAN'T. I CAN'T RISK IT. Y-YOU AREN'T REAL.
TO YOU WE'RE NOT. BUT TO US...THIS FEAR, THE UNCERTAINTY THAT WE'LL EVER SEE OUR HOMES..THAT'S REAL. IT'S REAL TO US.

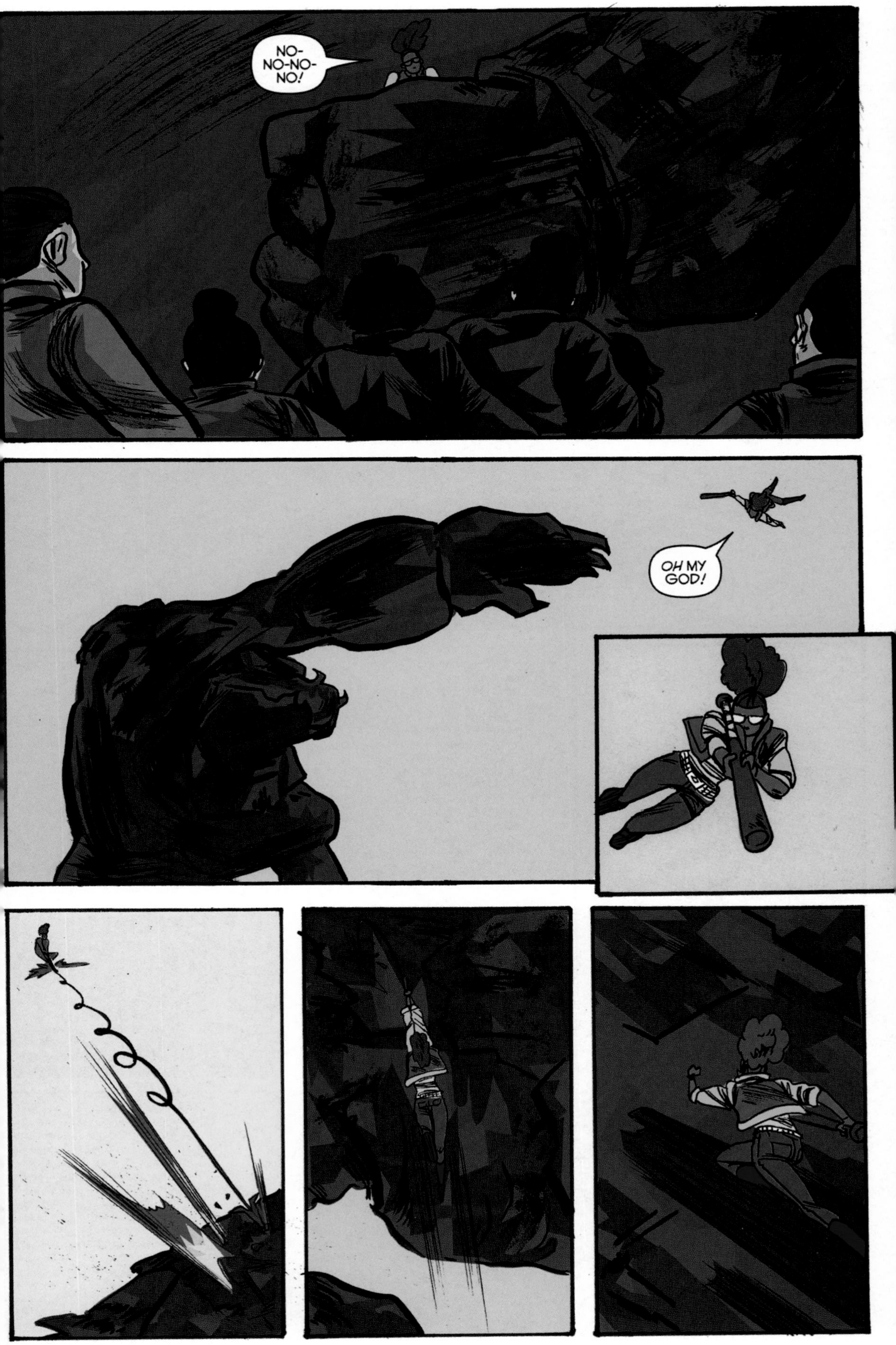
NO-
NO-NO-NO-
NO!
OH MY GOD!

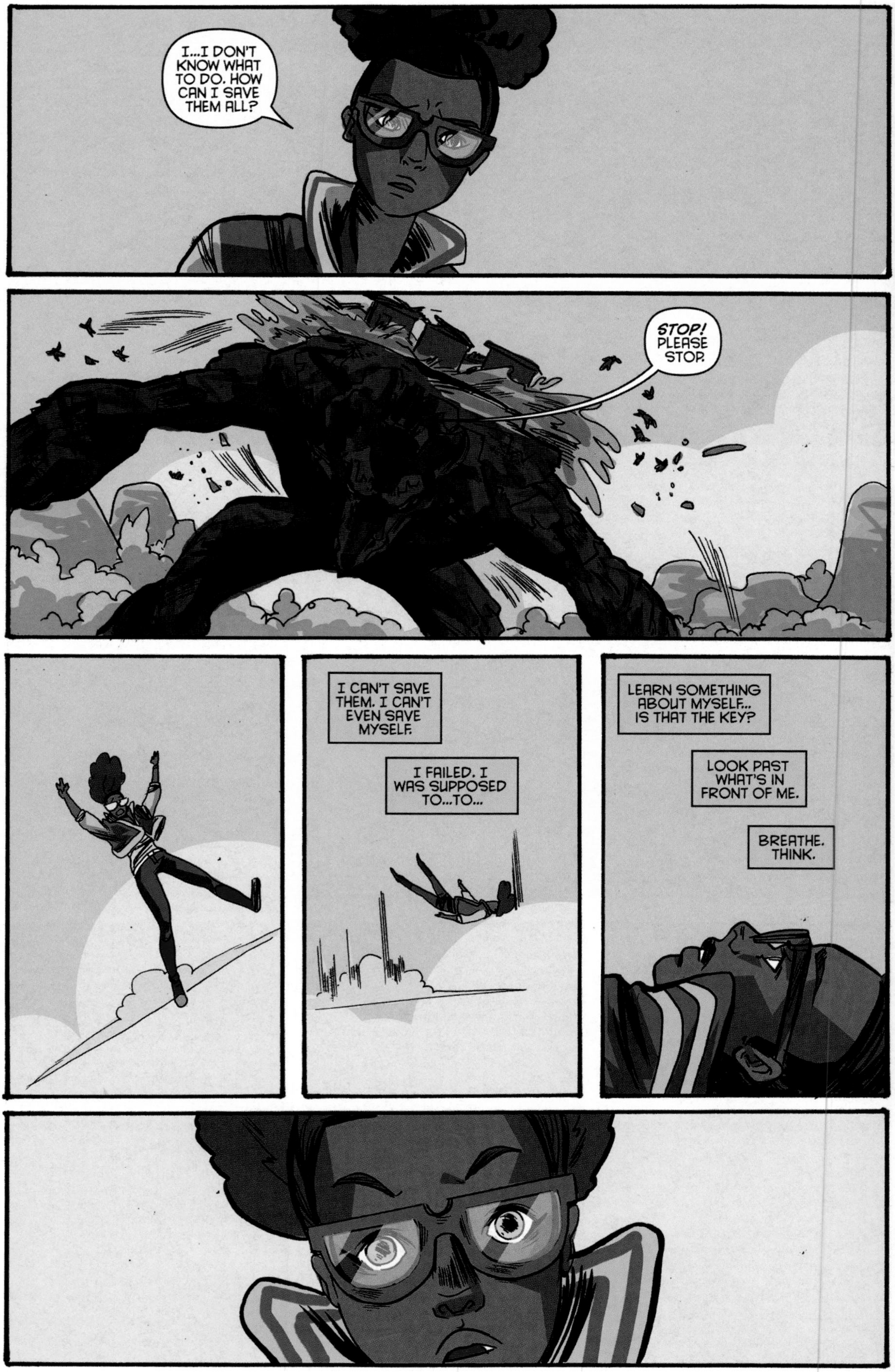
I...I DON'T KNOW WHAT TO DO. HOW CAN I SAVE THEM ALL?
STOP! PLEASE STOP.
I CAN'T SAVE THEM. I CAN'T EVEN SAVE MYSELF.
I FAILED. I WAS SUPPOSED TO...TO...
LEARN SOMETHING ABOUT MYSELF... IS THAT THE KEY?
LOOK PAST WHAT'S IN FRONT OF ME.
BREATHE. THINK.

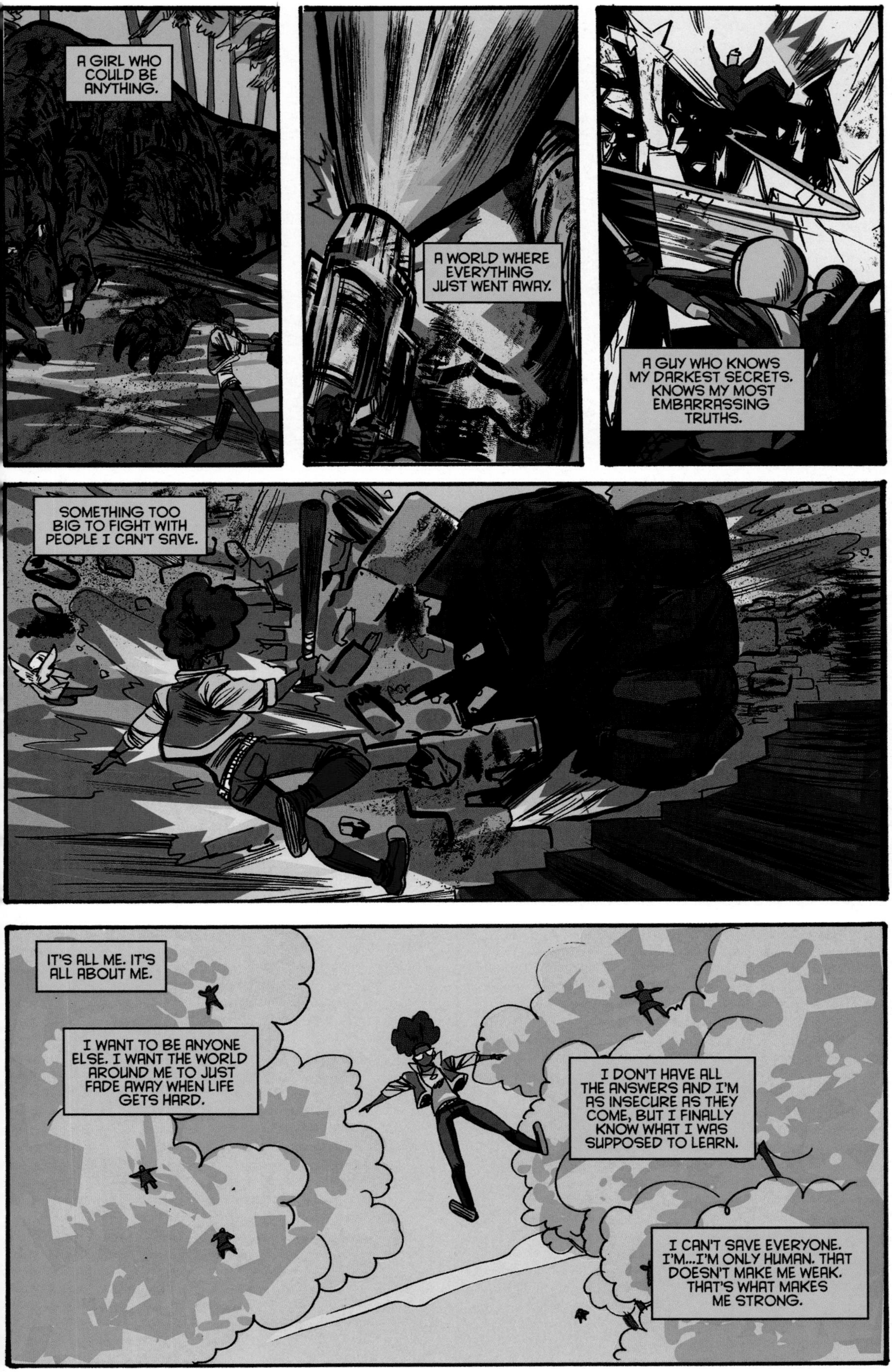
A GIRL WHO COULD BE ANYTHING.
A WORLD WHERE EVERYTHING JUST WENT AWAY.
A GUY WHO KNOWS MY DARKEST SECRETS. KNOWS MY MOST EMBARRASSING TRUTHS.
SOMETHING TOO BIG TO FIGHT WITH PEOPLE I CAN'T SAVE.
IT'S ALL ME. IT'S ALL ABOUT ME.
I WANT TO BE ANYONE ELSE. I WANT THE WORLD AROUND ME TO JUST FADE AWAY WHEN LIFE GETS HARD.
I DON'T HAVE ALL THE ANSWERS AND I'M AS INSECURE AS THEY COME, BUT I FINALLY KNOW WHAT I WAS SUPPOSED TO LEARN.
I CAN'T SAVE EVERYONE. I'M...I'M ONLY HUMAN. THAT DOESN'T MAKE ME WEAK. THAT'S WHAT MAKES ME STRONG.

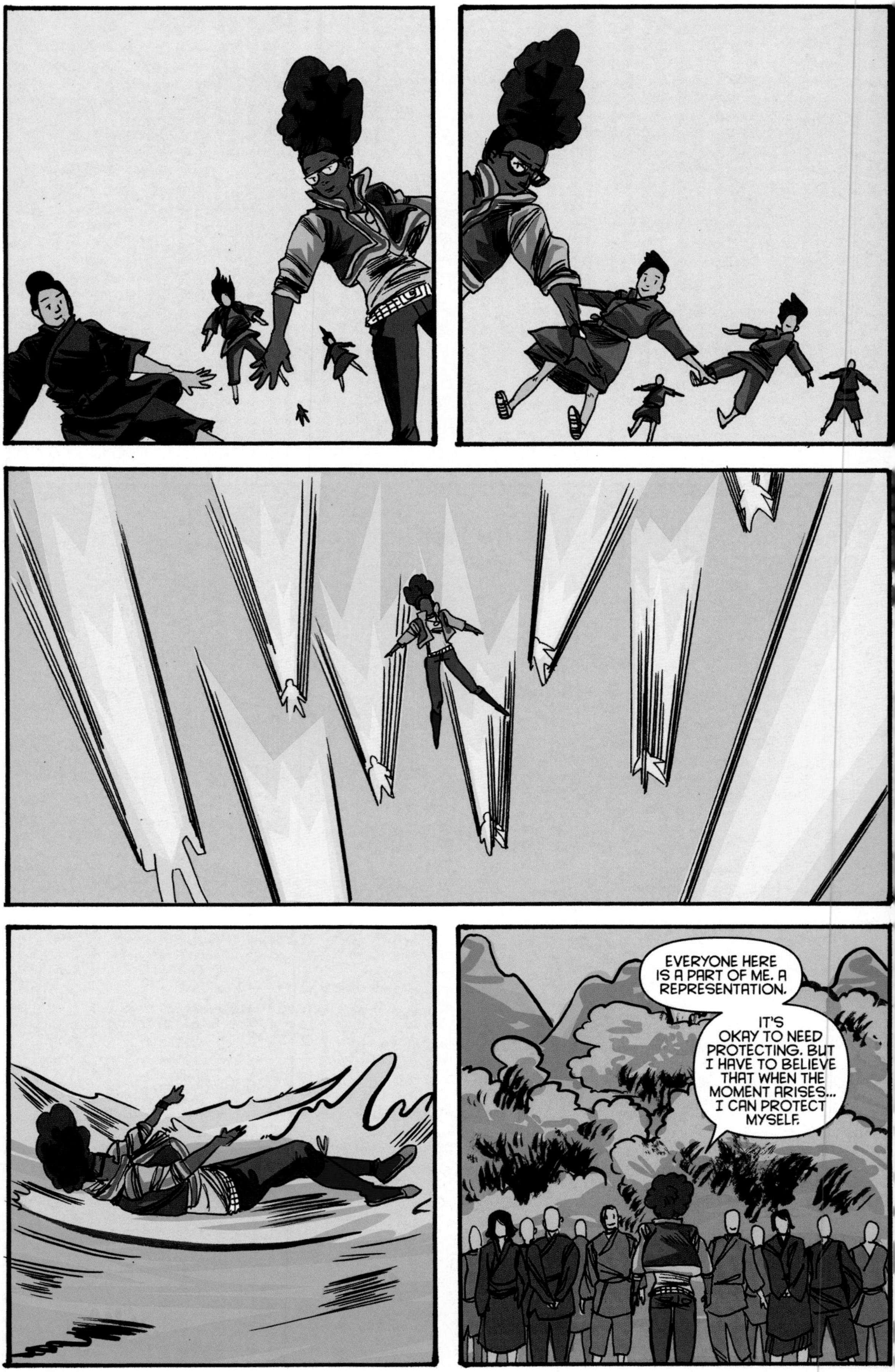
EVERYONE HERE IS A PART OF ME. A REPRESENTATION.
IT'S OKAY TO NEED PROTECTING. BUT I HAVE TO BELIEVE THAT WHEN THE MOMENT ARISES... I CAN PROTECT MYSELF.

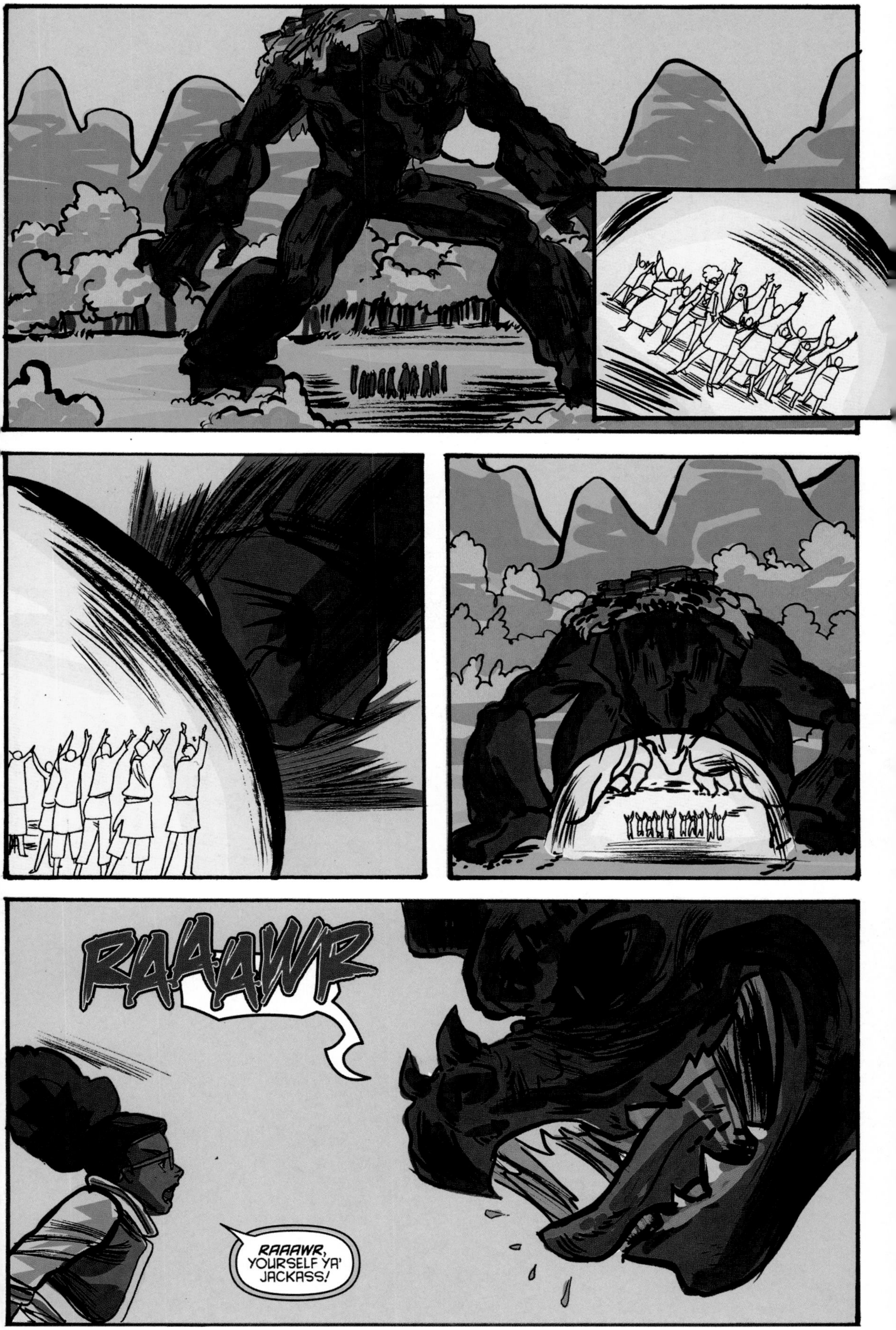
RAAAWR
RAAAWR, YOURSELF YA' JACKASS!

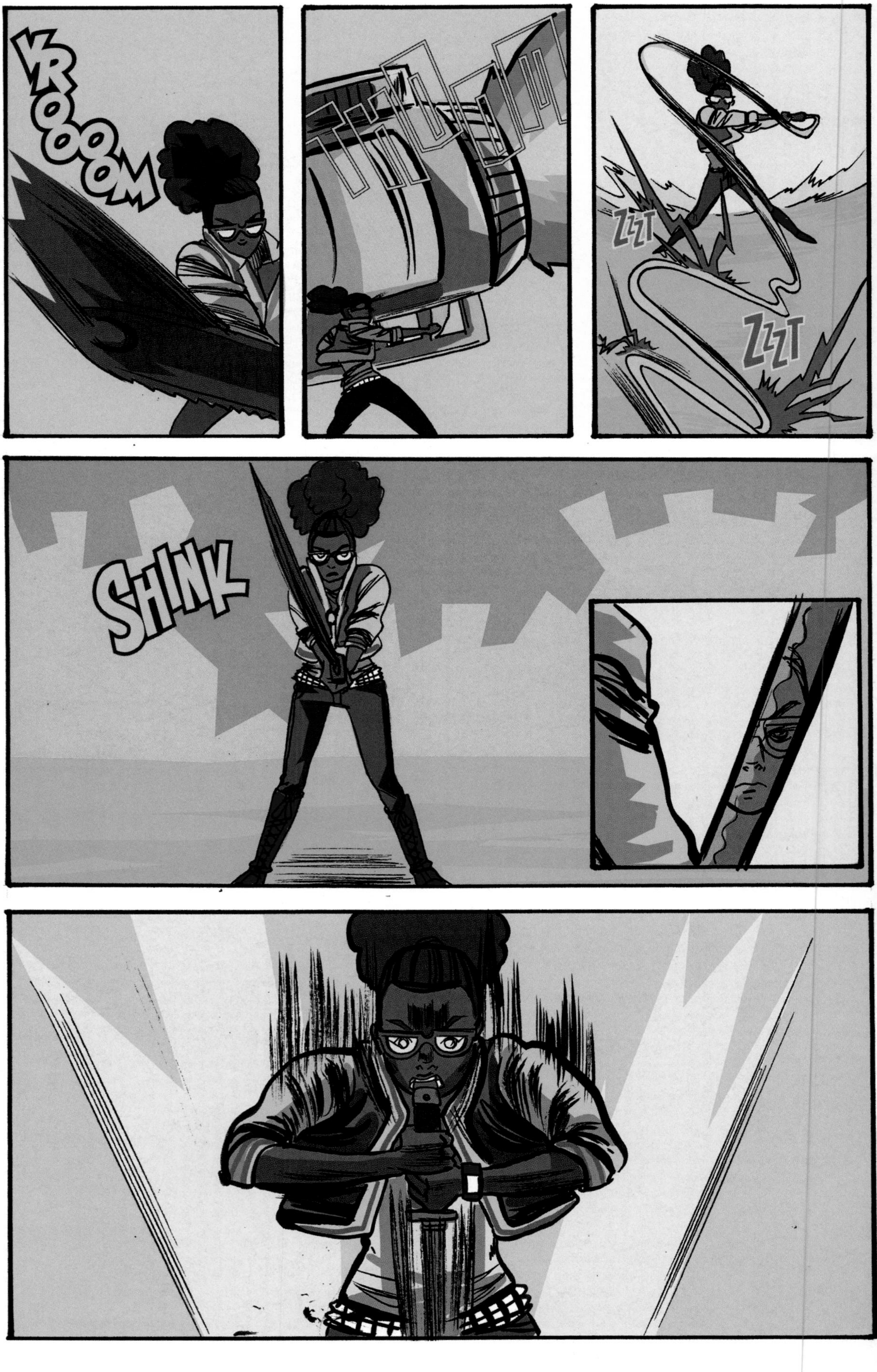
VROOOOM
THOOOM
ZZZT
ZZZT
SHINK

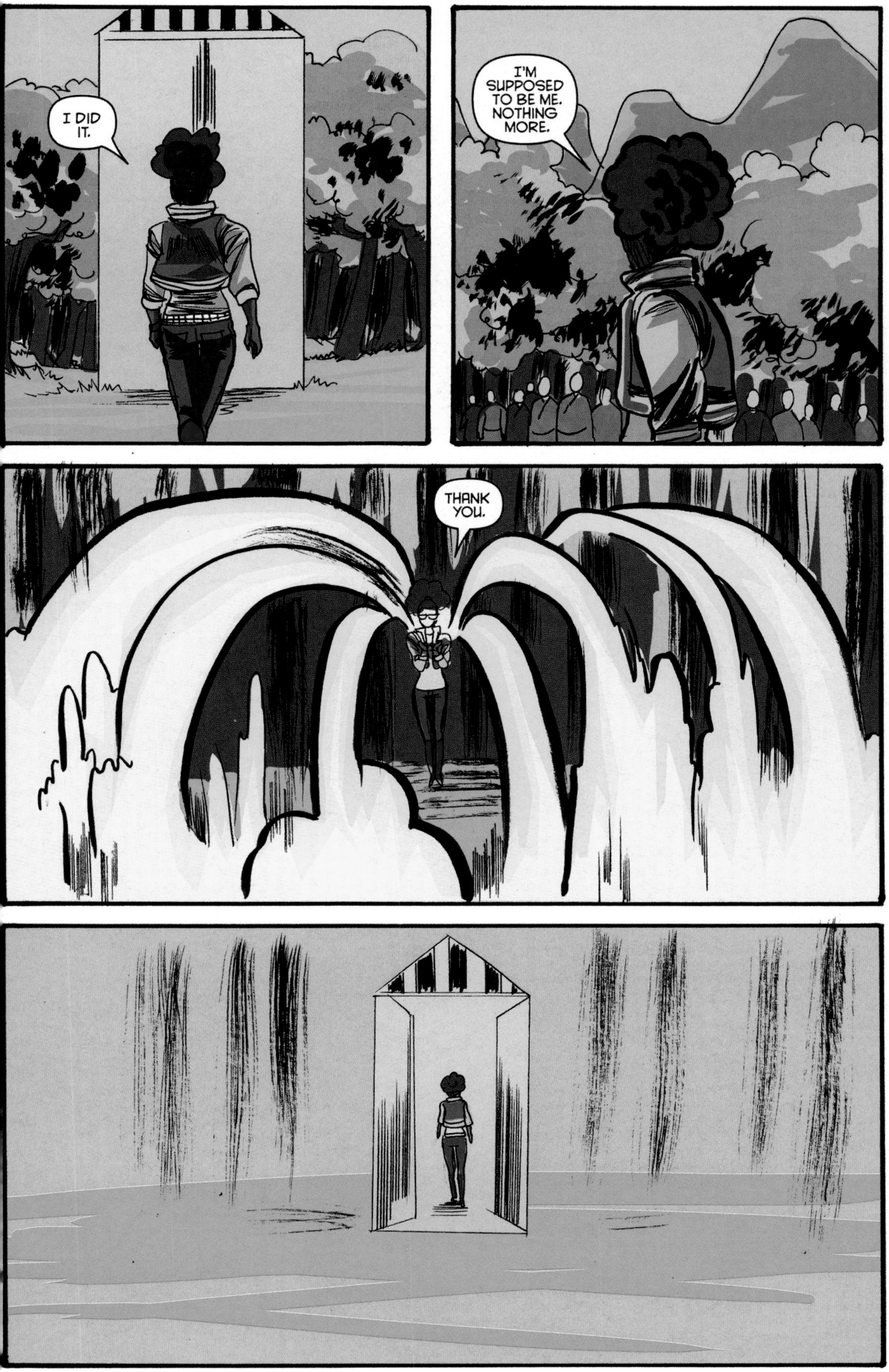
I DID IT.
I'M SUPPOSED TO BE ME. NOTHING MORE.
THANK YOU.

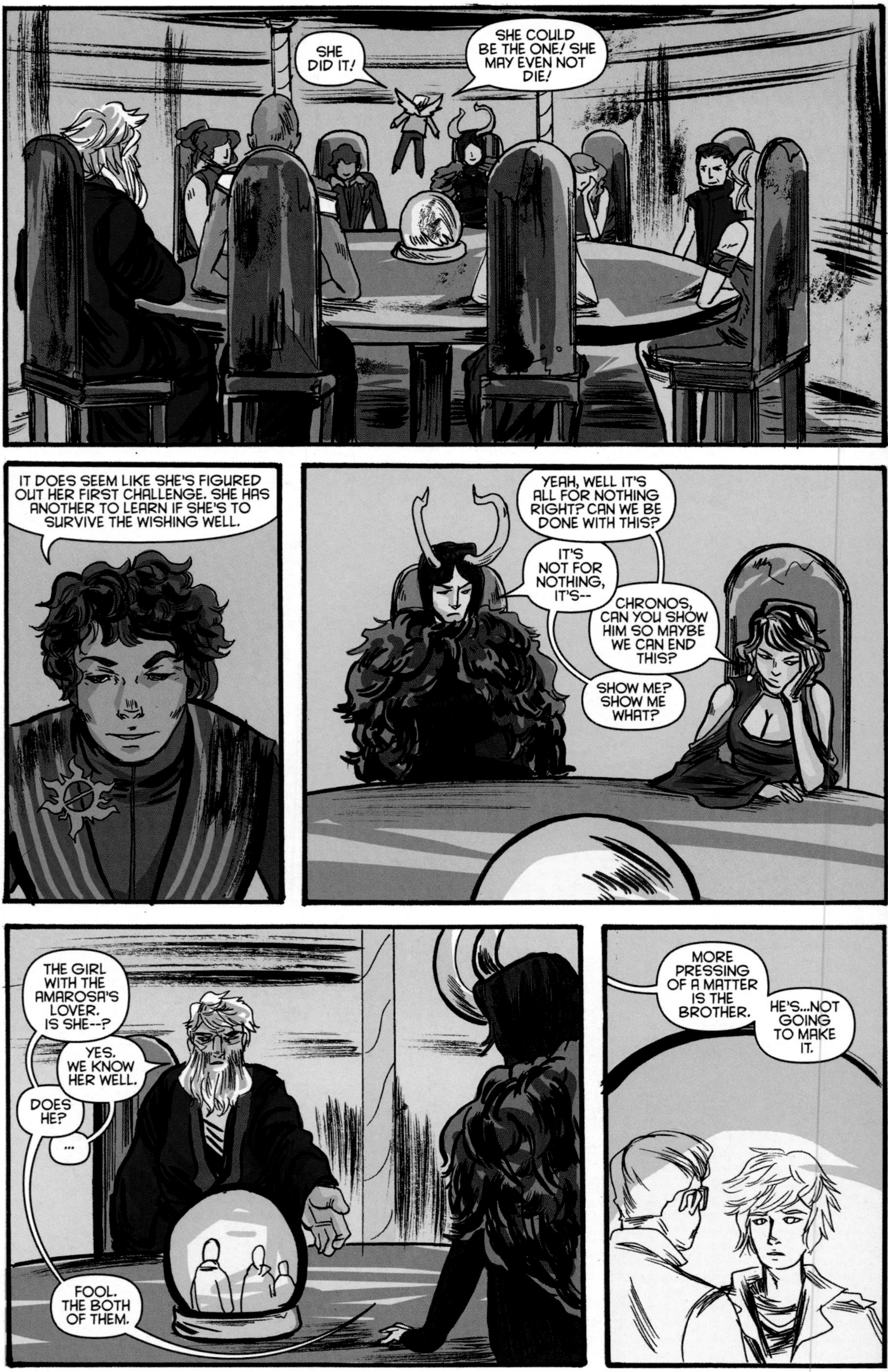
SHE DID IT!
SHE COULD BE THE ONE! SHE MAY EVEN NOT DIE!
IT DOES SEEM LIKE SHE'S FIGURED OUT HER FIRST CHALLENGE. SHE HAS ANOTHER TO LEARN IF SHE'S TO SURVIVE THE WISHING WELL.
YEAH, WELL IT'S ALL FOR NOTHING RIGHT? CAN WE BE DONE WITH THIS?
IT'S NOT FOR NOTHING, IT'S--
CHRONOS, CAN YOU SHOW HIM SO MAYBE WE CAN END THIS?
SHOW ME? SHOW ME WHAT?
THE GIRL WITH THE AMAROSA'S LOVER. IS SHE--?
YES. WE KNOW HER WELL.
DOES HE?
...
FOOL. THE BOTH OF THEM.
MORE PRESSING OF A MATTER IS THE BROTHER.
HE'S...NOT GOING TO MAKE IT.

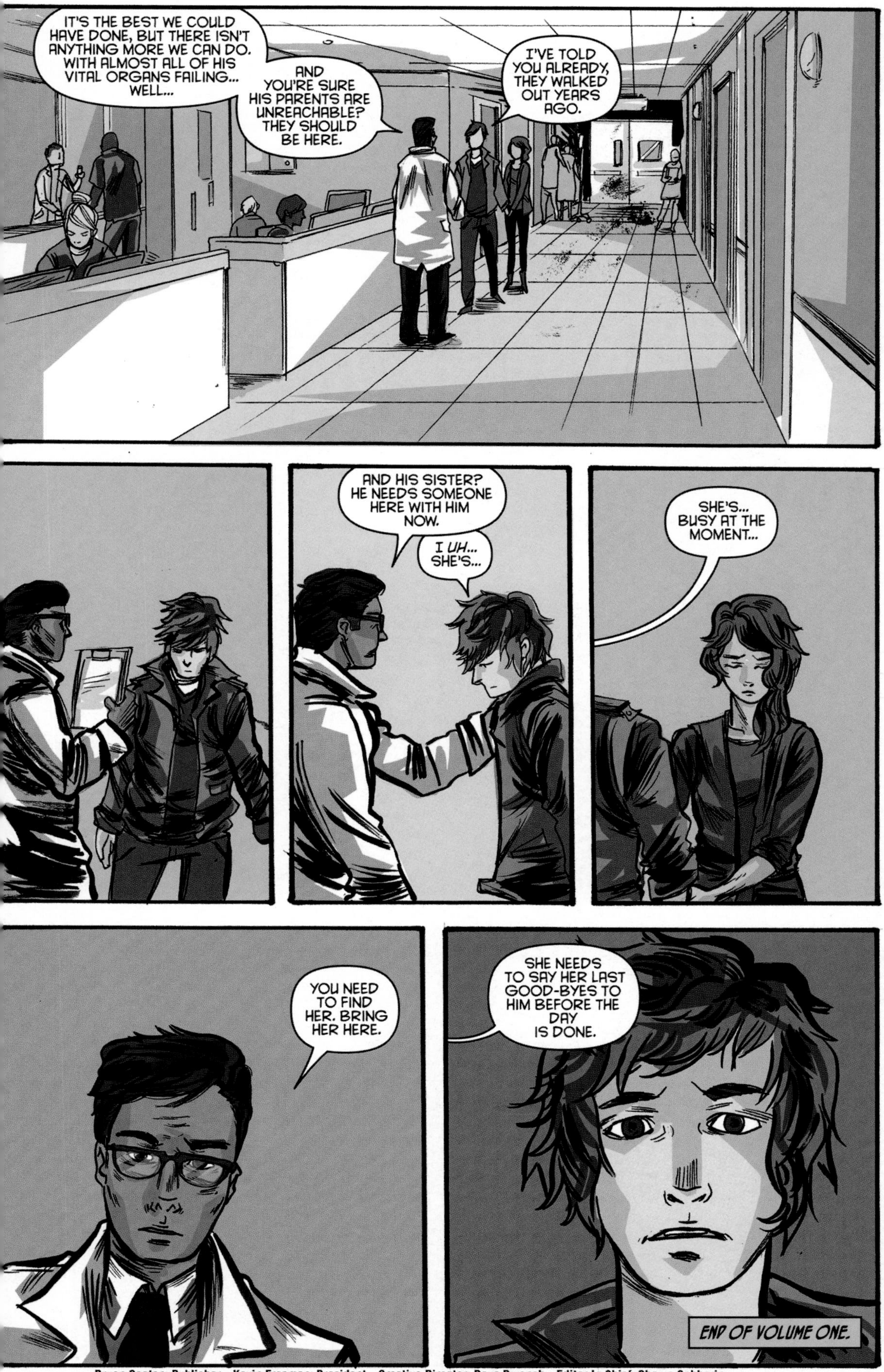
IT'S THE BEST WE COULD HAVE DONE, BUT THERE ISN'T ANYTHING MORE WE CAN DO. WITH ALMOST ALL OF HIS VITAL ORGANS FAILING... WELL...
AND YOU'RE SURE HIS PARENTS ARE UNREACHABLE? THEY SHOULD BE HERE.
I'VE TOLD YOU ALREADY, THEY WALKED OUT YEARS AGO.
AND HIS SISTER? HE NEEDS SOMEONE HERE WITH HIM NOW.
I UH... SHE'S...
SHE'S... BUSY AT THE MOMENT...
YOU NEED TO FIND HER. BRING HER HERE.
SHE NEEDS TO SAY HER LAST GOOD-BYES TO HIM BEFORE THE DAY IS DONE.
END OF VOLUME ONE.

Bryan Seaton: Publisher - Kevin Freeman: President - Creative Director: Dave Dwonch - Editor In Chief: Shawn Gabborin
Co-Directors of Marketing: Jamal Igle & Kelly Dale - Social Media Director: Jim Dietz - Kaiju: Chad Cicconi - Submissions Editor: Colleen Boyd

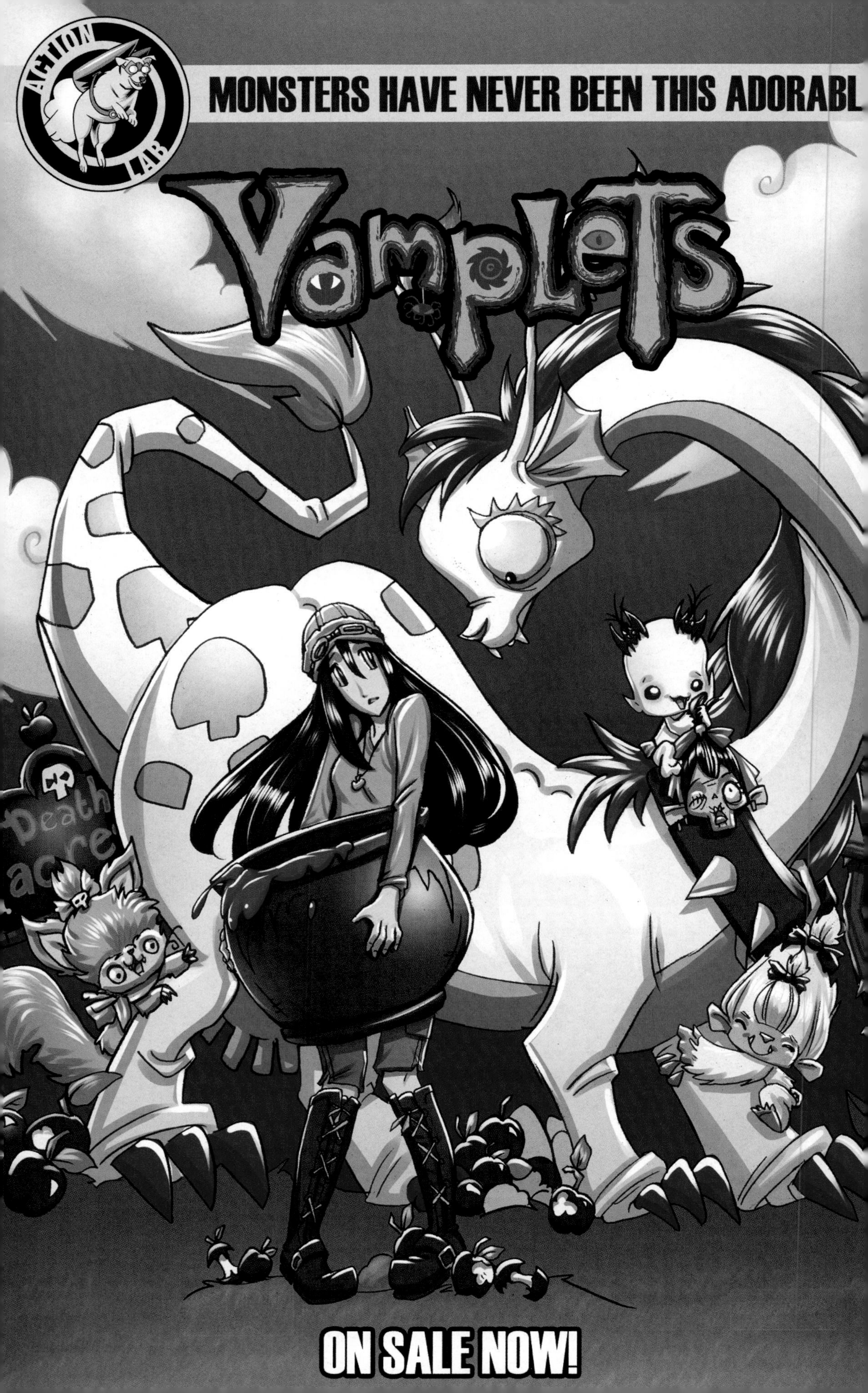
ACTION LAB
MONSTERS HAVE NEVER BEEN THIS ADORABL
Vamplets
Death acre
ON SALE NOW!

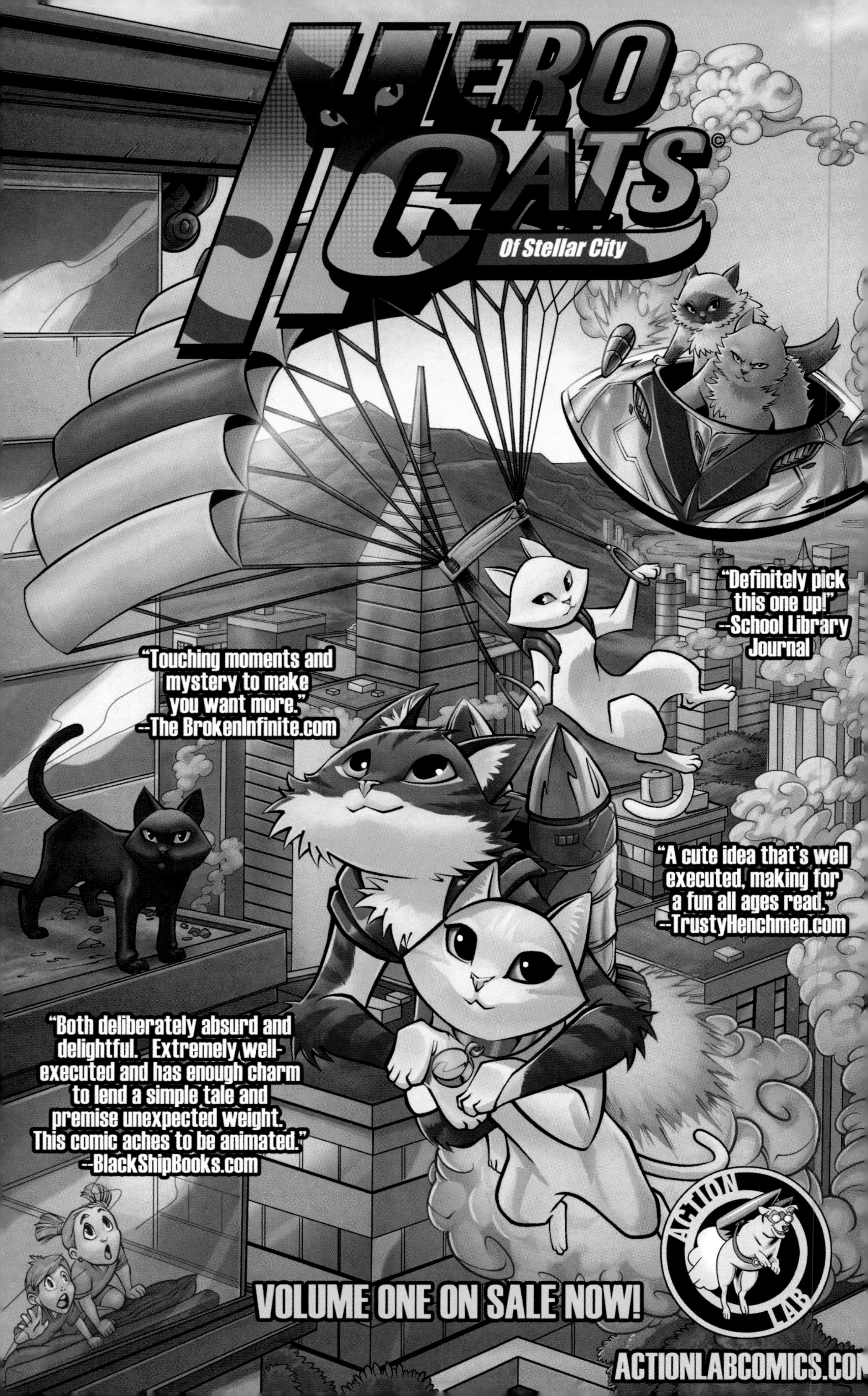
HERO CATS©
Of Stellar City
"Definitely pick this one up!" --School Library Journal
"Touching moments and mystery to make you want more." --The BrokenInfinite.com
"A cute idea that's well executed, making for a fun all ages read." --TrustyHenchmen.com
"Both deliberately absurd and delightful. Extremely well-executed and has enough charm to lend a simple tale and premise unexpected weight. This comic aches to be animated." --BlackShipBooks.com
ACTION LAB
VOLUME ONE ON SALE NOW!
ACTIONLABCOMICS.COM

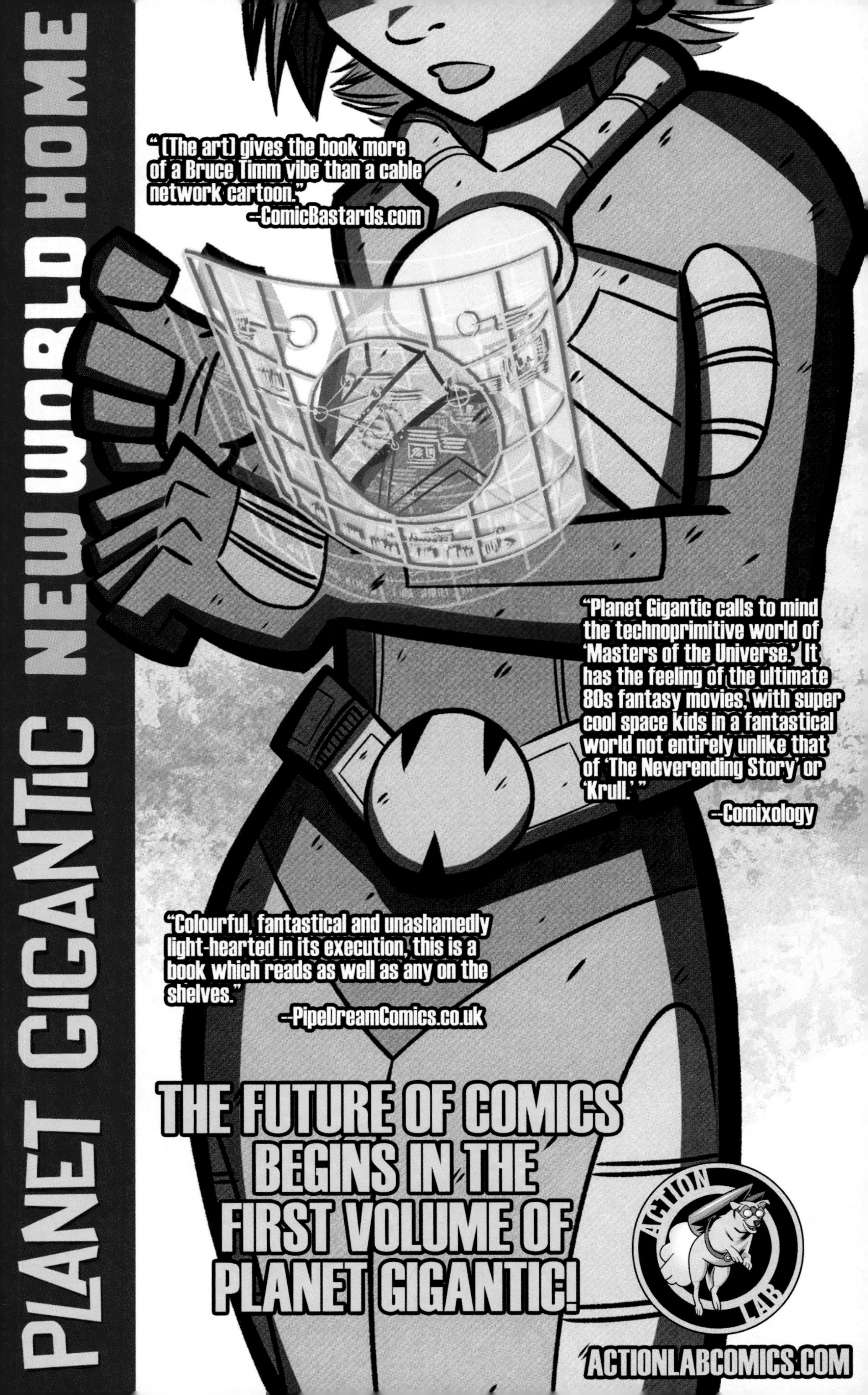
PLANET GIGANTIC NEW WORLD HOME
“(The art) gives the book more of a Bruce Timm vibe than a cable network cartoon.”
--ComicBastards.com
“Planet Gigantic calls to mind the technoprimitive world of ‘Masters of the Universe.’ It has the feeling of the ultimate 80s fantasy movies, with super cool space kids in a fantastical world not entirely unlike that of ‘The Neverending Story’ or ‘Krull.’ ”
--Comixology
“Colourful, fantastical and unashamedly light-hearted in its execution, this is a book which reads as well as any on the shelves.”
--PipeDreamComics.co.uk
THE FUTURE OF COMICS BEGINS IN THE FIRST VOLUME OF PLANET GIGANTIC!
ACTION LAB
ACTIONLABCOMICS.COM

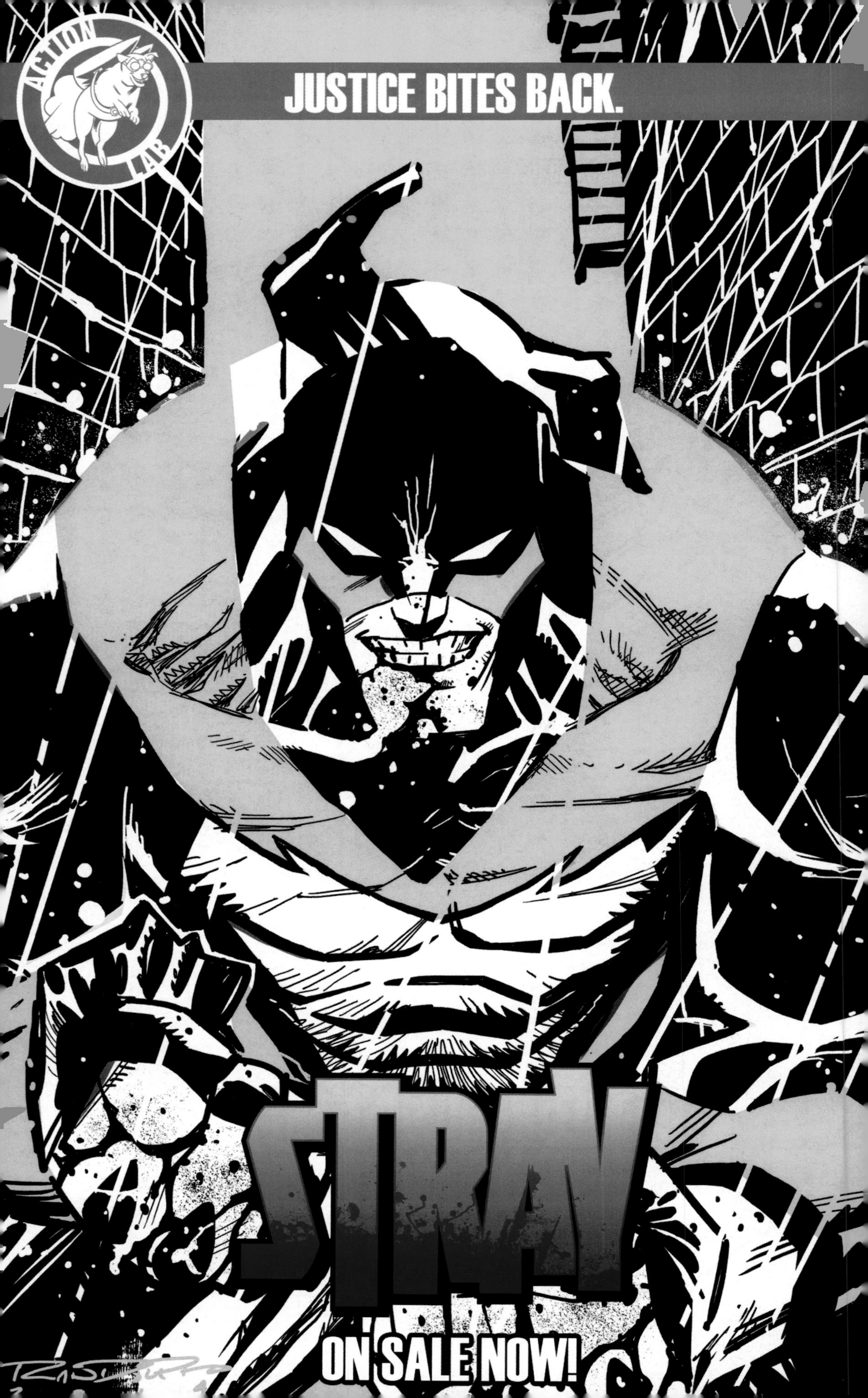
ACTION LAB
JUSTICE BITES BACK.
STRAY
ON SALE NOW!

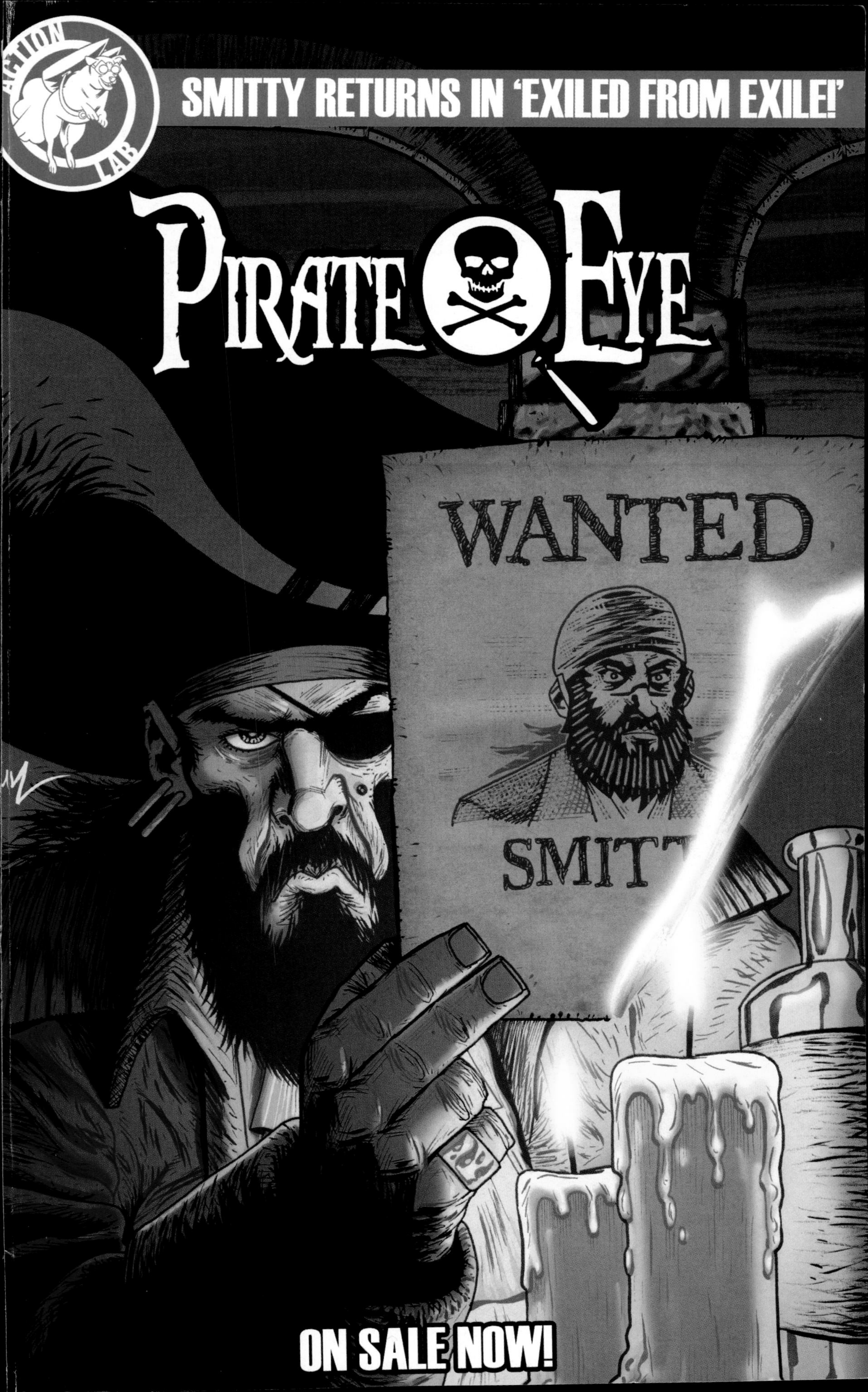
ACTION LAB
SMITTY RETURNS IN 'EXILED FROM EXILE!'
PIRATE EYE
WANTED
SMITT
ON SALE NOW!

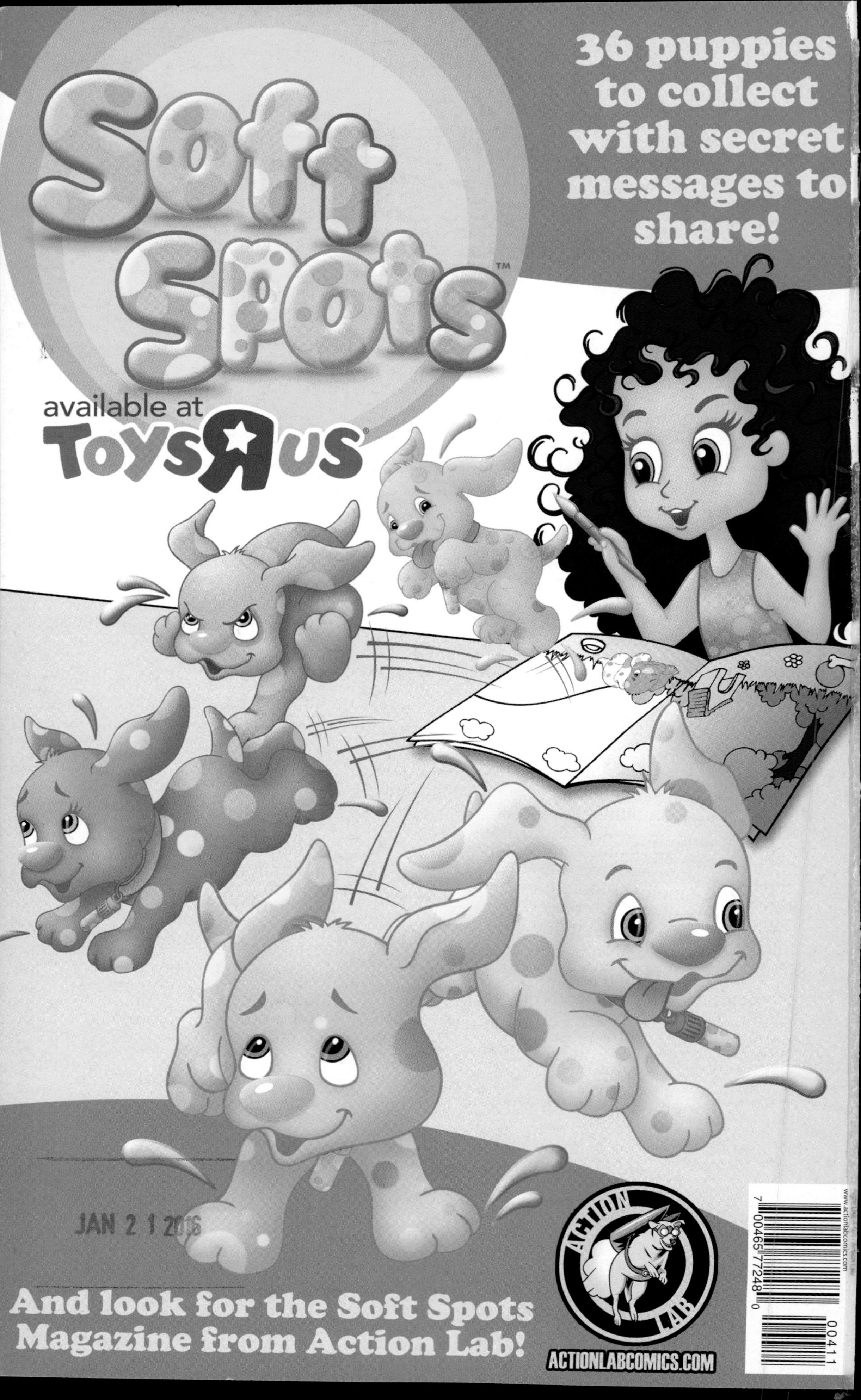
36 puppies
to collect
with secret
messages to
share!
Soft Spots™
available at
Toys R Us®
JAN 2 1 2016
And look for the Soft Spots
Magazine from Action Lab!
ACTION LAB
ACTIONLABCOMICS.COM
www.actionlabcomics.com
7 00465 77248 0
00411